COUNTERTRANSFERENCE

COUNTERTRANSFERENCE

Edited by
Edmund Slakter, M.D.

Jason Aronson Inc.
Northvale, New Jersey
London

Library of Congress Cataloging-in-Publication Data

Slakter, Edmund.
  Countertransference / by Edmund Slakter.
    p.   cm.
  Bibliography: p.
  Includes index.
  ISBN 0-87668-948-9
  1. Countertransference (Psychology)   I. Title.
RC489.C68S58 1987
616.89'14--dc 19   87-21478
                                                          CIP

Manufactured in the United States of America.

To Ruth, Eve, Paul, Mark, and Lynn—
without their patience, forbearance, and
understanding, this book would not have been written.

Contents

PART II: RECENT INTERPRETATIONS OF COUNTERTRANSFERENCE

PART III: QUESTIONING COUNTERTRANSFERENCE

Acknowledgments

I wish to thank Drs. Jacob Arlow, Harold Blum, Charles Brenner, Theodore J. Jacobs, Joseph Sandler, Charles Savage, Harold Searles, and Martin Silverman for the major contributions they have made to this book. It is a distinct privilege to be in the same profession with them.

I am also grateful to my many colleagues who, like those mentioned above, openly revealed their personal countertransferential experiences and permitted me to draw upon their disclosures.

I want to thank Lucy Freeman and Audree Siden for their inspiration and encouragement.

I am deeply indebted to Joan Acoccella for her perceptive editorial advice and to Marilyn Herelith for transcribing and typing the proceedings of The Regional Council Conference of the

Psychoanalytic Societies of Greater New York held at Princeton in June 1984.

Lastly, my very special thanks to my publisher, Jason Aronson Inc. In particular, I would like to thank Nicholas Radhuber for his editorial support and guidance through the publishing process.

New York City
July 1987

Contributors

Arlow, Jacob, M.D., Clinical Professor of Psychiatry, New York University Medical School; Supervising and Training Analyst at the New York Psychoanalytic Institute and at the Psychoanalytic Institute, New York University Medical Center

Blum, Harold, M.D., Clinical Professor of Psychiatry, New York University Medical School; Supervising and Training Analyst at the Psychoanalytic Institute, New York University Medical Center

Brenner, Charles, M.D., Clinical Professor of Psychiatry, State University of New York, Downstate; Supervising and Training Analyst at the New York Psychoanalytic Institute

Jacobs, Theodore, M.D., Clinical Professor of Psychiatry, Albert Einstein College of Medicine; Supervising and Training Analyst at the Psychoanalytic Institute, New York University Medical Center, and at the New York Psychoanalytic Institute

Sandler, Joseph, M.D., Training and Supervising Analyst in the Israel and British Psychoanalytic Societies

Savage, Charles, M.D., Chief Psychiatrist, the Veterans Administration Medical Center, Baltimore, MD

Searles, Harold, M.D., Supervisory and Training Analyst, Washington Psychoanalytic Institute, Washington, D.C.

Silverman, Martin, M.D., Clinical Associate Professor of Psychiatry; Supervising and Training Analyst at the Psychoanalytic Institute, New York University Medical Center

Part I
Countertransference Reactions

Chapter 1
The Question
of Countertransference

This book presents a comprehensive view of countertransference, a concept that in its present (though fluid) definition, denotes all those reactions of the analyst to the patient that may help or hinder treatment. Part I traces the historical evolution of the concept, from Freud's original remarks in 1910 to current views. Part II is a collection of recent papers on the theories and uses of countertransference. The third part of the book explores a number of questions surrounding the concept: Is the term *countertransference* in fact meaningful? What is the relationship between countertransference and other reactions, such as empathy? How does, and how should, countertransference operate in the actual practice of psychoanalysis? Should analysts refuse to accept as patients people they dislike? How much of the countertransference should be revealed to the patient? Does the specific nature of the countertransference cause the analyst to succeed with some patients and fail with others?

Countertransference is a vitally important psychoanalytic concept, yet until recently it was largely overlooked in the literature. This is probably because there was a general feeling that to expose one's countertransference was to expose one's weaknesses, both professional and personal. Traditionally, analysts have acknowledged its existence, but they tended to discuss it among themselves; to write about it was to invite critical assault.

This fear began to dissipate during the 1940s with the development of ego psychology, which encouraged analysts to examine all aspects of their technique, including their countertransference responses. Another crucial development occurring in the 1940s was the broadening of treatment to include narcissistic, preoedipal, borderline, and psychotic patients — patients who provoked strong feelings in their analysts and thereby almost forced the analysts to tackle the question of their responses. It is not surprising that many of the first writers to present new views of countertransference — Winnicott (1949), Heimann (1950), Little (1951), Racker (1957), Grinberg (1957, 1962) — were treating patients with very primitive ego constellations and identifications.

Freud himself rarely addressed the subject of countertransference. In the 23 volumes of his published writings, there are only a few scattered comments on the subject, comments indicating that, in general, he considered countertransference to be little more than a hindrance to the treatment process. This view dominated writings on countertransference until mid-century. Then, in 1949, the English analyst Donald W. Winnicott published his paper "Hate in the Countertransference," which was followed a year later by Paula Heimann's equally landmark work, "On Countertransference." The critical reversal in these two papers was the assertion that countertransference emanated not just from the analyst's unresolved conflicts but also *from the patient and the treatment situation*. Hence it need not be solely or even primarily a therapeutic obstacle. On the contrary, it was potentially a useful treatment tool.

During the 1950s, the ideas of the British school spread to America. Some analysts, like Annie Reich (1951), remained unconvinced and continued to reaffirm the traditional position that countertransference was predominantly a hindrance to treatment. Others, however, began to come around to the view that countertransference could help analysis. For the next three decades, these new so-called constructivists explored, in theory and practice, the presumed constructive power of the countertransference. Should analysts disclose their countertransferential reactions to their patients? If so, when, how, to what end, and with what effect on the patient? These were essentially the same issues Ferenczi (1920) had raised when he commented to Freud that the therapist has to prove to the patient through both words and actions that he cares.

Today, examination of the countertransference is still going on. The polarization that occurred in the wake of the Winnicott/Heimann revision has eased somewhat, with many theorists taking a middle position. But there are still two recognizable camps: the classicists, heirs of Reich, who are concerned with the potentially destructive effect of the countertransference, and the totalists, heirs of the constructivists, who, while acknowledging its dangers, emphasize its constructive uses.

In the context of this brief overview, it is perhaps illuminating to recall the history of the concept of transference. Originally, Freud (1910) also regarded transference as a resistance or obstacle to treatment. Yet he and his colleagues gradually came to see it as a medium not only for the patient's expression of his symptoms but also, and most importantly, for the revelation of his core conflicts. A similar destiny awaits countertransference—that is, once we analyze it, we will find that what seemed a wall is in fact a window.

Analysis of the countertransference affords us a unique means for studying the patient not as an isolated subject, but as one both acting and acted upon. For many years, psychoanalytic theory has centered on the *intra*psychic equilibria and the dynamism of the structural apparatus. Today, with a new focus on countertransference, we are also able to gain insight into the patient's *inter*psychic, or social, functions: what it is that determines the responses he evokes from others. The analyst who can tap, and move comfortably between, both these sets of dynamics is at a considerable advantage.

In addition, the countertransference has bearing on our concern with self- and object-representations, and how these coalesce in the formation of the self, the self-concept, and self-esteem. By examining the impact of the countertransference on the patient, we can see how the patient integrates such representations into that ultimate testing ground for mastery—the social self.

Thus, examination of the countertransference provides a healthy balance to the study of the individual as an exclusive, *sui generis* phenomenon—an analytic method that, however canonical, may promote an iatrogenic narcissism. Insofar as countertransference serves as an avenue for expressing and measuring the elements that have been integrated into the personality, and for testing its interpsychic functions, analysis of the countertransference allows the analyst to see the patient more realistically and encourages the patient to do the same.

Countertransference operates in varying degrees in almost every session. When we are unintimidated by its presence—that is, when we recognize and analyze it—we may find out what, in fact, it is. To what extent is the patient a truly transferential object for the analyst, as true transference relates to childhood figures? To what extent, on the other hand, does the patient represent for the analyst his own former patient–self, and the countertransference reflect unresolved transference–countertransference issues from the training analysis? When such questions are answered, we will be able to use the countertransference most constructively.

In the meantime, we must still use it. Countertransference represents, in part, a distillation of the personalities of both the analyst and the patient. For this reason alone, we must investigate it in all its aspects, including the most controversial. When we do so, we profit along with the patient.

Chapter 2
The History of the Concept

FREUD AND COUNTERTRANSFERENCE

It is ironic that Freud wrote so little on countertransference, for the case that he said launched him on his famous discoveries was filled with countertransference manifestations. For more than a year and a half in the early 1880s, Freud's friend Dr. Joseph Breuer treated for hysteria a patient he subsequently called Anna O. (She was Bertha Pappenheim, who later became one of Germany's leading volunteer social workers.) Both during and after the treatment, Breuer discussed the case with Freud in considerable and frank detail. Freud, Breuer later recalled, was "haunted" by the story, and eventually he persuaded Breuer to co-author with him a description of the case, based on Breuer's notes. The article, "On the Psychical Mechanism of Hysterical Phenomena, Preliminary Communication," was published in

1893, a decade after Breuer had stopped seeing Bertha. Two years later, in 1895, a fuller account appeared as a chapter of Breuer and Freud's book *Studies on Hysteria.*

Neither account reveals anything substantial about Breuer's feelings toward Bertha. Yet as Jones (1953), among others, has reported, those feelings were apparently strong, and Freud knew of them. For example, Breuer confided to Freud that he had not only hypnotized Bertha, but had fed her when she refused to eat. Sometimes he had also held his young patient's hand during their twice-daily sessions in the spacious old apartment on Liechtensteinstrasse, where she lived with her mother, brother, and dying father. When, during the holidays, the family moved to a rented summer house on the outskirts of the city, Breuer traveled there twice a week to see Bertha—a trip that took an hour by carriage each way. Sometimes he walked with her in the garden and conducted the session there. Breuer also told Freud how Bertha had once stood up in midsentence, run to a tree, and started to climb it. Quickly following her, Breuer caught hold of her hand. She then resumed her interrupted sentence as though nothing had happened. Later, when he hypnotized her and asked why she had run from him, she said that, having seen a large white bird trapped at the top of the tree, she had wanted to climb up and rescue it.

Prior to Breuer's treatment of Bertha, no doctor on record had ever devoted so much time or concern to the care of a hysterical patient. This fact and its implications were apparently not lost on Frau Breuer, for she asked her husband to stop seeing Bertha, and he agreed. The last session was not lacking in drama. Bertha threw herself on the bed (the indoor sessions were conducted in her bedroom) and started to thrash about, apparently in acute pain, as if giving birth. From her lips issued words intimating that Breuer was the father of her baby.

Breuer was understandably panicked. As he later remarked in both the article and the book, Bertha, in the entire year and a half of treatment, had never mentioned falling in love with a man, much less with him. In fact, he had been surprised that this attractive, charming, and passionate young woman seemed so sexually undeveloped.

Despite his horror in the face of Bertha's hallucination, the physician in Breuer took over. Recalling that hypnosis had calmed her during previous hallucinatory episodes, he tried it once again, and it worked. He then fled, never to return.

In mentioning the case to Freud, Breuer was possibly seeking the younger man's assurance that he had done all he could for his patient. Indeed, Breuer had accomplished much during the course of treatment: The paralysis in Bertha's arms and legs had disappeared, as had her headaches, persistent cough, and, until the last session, her hallucinations. She had also begun to eat again after having previously refused most food. In effecting these changes, Breuer had used hypnosis, which at that time was the treatment of choice for hysteria. Bertha herself, however, had taken the therapy one step further. After Breuer had told her, when she was under hypnosis, that she would feel better afterward—this assurance was a regular part of the procedure—the young woman had suddenly started to talk about certain painful memories and to reexperience the emotions that had originally accompanied them. Afterward, to Breuer's astonishment, Bertha's crippling symptoms vanished.

In telling Freud this, Breuer little knew that what Bertha called her "talking cure" would lead to the discovery of a direct causal relationship between repressed traumatic memories and conversion symptoms.

Breuer's sheer investment of time in Bertha, let alone the feeding and hand-holding, indicates the strength of his countertransference. (She may have reminded him of his pretty, young mother, who died when he was four.) Yet, as noted, these details of his countertransference feelings were omitted from Breuer and Freud's account of the case. Nor, apparently, did Freud realize their significance. He was certainly aware of the importance of the case. In 1909, in his famous lecture series at Clark University in Massachusetts, Freud gave Breuer and Bertha Pappenheim credit for the discovery of psychoanalysis. Yet in the explorations of the unconscious on which he embarked as a result of this case, it was the *transference* that he ultimately focused on as the critical therapeutic interaction in the treatment of neurosis. The countertransference was never dealt with—probably, as later analysts have suggested, because Freud simply could not face it.

He did, however, mention it in passing. The first reference occurs in "Future Prospects for Psycho-Analytic Therapy," from 1910:

> We have become aware of the "counter-transference" [Gegenüber-tragung] which arises in [the physician] as a result of the unconscious feelings and we are almost inclined to insist that he shall recognize this counter-transference in himself and overcome it. . . . We have noticed that no psychoanalyst goes further than his own complexes and resistances permit, and we consequently require that he shall begin his activity with a self-analysis and continually carry it deeper while he is making his own observations on his patients. Anyone who fails to produce results in a self-analysis of this kind may at once give up any idea of being able to treat patients by analysis. [pp. 141–142]

Two years later, in 1912, he described the analyst's use of his unconscious to understand the patient's unconscious:

> To put it into a formula: [the analyst] must turn his own unconscious like a receptive organ toward the transmitting unconscious of the patient. He must adjust himself to the patient as a telephone receiver is adjusted to the transmitting microphone. Just as the receiver converts back into soundwaves the electric oscillations . . . so the doctor's unconscious is able, from the derivatives of the unconscious which are communicated to him, to reconstruct the unconscious, which has determined the patient's free associations. [pp. 111–112]

This suggests the current theory of countertransference, but it stops far short of the idea that the analyst's unconscious may be a contributer as well as a receiver.

These two ideas—that the analyst's unconscious functions as a receiver of the patient's unconscious, and that anything beyond that (that is, any actual countertransference) constitutes a hindrance to treatment—dominated analytic thinking for the next 40 years. Indeed, during this time, most analysts, following Freud's lead, defined countertransference as any sign of analyst-to-patient transference that interfered with treatment. In Freud's own lifetime, such interference was generally understood to be seduction, real or symbolic. Thus when Ferenczi told Freud that he thought patients need proof that someone cared, and that, in addition to giving interpretations and helping rouse traumatic memories, he kissed his women patients, the shocked Freud advised him to give up such seductive behavior. Except for shaking hands in greeting and farewell, Freud believed in a strict hands-off policy.

COUNTERTRANSFERENCE BEFORE 1949

Most of Freud's successors, following his initiative, ignored countertransference, and those few who did comment on it — usually in passing, while writing on other subjects — almost never directly questioned the obstacle-to-treatment dictum. Yet over the years, these side excursions into the subject tended to occur more frequently, and one senses in them a growing awareness that countertransference might be more complex and, above all, more interactive than Freud had imagined.

Predictably, Ferenczi (1919) was one of the first to comment on the subject of countertransference, and in doing so he mounted the first critique of Freud's concept (1912) of analyst-as-mirror. Ferenczi warned that the effort involved in "mastering the countertransference" might prevent the analyst from giving the necessary free rein, or "free-floating attention," to his own unconscious processes, out of which arise empathic understanding of the patient. Ferenczi also pointed to what he called the *objective countertransference,* the analyst's emotional reactions to the real personality of the patient. As he put it, "the doctor . . . is always a human being," and his reactions, willy-nilly, will become part of the treatment process. This idea of the objective countertransference was later to be picked up and expanded on by many writers.

Ferenczi also recommended that as part of the therapeutic process, analysts should reveal in certain circumstances their feelings and also their mistakes to the patient — a suggestion unheard of then and still controversial today. Yet, Ferenczi added, the analyst must in general carefully control his emotions toward the patient and "correct" them when necessary, even if this means restricting the free flow of his unconscious. In this admonition we see Ferenczi circling back to Freud. At the same time, in pointing out the inevitability and importance of the analyst's feelings toward the patient and in suggesting that it might be therapeutic to reveal these feelings, he ventured far beyond Freud.

Ferenczi also went beyond Freud in his willingness to examine the origins of the countertransference. In his view, the patient, through his transference, induces certain feelings and attitudes in the analyst, some of them uncomfortable, and these countertransference conflicts are in turn picked up by the patient, causing him to pull back from the analyst. In this formulation, Ferenczi was probably the first to recognize negative countertransference and also to understand that it has as much to do with the analyst's reaction to the patient's transference as with the analyst's unresolved narcissism or oedipal conflicts. These ideas were later taken up by Winnicott (1949), Heimann (1950), and Little (1951).

Five years after Ferenczi, Stern published his paper "On the Countertransference in Psychoanalysis" (1924), the first essay actually devoted to the subject. In tracing the origins of the countertransference, Stern pointed to two elements. One was the analyst's own unresolved problems, which might cause him, when confronted by the patient's intense transference, to relinquish his therapeutic role, with possibly disastrous results. But a second and perhaps more important source, in Stern's view, was the patient's transference itself — an insight, as we have seen, that was foreshadowed by Ferenczi.

According to Stern, the analyst's ability to control the countertransference is determined by several factors. One is his own transference capacity. If this is strong — that is, if he can freely and deliberately meet the patient's transference with a transference of his own, allowing his unconscious to identify with the patient's unconscious — then he will be able to tolerate and analyze the patient's transference without undue interference from his own psychic history. The analyst's moment-by-moment, day-to-day personal fluctuations constitute a second and more prosaic determinant. During a stressful period in his life, he will have difficulty accepting and analyzing transference phenomena that he could easily handle in a calmer period. Here, and in his analysis of the sources of the countertransference, Stern is contributing to the gradual reconceptualization of countertransference as a complex, give-and-take process.

Two years after Stern, Deutsch (1926) argued that countertransference consists of far more than transference to the patient. The analyst's task, Deutsch claimed, is to receive the patient's associations, sift them through his own unconscious, and then process the relevant data intellectually. In the course of these operations, the patient's associations become an inner experience for the analyst, although at the same time he still recognizes them as belonging to the patient. This taking-in of the patient's associations is the basis for all intuition and also for intuitive empathy.

Like Stern, Deutsch sought to clarify the components of the analyst's countertransference. First, she writes, the analyst identifies emotionally with the patient's infantile ego. Then, as the patient transfers his feelings toward early objects in his life onto the analyst, the analyst identifies with these objects as well. Deutsch called this dual identification the "complementary" attitude and warned against confusing it with the analyst's conscious relationship to the patient.

Here we see Deutsch, too, inching her way toward a "constructivist" or at least preconstructivist view of the countertransference. The warnings against inappropriate use are still sounded. Yet, she maintains that as long as the analyst can shift comfortably between his identifications with the patient and his actual, conscious relationship to him, such identifications need not obstruct therapy; indeed, as we have seen, they are the source of intuition and empathy, without which therapy can hardly proceed.

Glover (1927) elaborated on Stern's idea that the patient helps to induce the analyst's countertransference reactions. Countertransference, Glover writes, may be understood in the context of stages within the analyst's psychosexual development. Therefore, by definition, it is subjective. Yet at the same time, it is a response to the patient, for the aspect of the countertransference that emerges at any given time is keyed to the patient's psychosexually fixated transference.

Glover also emphasized the distinction between counterresistance and countertransference. Counterresistance is the more mature reaction, arising from the analyst's oedipal stage, whereas countertransference originates in the earlier oral, anal, and phallic stages. In discussing these two phenomena, Glover reaffirmed Ferenczi's concept of *negative countertransferences*. These are direct reactions to the patient's negative transferences, and they often masquerade as positive feelings, such as enthusiasm or a sense of well-being.

Sharpe (1930) referred to the analyst's blind spots, noting that they can prevent him from understanding the patient's transference and its effect on him, in which case the analyst's own transference to the patient may be harmful. Whether this is happening or not can be determined from the nature of the gratification the analyst receives from the therapy. If failure does not depress him and if he is interested primarily in the patient's ultimate freedom to live a full life, then his transference to the patient can be useful. If, on the other hand, he is disturbed by failure or finds personal satisfaction in the patient's affects, then his transference may do harm. Like Deutsch, Sharpe, by isolating the ways in which countertransference can be damaging, was also identifying the ways in which it can be beneficial. Thus, with Deutsch, she moved in the direction of a bipartite view of countertransference as an objective/subjective and useful/harmful transaction—a view that is still very much alive in the analytic community today.

The next to expand on the possible benefits of countertransference was Hann-Kende (1933), who introduced the idea that, through self-analysis of countertransferences, the analyst could sublimate his libidinal and destructive tendencies toward the patient. Countertransference might then make it easier, not harder, for the analyst to cope with a patient's transference.

These tentative moves in the direction of a constructivist view were, however, still offset by warnings of danger. For example, Wilhelm Reich (1933), writing in the same year as Hann-Kende, stressed the harm that could be done by an analyst unaware of his own emotional difficulties. Reich suggested that instead of using the countertransference to understand the patient, the analyst should rely on intuitive comprehension, or *empathy*. As this recommendation indicates, Reich saw a clear distinction between countertransference and empathy. Today, we see them as inextricably linked.

Strachey's contribution (1934) to the theory of countertransference was his discussion of *mutative interpretation*, a term he coined to describe an intervention in which the patient comes to understand some aspect of the transference in terms of a current cathectic investment in his relationship with the analyst. Strachey began by noting how small a proportion of the literature was devoted to treatment methods. Analysts, he wrote, "do not seem to know much about what interpretation is or how it works." Furthermore, they are constantly being drawn away from interpretation into other, less effective interventions, such as advising, questioning, and reassuring. Or they will give interpretations that are less to the point: extratransferential, nonimmediate, inexact. By contrast, mutative interpretation goes to the heart of the transference (hence of the neurosis), and the patient responds, as the term indicates, by actually changing. Such interpretations, Strachey notes, constitute only a small part of therapy, but they are the part that most deeply affects the patient.

Strachey recognized, for the first time in the literature, the existence of *mutuality*, or the interaction between the patient and the analyst, and deemed it essential to therapeutic effectiveness. The mutative interpretation is by definition aimed at the transference, and it is only in the emotional force-field between the two participants that the cognitive insights produced by the mutative interpretation can lead to actual change. Stressing the interaction, Strachey went on to note that the mutative interpretation is critical for the analyst as well as for the patient. In giving such an interpretation, the analyst is coming perilously close to the unconscious, and he makes himself the direct target of the patient's id energy. In doing so, he puts to the test his relationship with his own unconscious impulses.

Here Strachey is hinting at the connection between interpretation as an interactional process and countertransference. (Indeed, we may ask whether mutative interpretation is possible without countertransference.) Strachey minimized the usefulness of other therapeutic procedures, such as suggestion, reassurance, and abreaction. Still, his insistence on mutative interpretations as "the ultimate operative factor" and his recognition that this technique is interwoven with the analyst's use of his own countertransference were among his most outstanding and heuristically valuable contributions, and other analysts quickly adopted them.

Low (1935) was one of the first to extend Strachey's ideas. In her view, Freud's assumption that the analyst could always recognize and then cope with the operations of his own unconscious during treatment was a fantasy—nor, she implies, would such mastery even be desirable. Instead of trying to exclude his emotional reactions from therapy, the analyst should use them in order to arrive at correct interpretations; indeed, it is primarily through such subjective operations that this can occur. In other words, the analyst's direct and free contact with his emotions leads to the very insights that cause the patient to feel understood and, consequently, to make the effort toward change.

Low also saw these emotional processes on the part of the analyst as a kind of introjection and projection that the analyst directs toward the patient's material. This notion was examined more deeply in the 1950s, especially in papers on projective identification (Racker 1953, 1957, Grinberg 1957).

Balint and Balint (1939) addressed the effect the analyst's personality and background might have on the patient's transference. They pointed out that there are many subtle ways in which the analyst gives out information about himself—for example, through his office furnishings, the way he begins and ends the session, or the frequency and style of his interpretations—and that patients quickly pick up these clues. The Balints added, however, that most of their patients simply proceeded with their own, unilateral transference, "almost undisturbed" by signs of the analyst's countertransference. The Balints thus minimized the effect of the countertransference. At the same time, their use of the word "almost" is significant—an acknowledgment of at least some slight countertransferential effect. Furthermore, in pointing out the analyst's unintentional self-revelations, the Balints added to our understanding of what constitutes countertransferential phenomena.

Fliess (1942) positioned himself between the hardliners and the revisionists. On the one hand, he reiterated the negative view of countertransference. Countertransference, he writes, occurs when the analyst repeats an infantile response, substituting the patient for his infantile object. On the other hand, Fliess anticipated current thought on countertransference by expanding on Reich's idea of the importance of empathy.

For Reich's "intuitive comprehension" Fliess substituted *trial identification*. This, he said, was similar to empathy, but whereas empathy was an emotion—that is, static and passive—trial identification was an activity: the analyst, as he listens to the patient, explores in himself states of mind akin to the patient's so that he may understand him better. Implicit in this formulation is the assumption that the analyst can distinguish, and voluntarily shuttle between, these identificatory states of mind and his objective analysis of the patient's material.

Fliess thus encouraged the analyst to consciously permit himself to use all the feelings aroused in him by the patient. Today we would say that, whatever his warnings about the dangers of countertransference, he was actually recommending its constructive use.

De Forest (1942) also advocated using countertransference in the treatment. In her view, the development of an emotional relationship between patient and analyst is inevitable. The difference between their feelings—and this is important for therapeutic success—is that the analyst, unlike the patient, understands his own reactions. He should then disclose his reactions to the patient: both the responses that arise from his own life (these feelings expose the patient to the reality situation) and the responses that he traces to the patient's resistances. Coming from Ferenczi's analysand and biographer, these recommendations have a familiar ring.

Such positive views remained, however, a minority position. The general feeling, well into the 1940s, was against the positive use of countertransference. For example, Sandor Lorand, in his book *Technique of Psychoanalytic Therapy* (1946), devoted an entire chapter to countertransference—and in the process described it in greater detail than anyone before him—but his views on the subject were almost entirely negative. Conceding that countertransference might arise as a reaction to the patient's material, he nevertheless emphasized that its ultimate source lay in the analyst's unresolved anxiety, narcissism, or emotional immaturity, and accordingly that it could play no beneficial role in treatment. As Freud had stated, it was to be analyzed out.

NEW VIEWS ON COUNTERTRANSFERENCE

With the publication of Winnicott's paper "Hate in the Countertransference" (1949), ideas about countertransference underwent a profound change. The time was ripe for revision. The analytic community was growing, new journals were proliferating, and analysts everywhere were subjecting past theory and technique to critical review. Freud himself did not escape such scrutiny. For example, some writers began to ask, contrary to Freud, whether psychoanalysis could help or even "cure" psychosis, and whether to attempt such treatment. Hence, a number of psychotics and borderline personalities were taken into therapy—a development that led to a serious exploration of the boundaries of technique, including countertransference.

Winnicott's stated goal in his paper was to examine the countertransference aspects of working with psychotics and antisocial personalities. He begins by acknowledging the subjective and idiosyncratic components of the countertransference. He then makes a sharp distinction between such feelings and what Ferenczi (1919) called the *objective countertransference*, or "the analyst's love and hate in response to the actual personality and behavior of the patient." In the analysis of psychotics and antisocial personalities, such objective reactions may be very powerful, and the therapist must be able to sort them out, study them, and keep them stored for use in interpretation. Above all, he must not deny them. In Winnicott's view, the analyst's main task is to maintain objectivity in respect to all the material presented by the patient; to feel hate, when it has been provoked, is part of that objectivity. Indeed, Winnicott claims, in certain stages of treatment the patient may actually seek the analyst's hate, and if he does, he must be allowed to reach it.

Winnicott relates this situation to the normal mother–child interaction. A mother, he says, must be able to hate her child, and this hate is objective, for the infant often misuses and fails to appreciate her. Indeed, it is the absence of such hate that undermines the typical child adoption situation. A child without parents is always unconsciously looking for them, and in doing so, he is looking for someone to hate him as well as to love him. But in the typical, "sentimental" adoption situation, the guardians can tolerate in themselves only loving feelings toward the child. Hence, by a seeming paradox, the child cannot feel loved by them, for in order to feel loved he must feel that he can be hated as well.

The same rule applies to the analytic situation. Like the

orphaned child, the patient seeks and must be able to reach objective hate; otherwise, he feels he cannot reach objective love. He also needs the analyst's hate in order to tolerate his own, and to overcome his resistances to maturation. In Winnicott's paper these observations were limited to the treatment of psychotics and antisocials, but many analysts have since found them applicable in some measure to all patients.

Among Winnicott's main contributions was his rejection of Freud's vision of the analyst as a mirror. In its place he submitted another ideal, that of the analyst who, existing as a person in his own right, *reacts* to the patient and, albeit aware of the counter-transferential nature of these reactions, uses them therapeutically. In other words, whereas Freud denied the existence of strong feelings in the analyst, Winnicott said that all analysts had them, were entitled to have them, and should make them part of the treatment process. Previous writers, as we have seen, had adumbrated this position. Winnicott stated it unequivocally and thereby made a radical break with all former theory of countertransference.

The next breakthrough came the same year when Paula Heimann read her paper "On Countertransference" at the 16th International Psychoanalytic Conference in Zurich. Heimann's ideas on the nature of countertransference were revolutionary. First, reasoning that the prefix *counter* implies additional elements, she broadened the definition of countertransference to mean not just the analyst's transferences but *all* his feelings toward the patient, including elicited reactions, which in Heimann's view, as in Winnicott's, constituted the most significant part of the countertransferential response.

Second, Heimann reappraised the value of the countertransference in the treatment situation. Taking on Freud directly, Heimann argued that his demand that the analyst always recognize and master countertransferential feelings not only suggested that the countertransference was bad—something the analyst must defend himself against—but also implied that the ideal treatment posture was one of relative detachment. On the contrary, Heimann argued, countertransference is both inevitable and desirable, for—and this is the crux of Heimann's contribution—it can serve as "an instrument of research into the patient's uncon-

scious." Since the countertransference is in large measure elicited
by the patient, it can be seen as his creation; it is "a part of the
patient's personality." Thus understood, the countertransference
becomes an aid not for understanding the analyst, but for
understanding the patient. Indeed, Heimann argued, if the analyst
does not consult the countertransference, his interpretations will
be incomplete and possibly insensitive.

In one respect Heimann took a conservative position: She
advised against disclosing countertransferential reactions to the
patient. Otherwise her approach was totally revisionist. Not just
Freud's, she asserted, but all previous views of countertransference were incomplete. What was needed was an intense investigation of countertransference as a sensor of the patient's psychic
processes. Such research, she believed, would ultimately reveal
how the nature of the countertransference at any given moment
corresponded to specific unconscious impulses and defenses operating at that moment in the patient's mind.

Heimann's paper differed from Winnicott's in its emphases. He
was concerned with psychotics and antisocials; she, with all
patients. He took on the special problem of hate; she was
concerned with the entire range of countertransferential feelings.
He was a discloser; she was not. He was more interested in the
countertransference as a facet of the patient–analyst relationship;
she, in the countertransference as a reading of the patient's
unconscious. But both insisted on the objective, elicited nature of
the countertransference and, consequently, on the absolute necessity of employing it in treatment, rather than screening it out. As
we shall see, these assertions had a decisive effect. As long as
countertransference was viewed as a sign of pathology or an
interference to treatment, there was little motivation to study it.
Now, with Winnicott and Heimann, the door was opened to a
serious investigation of the subject. The "constructivist" position,
although by no means uncontested, had been established.

In her book *Principles of Intensive Psychotherapy,* Frieda
Fromm-Reichmann (1950), who worked almost exclusively with
psychotics, cautiously endorsed the new view. She pointed out that
the psychotic's verbalizations, behavior, and transference arouse
in the analyst a strong countertransferential emotion, principally
anxiety. Consequently, the analyst's investigation of the counter-

transference should constitute a critical part of all work with psychotics. Taking her cue from Heimann, Fromm-Reichmann advised against burdening the patient with disclosures of counter-transferential feelings. The analyst should, however, recognize and accept these feelings as part of his own humanness. In the same way that the patient's transference/parapraxic processes derive from his relationship with significant others throughout his past life, so does the analyst bring to the treatment his total being, his "past-in-present." Only to the extent that he remains aware of this, through continued self-analysis, will he function effectively.

Influenced by Winnicott and Heimann, Little (1951) elaborated on the Balints' remarks (1939) about the analyst's influence on the patient's transference. The Balints, it will be recalled, noted only a small effect on their own patients. In contrast, Little found that patients are significantly influenced by the analyst's countertrans-ference.

Little's chief contribution was her exploration of the interac-tional aspect of the countertransference. The unconscious, she noted, is the repository of both normal and pathological elements. In the same way that not all our conscious processes are "normal," not all repression is pathological. The entire patient–analyst relationship is a mix of normal and pathological, transference and countertransference, with specific conflictual characteristics of the individual patient and the individual analyst thrown in. Thus, just as every transference is different from any other, so every countertransference is different from any other. Moreover, the countertransference, like the transference, changes as the two participants and the external environment change.

What is it in the treatment, Little asked, that pushes the patient toward wellness? The decisive factor is the combined id urges of the two participants. This meshing in turn depends on the analyst's ability to achieve "a special kind of identification" with the patient (a phenomenon that might also be called empathy). But this identification has its complications. Both consciously and uncon-sciously, the analyst wants the patient to get well and identifies with him in his desire to do so; that is, the analyst identifies with the patient's ego. At the same time, the analyst also unconsciously identifies with the patient's superego and id in their prohibitions against getting better. He may thus unwittingly exploit a patient's sickness for his own libidinal and aggressive purposes. These countertransference cues will be quickly picked up by the patient, to the detriment of therapy.

A related countertransferential hindrance has to do with the analyst's reparative need. After a patient has been in treatment for some time, he usually becomes the analyst's love object, one to whom the analyst wishes to make reparations. But when partially repressed, these reparative impulses can be subject to the repetition compulsion. The analyst, in other words, may want to make the patient well again and again, which means making him ill again and again in order to have something to make well. In consequence, treatment will suffer.

Little went further than any of her predecessors (with the exception of Ferenczi and De Forest) in advising that the analyst occasionally admit to mistakes. Such openness, she believed, would increase the patient's confidence in the analyst's honesty and good will. But she, too, counseled moderation; rather than unloading "confessions" on the susceptible patient, it might be sufficient simply to mention to him the analyst's need to scrutinize his own countertransferential reactions. What is important is that both analyst and patient recognize that these reactions exist.

Little developed some of these ideas in a later paper in 1957. Again she was concerned with the components of a successful analysis and with the role of the analyst's feelings therein. She concluded that success, at least for the analyst, depended on how well the analyst could cope, both inside and outside the treatment, with his own paranoid anxieties—anxieties inseparable from his work—and with his own depression.

To Little, then, analysis is, above all, an interaction. Consequently, the position of the analyst is changed. No longer is he the Freudian mirror, reflecting the patient's problems. On the contrary, the patient holds the mirror up to the analyst, and the analyst sees in it his own subjective self. Evicted from his safe position, the analyst now has the burden of coping with his own paranoid and depressive feelings, of recognizing his mistakes and even, at times, admitting to them. This new formulation—the interactional view of treatment and the consequent dethronement of the analyst—had a profound influence on later writers.

Not everyone was convinced, however. Annie Reich (1951), for example, swiftly came to the defense of the traditional view, stating emphatically that countertransference was *not* a therapeutic tool: It could not be used as a means either for understanding the patient or for communicating with him. Small wonder, then, that Reich warned her colleagues away from Little's recommendations regarding disclosure. However grounded in basic analytic thought, revelations of countertransferential feelings did not fall within the boundaries of analytic technique. To indulge in them would mean foregoing any attempt to understand the interaction of the psychic structures and the operation of the defenses—any attempt, in other words, to analyze and correct ego pathology. Instead, the analyst would be trying to work directly with the id, thereby disregarding Freud's most important formulation regarding the aim of analysis: "Where id was, there shall ego be."

Reich was not simply against revealing countertransference. Like Freud, she believed that countertransference reflected the analyst's permanent neurotic problems and thus could seriously obstruct treatment. She cited the example of an analyst who tended to fall in love with young and attractive female patients. His second analysis revealed that he was not really interested in these women; rather, he wanted to identify with them and thus be made love to by the analyst—a gratification of homosexual transference fantasies that had remained unexplored in his first analysis. Other examples of countertransferential interference pointed up by Reich were unconscious aggression, which could cause the analyst to be overconciliatory, and unconscious guilt, which could be expressed as boredom or overeagerness.

Despite these reservations, Reich acknowledged that countertransference was necessary if analysis was to work. Without it, the analyst would lack the ability and the interest to treat the patient. But, she insisted, it had to remain in the background, existing only as traces within the analyst of "the original unconscious meaning of analyzing."

Reich's remarks constituted a restatement of the claims of ego psychology—of psychoanalysis as analysis of defense—and an effort to ward off the seductive, regressive pull of id psychology. After Reich, the battlelines were drawn. While some contributors still tried to stake out a middle ground, most aligned themselves either with traditionalists such as Reich or with the newly established "constructivist" position forged by Winnicott, Heimann, and Little.

Gitelson (1952) responded to Little's cues and focused on the analyst, differentiating three elements in his response to the patient. The first—not to be considered transference—consists of the analyst's intellectually sublimated curiosity, his capacity for empathy, and his wish to be helpful. The second element, which should be classified as the analyst's transference, consists of his entire range of reactions to that particular patient and, as such, includes residual neurotic conflicts. In general, these two types of response are already in operation at the start of treatment. In contrast, the analyst's third set of responses, his actual counter-transference, arises only later, within an established treatment situation. This countertransference consists of the analyst's reactions to the patient's transference, to the material the patient brings in, and to the patient's response to him as a person. In view of the patient's extreme sensitivity to these countertransference reactions, Gitelson felt that acknowledging and discussing them might be advisable.

Ten years later, Gitelson (1962) appeared to become more conservative in his views on countertransference. Therapy, he wrote, can influence only the ego. Therefore, interpretation of defense is the prime treatment tool; countertransference, though invaluable, should be used solely in a supportive manner. This change in Gitelson's position reflects the problems analysts encountered as they began to study countertransferential phenomena. In the first flush of discovery, the elements of the counter-transference and the ways in which it should be used seemed obvious, undeniable. Later, after closer investigation, these matters became less clear, and the writers, consequently, more cautious.

Picking up where Gitelson left off in his earlier paper, Benedek (1953) maintained that the patient intuitively understands the analyst's feelings. If the analyst is also able to understand them, he can use them to further the therapy; if not, they will hinder treatment. For Benedek, these considerations elevated the analyst's personality to a position as the critical element in the treatment process—the element that would make or break the analysis.

In a paper of the same year, Racker (1953), shifting the

emphasis slightly, attempted to focus on the countertransference process itself as well as on the analyst's personality. Having trained with Klein and Winnicott, among others, Racker wanted to look at countertransference operations differently. Since countertransference was induced, for the most part, by the patient's transference, personality, and behavior, it presumably should lead the analyst to vital information about the patient. How, then, did it happen, as so many claimed, that the countertransference interfered with treatment? The answer, Racker believed, was insensitivity on the part of the analyst.

An essentially psychotherapeutic striving is innate in everyone, he writes, and this striving can be seen, albeit in repressed form, in every patient. Failure on the part of the analyst to recognize these feelings in the patient accounts for the patient's unconscious resistance to treatment more than anything else in the treatment situation. The analyst must acknowledge their existence, regardless of any departure from classical theory and technique. Here Racker positions himself directly opposite traditionalists such as Reich.

Subsequently, Racker (1957) turned his attention to additional countertransference difficulties, stemming, he claimed, from the training analysis. What he was interested in were the defenses that caused analysts to avoid writing on countertransference and, even more importantly, prevented them from recognizing its manifestations during treatment. He attributed these failures to analysts' rejection of their own countertransference, a rejection traceable to unresolved struggles with primitive anxiety and guilt.

These struggles, Racker argued, originate in infantile ideals that have not been adequately explored in the training analysis. To function effectively, an analyst must lay aside such ideals and accept the fact that he is still a child and a neurotic as well as an adult and an analyst. When he does so, he will be able to overcome regressive tendencies toward splitting and projection. Consequently, when his patients, in ridding themselves of a toxic introject or some unwanted part of themselves, identify him with the split-off part of their personality, he will be able to overcome the temptation to engage in counterprojective processes (*lex Talionis*, an eye for an eye). This will leave him free to analyze the transference-countertransference content and to formulate an interpretation.

Racker's recognition of the dangers of refusing to acknowledge the patient's striving for health represents a brilliant insight into the countertransference process, as does his discussion of how grandiose ideals, having escaped the training analysis, can cause the analyst to retaliate against patients who injure his narcissism. With both of these observations, Racker once again raised the problem of the analyst's conflicts, just as, in assuming the universality both of the Talion principle and of projective identification, he linked the analyst's unconscious processes with that of the patient's. Racker's insights were part of a trend during the 1950s and 1960s of analysts using countertransference as a way of closing the gap between themselves and their patients.

THE SHIFT TO AN INTERACTIONAL APPROACH

Tower (1956) was one of the first American analysts to offer an extended description of the intensely interactional nature of the countertransference. Countertransference, Tower claimed, must be distinguished from the analyst's habitual characterological attitudes, as well as from defects in his perception or experience. True countertransference, like transference, is an unconscious process based on the repetition compulsion (Little 1951) and stemming from critical experiences with significant persons in the past — most especially from childhood.

Tower argued that some form of countertransference, even a neurosis, develops in every analysis, as the counterpart to the transference neurosis. The two processes run parallel to each other and are interdependent, for the patient's resolution of the transference depends significantly on the analyst's resolution of his own countertransference syndrome.

In Tower's view, there is no longer the question of "analyzing out" the countertransference. It is intrinsic to the analysis, part of the combined unconscious work of analyst and patient. Tower suggested that at its deepest level the analytic situation probably follows the prototype of the mother–child symbiosis described by Benedek (1953), characterized by active libidinal exchanges between patient and analyst through unconscious, nonverbal communication. Thus the patient *does* affect the analyst, and profoundly. In the successful analysis, the patient not only bares his own worst impulses but probably tries to make the analyst do the same, partially in order to test the analyst and partially to unmask him as a fallible human being. Tower strongly recommended that analysts recognize this interchange and study their role in it. By doing so, they would learn to separate the defensive and acting-out elements of the countertransference from the constructive ones and thereby establish a scientific base for evaluating technique.

Tower thus picked up Winnicott's (1949), Heimann's (1950), and Little's (1951) suggestions regarding the therapist's humanness and expanded them into a more radical formulation. In her view, the analyst's vulnerability becomes a central element, and analysis becomes a dual process, with the patient and the analyst regressing together and doing their most important work on an unconscious level.

Money-Kyrle (1956) also saw the analytic process as a fluid interaction between patient and analyst. Through the patient's verbal and nonverbal communications, the analyst absorbs the patient's mind state and sees it as an expression of his own unconscious fantasies, which he then projects onto the patient by forming an interpretation. This process is kept going as long as the analyst repeatedly recognizes the connection between the emotions he has absorbed and his own unconscious fantasies. By the same token, it is halted as soon as he fails to recognize this interplay.

Thus, in Money-Kyrle's view, the countertransference is not the effect of repressed or dissociated elements of the analyst's character; rather, it is his inevitable and normal response to the patient's presentation. Its sympathetic nature is based on the analyst's concern for the patient, which in turn arises out of his need for reparation and his natural tendency to see the patient as "the child in himself." These observations, based on Racker (1953), added little to the theory of countertransference, but Money-Kyrle was able to substantiate Racker's observations with extensive clinical data. He also anticipated Kernberg's observations (1965) on the therapeutic role of the analyst's "concern" for the patient.

The following year, Grinberg (1957), adapting Klein's concept (1946) of projective identification, coined the term *projective counteridentification* to refer to that aspect of countertransference that is based on the unconscious interaction between patient and analyst. The intensity and pathological character of the patient's projective identifications vis-à-vis the analyst cause the analyst to react, in turn, with projective counteridentification. That is, the patient, through his projections, induces different roles, affects, and fantasies in the analyst, who then unconsciously and passively plays and experiences them.

In a later paper, Grinberg (1962) elaborated on the subject of projective identification as it operated in analysis. Projective identification, he writes, consists of the omnipotent fantasy that undesirable parts of one's personality or of internal objects can be split off and projected onto an external object, and then controlled in that object. Under normal conditions, projective identification determines the person's empathic relationship with the object, not only because it allows him to put himself in the place of the other — and thereby to better understand the other's feelings — but also because of what it brings out in each of them. The process is reciprocal. The projector's attitude, the way he looks at the object, how he speaks, what he says, his gestures, allow the object to read the content of the projection, respond to it emotionally, and counter with projective identifications of his own. The result is an emotional interchange.

In treatment, the analyst's response to the patient's projective identifications will depend on his degree of tolerance. One possible scenario is for him to make himself the "active" subject of the patient's projections, in which case his response will follow three steps. First, he will selectively introject the different aspects of the patient's verbal and nonverbal material, with their corresponding emotional charges. Then, he will work through and assimilate the identifications of the patient's inner world. Finally, he will project the results of this assimilation through interpretation.

Alternatively, the analyst may make himself the "passive object" of the patient's projections and introjections, in which case one of two things will happen. Either the patient's conflicting material will reactivate or intensify the analyst's own conflicts and anxieties, thereby informing his response, or his response may be independent of his own emotions, appearing as a direct reaction to the projections themselves.

Elaborating on the theme of the dual analysis (Tower 1956), Searles (1958) described the nature — and possible danger — of the patient's therapeutic efforts vis-à-vis the analyst. Just as the analyst discovers the patient, so, too, Searles observes, does the patient discover the analyst, and a good deal of what he discovers is true: "There is an element of reality in all the patient's distorted transference-perceptions of the analyst," Searles writes. And once he begins to understand some of the analyst's unconscious conflicts, the patient will often try, unconsciously, to act as the analyst's analyst (Searles 1975). In itself, there is nothing wrong with this striving to "cure" the analyst. On the contrary, it is based on the mother–infant symbiosis that in normal development — and in analysis — is the foundation for later individuation. But as Searles notes, an unhealthy mother–child relationship can result in the child's never being released from the symbiosis, in which case he never truly becomes an individual. Instead he becomes a "symbiotic therapist, whose own ego-wholeness is sacrificed throughout life . . . to complementing the ego-incompleteness of the mothering person." By the same token, analysis can be undermined if the patient is not released from his symbiosis with the analyst.

Searles coined the term *therapeutic symbiosis* to describe both the ambivalent and preambivalent types of symbiosis in the patient–therapist relationship. Both, he claimed, were traceable to the very early mother–child relationship, before enough hate had accumulated to disrupt their oneness and establish a pervasive ambivalence.

In making explicit Tower's implicit notion of dual analysis and in exploring this process, Searles was the first to see how the analyst's failure to recognize the countertransference could, like a mother's poor relationship to her child, stunt the patient's (child's) development into a separate individual. In his discussion of the patient–therapist and mother–child symbiosis, Searles anticipated some of Mahler's later work (1963) on separation–individuation.

In keeping with the gradual shift toward a constructivist point of view, Karl Menninger (1958) in his book *Theory of Psychoanalytic Technique*, declared that countertransference was "dangerous only when it is forgotten about." Menninger distinguished between the countertransference that arose in the analyst's work in general and that which occurred only with specific patients. He believed that when recognized by the analyst and not resisted, patient-specific countertransference reactions were of value in understanding the patient's transference. When unrecognized, however, they could cause the analyst to behave in ways that would ultimately undermine the analysis.

During the 1960s and 1970s, a number of analysts attempted to take into account what they saw as the bipartite nature of the treatment situation. Specifically, they tried to balance the realistic, or objective, aspect of the therapeutic relationship (and of the analyst's feelings) with its more unconscious, interactive quality and to examine how each of these elements influenced the countertransference. Spotnitz (1963), for example, reported that in treating severely disturbed schizophrenic patients, he had made extensive use of the "objective countertransference" (Ferenczi 1919). It induced feelings that helped the analyst understand the patient and enabled the analyst to make emotionally charged interventions that could resolve the patient's resistances to mature communication and functioning as well as immunize the patient against repeating self-defeating patterns of behavior. Using this technique, Spotnitz was one of the first to demonstrate clinically the validity of Ferenczi's ideas about countertransference.

Kernberg (1965) stressed the vital need for the analyst to possess a "capacity for concern." This capacity does not simply enable him to recognize the patient's destructive and self-destructive impulses; it empowers him to identify, to neutralize, and thereby to resolve aggressive and self-aggressive conflicts in the countertransference.

Kernberg's notion of concern, as he explains it, is broader than the traditional concept of empathy. Whereas empathy designates mainly the ability to feel what the patient feels at any given moment, "concern" goes beyond that, involving an overall, ongoing regard for the patient's welfare. Such concern, in Kernberg's view, is present in any successful analyst, and it must exist as a protection against countertransference-based regression in the analyst. This "totalistic," or interactional, view of analysis was expanded by Kernberg in many subsequent writings on the treatment of borderline and narcissistic patients.

Bleger's contribution (1967) to the theory of countertransference developed from his discussion of what he called the therapeutic *frame*. The psychoanalytic situation, he writes, involves two components: a process that the analyst studies and interprets, and a frame, or nonprocess, made up of constants within the boundaries in which the process occurs. On the analyst's side, the frame consists both of his own personal style (for example, how he speaks, when he pauses, how he sits and moves), and of the therapeutic setting (the lighting in the office, the noises on the street, the presence or absence of a secretary or maid). By dint of being habitually reencountered and therefore taken for granted, this frame seems to be nonexistent or at least unimportant. It is only when the frame is altered that its importance is revealed, for any such alteration can force a crisis in the patient's nonego.

The reason for this upheaval is that the external frame corresponds to the patient's internal frame, his most regressive, most psychotic part, "his primitive fusion with the mother's body." Therapeutic change cannot occur unless this internal frame is analyzed, but in order for this to happen, it is critical that the analyst's frame remain stable. It "should be neither ambiguous, nor changeable, nor altered," Bleger writes, for only within the stability of the analyst's frame can the patient reestablish contact with his own frame (the original symbiosis) in order to change it.

Here we see Searles' concept (1958) of the therapeutic symbiosis being expanded to take into account those extra-analytic countertransference factors first noted by the Balints (1939). In Bleger's insistence on the importance of these factors, there lies an indication of the increasing weight now being given to countertransference.

Greenson (1971), elaborating on a theme that surfaces repeatedly in the history of countertransference theory, pointed out that the analytic relationship cannot be viewed solely in terms of transference and distortion. There is a genuine, realistic, nonfantasy relationship between patient and analyst, and this relationship is critical to the resolution of the transference neurosis, for interpretation alone will not resolve it. Greenson's paper does not deal directly with countertransference, yet his notion of the real relationship between patient and analyst does bear indirectly on the subject. A relationship such as Greenson describes involves numerous opportunities for the analyst to have less than neutral, objective reactions—in other words, to have countertransference reactions—to the patient. Greenson's emphasis on the therapeutic role of this relationship is thus a tacit vote for the constructive use of countertransference.

Feiner (1977), in what he called an "ultimate extension" of Freud's ideas on self-analysis, writes that "the key to the analysis of the patient resides in the analysis of the analyst, during the analysis," and that in this process the analyst should partially dispense with the traditional requirement of differentiating what is usable from what is not. In truth, Feiner writes, the usable, or "normal," elements in the analyst's character structure are inextricably interwoven with the unusable, or "neurotic," elements. Furthermore, "neurotic" feelings, such as anxiety, can also further analysis if they are recognized and mastered. What is essential is the self-analysis, and if that involves countertransference reactions, they, too, can be understood and then used to understand the patient.

In a 1978 paper, Langs returned to the subject of the frame (Bleger 1967). Proceeding according to an emphatically interactional view, Langs claimed that the countertransference could not be discussed in isolation, as a fact about the analyst, but only within a bipersonal field. The analyst, he writes, performs three major functions in regard to the patient: (1) he manages the framework and holds the patient, (2) he contains and metabolizes projective identifications, and (3) he interprets the patient's symbolic associations, projective identifications, and his attempts to destroy meaning.

All these functions are subject to influence by the analyst's unconscious countertransference fantasies. Under the third function, for example, missed interventions and inappropriate silences may be a function of the countertransference. But according to Langs, it is the first function that is the most neglected in the arena of countertransference expression. Because most analysts themselves have been analyzed within a bipersonal field whose framework has been modified (that is, by the intrusion of the requirements and mechanisms of the institute), it is in the management of the framework that they are most likely to ignore their countertransference operations. They will readily monitor their verbal interventions for countertransference-based distortion, but they forget the more subtle, seemingly extra-analytic aspects of their behavior that constitute the frame.

To maintain a secure framework, the analyst must be able to tolerate the patient's regression and related primitive communications, to renounce his own countertransferential needs for gratification, and be able to accept and manage his own (albeit limited) regression and anxiety, which are inevitable in the treatment situation. Security in these areas will enable him to adhere to the ground rules that constitute the frame. According to Langs, these include having an office separate from his home, always starting and ending a session on time, never taking notes or answering the telephone during a session, never eating in the patient's presence, and keeping his private life entirely private. When the analyst breaks any of these rules, he is demonstrating countertransference. And the more often he breaks them, the more difficulty he will have in understanding his reasons for doing so and hence in conducting a successful analysis.

Langs speculates that negligence in maintaining the frame may be related to anxieties on the part of the analyst regarding the patient's hold on him. For some analysts, the patient's hold generates an unconscious threat. Whatever the perceived danger — it may be related to fears of intimacy, or of seduction or aggression, or it may be a dread of the necessary therapeutic regression — these analysts will defend themselves by unconsciously attempting to disturb the patient's holding capacities. Countertransferential barriers are thus placed between the analyst and the patient, and the latter is denied the gratification that, together with insight and positive introjective identifications, he requires in order to achieve adaptive structural change.

As in Bleger (1967), Langs' main point is that the frame must remain fixed and undisturbed. However, whereas Bleger's emphasis was on the primitive analogues to the frame in the patient's unconscious, Lang stresses the analyst's unconscious, the various countertransference reactions that could cause him to disrupt the frame and thus block the patient's progress.

Issacharoff and Hunt (1978) introduced the term "beyond countertransference" to refer to the shared experience and understanding that constitute the therapeutic relationship. The purpose of the term, according to the authors, is to go beyond a model that divides the patient/subject from the analyst/observer-reactor, and transference from something "counter" to it, and instead to posit a truly unitary model.

Issacharoff and Hunt cite the example of a young man who was in both individual and group therapy. After the group had lost several members, the young man asked the leader whether it would be discontinued. The leader asked what prompted this question, and the young man replied that during a recent session in individual therapy, his analyst had suggested that at the age of 2 he had been psychologically abandoned by his parents. The analyst's statement, he said, had profoundly impressed him. He described it as a Rosetta Stone, for it suddenly allowed him to understand many events in his life, including, at the moment, his response to the loss of members in the group.

This breakthrough, the authors suggest, was the result of the analyst's ability to truly share the patient's inner experience in a manner "beyond countertransference." The patient had brought into treatment a lifetime of fragmented experiences of abandonment and isolation, along with fragile defenses constructed to ward off the pain of the original loss. What enabled the analyst to get past the defenses and reconstruct the infantile loss was her (the analyst's) recognition, inside herself, of a shared experience. Recognizing it, she could articulate it by saying to him (the patient) that his parents abandoned him when he was 2 years old. She was not just identifying the critical trauma, but communicating to him her shared experience of it. At that moment she was, in effect, inside him, saying, "I know what happened to you. I recognize it, I am with you." In consequence, she was able to create a new reality involving both of them, and a new locus of control. Previously, his terror over the original trauma had caused him to fragment his experiences. Now, armed with this new truth, he could organize his experiences around it and thus bring them into perspective.

The analyst who wishes to operate "beyond countertransference" is, however, faced with a difficult task. He must grope in darkness for the patient's deep structure, overwhelmed with data and, unsure of what is fundamental and what is epiphenomenal, trying to comprehend the inner workings of the system. Furthermore, he must deal with the awareness that his own personality is influencing the way he visualizes that structure.

The analyst's personality, as Issacharoff and Hunt see it, is an important agent and the basis of his empathy. It is through his empathy—the recognition that he and the patient share some parts of their selves—that the analyst sets in motion the interpersonal event whereby his and the patient's historical truths validate each other and create a new truth, one that integrates the therapist's will to be helpful with the patient's will to get well (Racker 1953). At the same time, the analyst must make careful use of his personality. Empathy, as the authors see it, operates via what Racker (1957) called "concordant identifications": The analyst allows the patient to create in him the patient's various emotions, attitudes, wishes, and fears. But having taken in these fragments from the patient, the analyst must not just experience them but understand what they reveal about the patient and then give them back to the patient for reintegration. In other words, he must analyze the countertransference.

These cautions notwithstanding, Issacharoff and Hunt's "beyond countertransference" model is still a radically interactionist view. The patient's "new truth" can only come through the sympathetic reactivation of the analyst's own history in response to the patient's. Hence the analyst, as a person, is deeply involved in the patient's gradual reintegration, and he, too, is changed by the experience.

Returning to the subject of psychotic patients, Giovacchini (1979), like others before him, noted that many analysts experience extreme discomfort in dealing with psychotics, who are adept at stimulating disruptive impulses in the analyst. Such feelings may be so threatening that the analyst will erect rigid defenses against them. For example, he may convince himself that such patients are psychoanalytically untreatable. In some cases this conclusion is probably correct, although even in those cases the conclusion may be based not so much on a rational assessment as on irrational countertransference reactions.

To prevent this from happening, Giovacchini advises, analysts should try to learn all they can about their countertransference responses. The higher state of ego integration they will then achieve should enable them to be more effective with a broader range of patients. For along with those psychotics who *are* psychoanalytically untreatable, there are probably many who could be helped by analysis and who, by virtue of the strong reactions they provoke, could help analysts to confront and deal with their own "sensitivities." Giovacchini offers a hypothetical case. An analyst takes on an "untreatable" schizophrenic. The situation changes during the therapy when, through his provocations, the patient helps reveal to the analyst his countertransference. In doing this, he teaches the analyst how to treat him. As Giovacchini puts it, "we treat the untreatable in order to receive treatment ourselves." Through this interaction, the analyst learns more about the earliest developmental phases in everyone and thereby decreases the number of items on his list of conditions that seem to contraindicate analysis. He may also, as Giovacchini implies, master belated conflicts that have escaped the training analysis.

As we have seen, the history of the concept of countertransference is closely and necessarily linked with the widening scope of treatment. Building on the work of others in treating psychotics, particularly Searles (1958), Giovacchini contributed to the reciprocal process whereby experience in treating severely disturbed patients has advanced our understanding of countertransference while our increased understanding of countertransference has in turn enabled us to accept more patients of this kind. If only for the furtherance of this latter goal, the gradual integration of countertransference into psychoanalytic method over the past few decades may be viewed as a hopeful development; these patients, as Giovacchini notes, "have, for the most part, known only suffering and misery," and there are, as yet, no other effective treatments for them.

In the same year as Giovacchini's paper, McDougall (1979) called attention to the unique value of the countertransference in treating psychotic patients. When the critical trauma in a patient's life has occurred before the child can communicate verbally, its nature is very difficult for the therapist to detect and may in fact be accessible only through the countertransference. In this very early period of the child's life, he sees the mother as a subsidiary part of himself. Severe trauma in this period will perpetuate the delusion, and this is what has happened in the case of the psychotic. The patient, McDougall writes, remains "outside himself" in analysis as in everyday life, and he therefore treats others, or the analyst, as vagrant segments of himself, which he naturally attempts to control.

This evokes in the analyst a countertransference very different from that which typically occurs in the treatment of neurotics. For the neurotic, the analyst becomes a target for the projection of his inner objects, and within these projections the analyst can read the patient's conflicts. But with the psychotic, who is treating the analyst as a split-off part of himself, such messages are much harder to hear. Indeed, at first the analyst may feel that he is not hearing anything beyond a discharge of tension. He is like the mother who is trying to discover the reason for her baby's crying. Because the baby, at this early age, has little identity beyond what he represents to her, the mother must interpret his cries and assign them meaning—that is, convert them into communication. Similarly, the analyst must try to decode the signs of distress that underlie the psychotic's angry or confused communications. If he succeeds, he has a chance to lead the patient to discover, as the mother does with her baby, who he is.

But in order for this to happen, the analyst must be very sensitive to the countertransference. In the first stages of treatment with a psychotic patient, the analyst will often feel severe doubts about his professional abilities, as well he might in the face of the patient who seems to make no progress and who responds to his efforts to understand as if they were hostile onslaughts. These countertransference feelings—self-doubt and accompanying resentment—can create in the analyst an "inbuilt resistance," making it hard for him to hear what the patient is communicating. The countertransference, then, is not just a key to understanding the psychotic, but a grave potential source of refusal to understand. Hence it has unique importance in this treatment situation.

In working with psychotics, McDougall says, the analyst should be wary of using the technique of expectant silence. Whereas for the neurotic such silence may spell hope, for the psychotic it is more likely to mean desolation. What the psychotic needs, above all, is to feel that others perceive him and that he is, therefore, really alive. Silence, then, is precisely what he doesn't need. McDougall also claims that transference interpretations are out of place with psychotics because they are likely to continue the pattern of mutual misunderstanding and distortion set up in the first mother–child communications. Like the expectant silence, the transference interpretation, instead of opening up a space for the emergence of long-buried feelings, may open up a void—"the silence of the primal unconscious, psychic death, nothingness." This is not to imply that the psychotic's primal repression has stifled his feelings altogether. His feelings are alive, and being expressed, in the form of "action–communication," or language as act. It is the analyst's job to help the patient convert these action-symptoms into language. If he can do so, the patient may be able to undergo a true analytic process.

In a recent paper, Schafer (1985) argued that the analyst should recognize that the patient's interpretations of events may be plausible to varying degrees. Citing the theories of Gill (1979), Schafer reiterates Gill's assertion that when conventional Freudians use the concept of distortion, they are making themselves privileged authorities on the nature of reality. As a sign of respect for the patient's reality testing, Gill recommended that the analyst adopt a pluralistic view of reality. He would then be pushed into confronting his many countertransferential contributions to the treatment relationship—in other words, his own distortions of reality.

Agreeing with Gill, Schafer suggests that analytic authoritarianism may derive in part from fears about identifying with the patient. In an earlier paper (1959), he described how the analyst constructs an internal image of the patient that grows more complex with more knowledge. Eventually, the image becomes a substructure within the analyst's ego—one that he can draw upon each time the patient stimulates him. The incorporation of this image signifies that the analyst has effected an identification with the patient. As Schafer points out in his recent paper, however, such identification may pose an unconscious threat to the analyst and he will defend himself by making himself an authority on the nature of reality, thereby setting himself against the patient. Schafer does not actually recommend an abdication of authority. Analysis, he writes, must still focus on the patient's resistance and repression. At the same time, analysts are obliged to make themselves more aware of how their own countertransference is helping to form the "reality" that they hold up to their patients.

With this recommendation we see an extension of the largely anti-authoritarian thrust of countertransference theory. The more attention that is given to the analyst's feelings and to the "real" relationship with the patient, the less right the analyst has to the mantle of paternal authority conferred on him by Freud. This loss of status is both timely and, one hopes, beneficial. The recognition of the influence and potential usefulness of the analyst's emotions may produce a more realistic authority. In any case, it should produce a greater competence, which is, after all, the proper foundation of authority.

Part II
Recent Interpretations of Countertransference

Chapter 3
Countertransference as Compromise Formation

Charles Brenner, M.D.

Freud discussed the concept of countertransference at some length in 1915 in his paper on transference love. What he meant by it was, if an analyst responds to a patient's transference love by falling in love with her, that is countertransference. Current interest in the concept dates back less far, however — some thirty years, perhaps. The most frequently quoted seminal article on countertransference is the one by A. Reich, which appeared in 1951. Her definition is considerably broader than Freud's original one. It is that countertransference "comprises the effects of the analyst's own unconscious needs and conflicts on his understanding or

Presented at the Regional Conference of Psychoanalytic Societies of Greater New York at Princeton, New Jersey, June 8–10, 1984, as part of a panel discussion chaired by Dr. Edmund Slakter. It also appeared as an article in the *Psychoanalytic Quarterly,* 1985, 54(2):155–163.

technique" (p. 26). This definition is still a good one, but only if it is taken out of the context of the article in which it appeared. From the context it is obvious that Reich meant only the unfavorable, harmful, deleterious effects of an analyst's unconscious needs and conflicts on his or her understanding and technique.

We all agree, from the writings of many colleagues on the subject, that countertransference is not necessarily harmful or disadvantageous. Followers of Melanie Klein have gone so far as to call countertransference an ego function, in fact, *the* ego function that makes analysis possible. For them, it seems, countertransference is synonymous with intuition or empathy (Heimann 1977). But, when we are asked to give clinical examples of countertransference, we know that what we are being asked for is examples of the kind of countertransference Reich was referring to, the kind that interferes with the conduct of an analysis or makes it impossible altogether.

What I have to say on the subject is from the other side of the fence. I want to put examples of the kind of countertransference which interferes with analysis in proper perspective. My thesis is this. Countertransference is ubiquitous and inescapable, just as is transference. There is, truly, no need for a separate term. Countertransference is the transference of the analyst in an analytic situation (Brenner 1976, McLaughlin 1981). Becoming an analyst, practicing analysis, necessarily involves, for each individual analyst, derivatives of that analyst's childhood conflicts. There is nothing pathological or neurotic in this. It is, in fact, as inevitable for the profession of analysis as it is for the choice and practice of any other vocation. The choice of analysis as a vocation is as much a normal compromise formation, a normal outcome of conflict over childhood drive derivatives, as is the choice of any adult occupation. It is when pathological compromise formations appear in an analyst's professional activity that analytic work may be disturbed. Instances of countertransference which interfere with analysis are examples of pathological or neurotic compromise formation.

The following considerations are important to an understanding of how this happens. Childhood drive derivatives which give rise to anxiety, to depressive affect, or to both, cause conflicts which result in compromise formations. Such compromise formations are a blend or mixture of several components. One component is wish fulfillment, i.e., gratification of the drive derivative. Another is the unpleasure aroused by the drive derivative in the form of anxiety and depressive affect. Still another is defense, aimed at reducing or eliminating altogether the unpleasure just referred to. Another is various manifestations of superego functioning. All of these are components of every compromise formation which results from conflict over childhood drive derivatives. It is important for us to keep these facts clearly in mind in discussing countertransference for the reason that every instance of countertransference is a compromise formation. It is equally important to remember that childhood drive derivatives persist throughout life. They never disappear. Neither do the conflicts to which they give rise. When you resolve a dispute between individuals, between different persons or even between nations, the dispute disappears. Harmony reigns. An intrapsychic conflict is never resolved in that sense. The conflict never disappears. What happens is that the compromise formations arising from the conflict are altered in the direction of normality. Instead of a pathological conflict one has a normal one. From a practical point of view the change—so often called resolution of conflict—is a very important one. It is the difference between sickness and health. It is what we hope for as the outcome of a successful analysis. But the conflict has not gone away. Its outcome is different, but the conflict is still as much there as ever. At least after very early childhood, the mental life and behavior of every human being is largely determined by conflict and compromise formation.

In all of this we take into account the influence, the effect of a child's environment, particularly of the people in its life. Every childhood drive derivative, every wish for drive satisfaction, has to do with a particular person or persons, with particular memories, with a particular form of pleasure, all of which are unique for that child. Moreover, a child's objects and environment may be favorable or unfavorable in their effect on its mental life. We have even a special name for circumstances which are specially unfavorable—we call them traumatic events. In other words, conflicts and compromise formations in childhood are shaped in part by external or environmental factors. A trauma or its opposite can alter a compromise formation in the direction of pathology, if it is a psychic trauma, or in the direction of normality, if the reverse. And, I should add, the same is true in later life, though we know that in later life compromise formations are less dependent on external circumstances than they are likely to be in early childhood; that is, we know that in older children and in adults what is of principal importance in psychopathology is what we call intrapsychic conflict—the effect of what went on in childhood psychic life and psychic development.

How does this apply to the problem of countertransference? It applies in this way. First, being an analyst is, for each one of us, an instance of compromise formation. Second, one's relationship with every patient, as with every person of any importance in one's life, is also a compromise formation. Third, current events in our lives can influence our conflicts and thus change our own compromise formations. By this I mean that whatever is happening in one's life, including the conflicts, transference wishes, and behavior of one's patients to which one is exposed in one's professional work, can, under unfavorable circumstances, change one's actions as an analyst and one's understanding of one's patient from what is analytically desirable to what is analytically undesirable.

Let me expand on each of these three points in turn. The first is that to become an analyst, to practice analysis, is an instance of compromise formation. This is a statement whose truth should be apparent to each of us from personal experience, so what I say about it will probably sound so familiar as to seem trite.

What drive derivatives are gratified by being an analyst? Different ones for different analysts, of course, but one which often plays a part is the wish to see another suffer. We make our living, as do all doctors and therapists, from the sickness and suffering of other people. As analysts we spend our days watching them suffer. Another common wish that is satisfied by being an analyst is sexual curiosity. To know what one's parents do in bed, to learn all about it, to participate in the primal scene, at least as onlookers, are childhood wishes that are regularly gratified by working as an analyst.

You will interject that neither these nor any similar wishes of early childhood are gratified by being an analyst in their childish version without modification. You will point out that only sublimated, highly modified versions of these wishes are allowed expression in one's analytic work. If you do, I shall agree, for that is precisely my point. As it appears in an analyst, the childish wish, e.g., to watch another suffer, is overlaid with reaction formation. As an analyst one is anxious lest one hurt a patient, or let the patient suffer more or longer than necessary. One is guilty and remorseful at having failed to relieve a patient's suffering in time, not happy at the opportunity of looking on at it. Thus depressive affect and anxiety play their parts as well as the drive derivative that has evoked them. So, too, does the defensive activity aimed at avoiding the unpleasure of depressive affect and anxiety. One reason that analysts read and study and go to regional meetings and listen to each other talk about psychoanalysis for hours on end is to be better able to relieve their patients' suffering and thus avoid or minimize in themselves the anxiety and depressive affect which are part of the normal compromise formation that being an analyst is. They repress their wish to watch others suffer, they disown any such wish, they attribute it to others whenever possible, they emphasize the opposite wish—to help, to cure—they identify with great healers, like Freud, and with lesser ones, like their own analysts and teachers. In short, they defend against the wishes that cause them anxiety and depressive affect in every possible way. Finally, analysts do all they can to live up to their own moral demands. When they fail to do so, they feel guilty, remorseful, self-punitive. Lesser degrees of superego activity may result in feeling burdened by one's work, dissatisfied with what it means to be an analyst, complaining to the world about how hard we analysts have to work, how inadequately we are paid compared with others less deserving than ourselves, and so on.

All of this demonstrates, if demonstration be needed, that the practice of analysis is a set of compromise formations among drive derivatives of childhood origin, anxiety and depressive affect, defense, and superego manifestations. Interestingly, with some patients one enjoys one's work more than with others. If a patient fails to improve, if a patient suffers much, one may feel more anxiety, more self-reproach, in a word, more unpleasure in analyzing that patient than in working with another who suffers less and improves more rapidly. Here again the reasons must vary from analyst to analyst, but I venture to say that in every instance the different feelings about analyzing different patients are the result of a change in the compromise formations which led each of us to practice analysis in the first place.

Suppose, for example, that a wish to watch another person suffer is one component of the compromise formations. This wish is associated with unpleasure, i.e., with anxiety and depressive affect, and defenses are operative to reduce the unpleasure, say by reaction formation. Then the compromise formation can be expressed in words such as these: "I can enjoy watching a patient suffer if I'm doing it to relieve the suffering. Then I can feel pleasure in what I'm doing and not feel guilty about it." If a patient cooperates by improving as a result of one's efforts, it "helps" one to feel good. If not, just the opposite. One feels not so good. Sometimes one feels more or less bad.

All of this can be within normal limits. One can feel, within normal limits, less comfortable, less happy, working with one patient than with another. Obviously, the example I have picked is only one among very many. I do not mean for a moment that unpleasure in working with a particular patient is always a function of increased or continued suffering on the patient's part that exacerbates the analyst's conflict over watching someone suffer. It can just as well be related to libidinal wishes, to competitive ones, or to a desire for omnipotence, to name but a few. My point is simply that the circumstances of one's analytic work, e.g., the nature of a patient's problems, can shift an analyst's conflicts enough to change one or another aspect of the analyst's compromise formations. If the change is a minor one, we consider it to be normal, by which we mean, in such case, only that it is frequent enough to be commonplace and small enough in degree to cause little hindrance in one's work.

Implicit in this view of countertransference is the fact that countertransference is what makes an analyst's professional activity possible. Were it not that being an analyst offers each of us the particular combination of drive gratification, defense, and superego functioning that is characteristic for our particular compromise formations, none of us would be an analyst. We would be doing something else, whatever it might be. The assertion of some colleagues (e.g., Heimann 1977) that countertransference is what makes psychoanalysis possible has in it a kernal of truth, though not what they mean when they say it. Countertransference is not a synonym for intuition or empathy, which is their idea. It is a set of compromise formations which expresses the conflicting and cooperating psychic tendencies at work in the mind of an analyst in his professional capacity. And, just as some circumstances, in particular some patients, make analysis less enjoyable and less easy to do well, other circumstances, in particular other patients, make analysis more enjoyable and easier to do well for a particular analyst.

As I said at the start, my purpose is to put in proper perspective those cases of countertransference in which an analyst becomes unable to analyze for reasons having to do with the analyst's own psychic conflicts. They are cases in which something has happened to shift the balance among the components of an analyst's conflict over the drive derivatives being gratified by practicing analysis so that the resulting compromise formations preclude adequate analytic understanding and appropriate analytic behavior. The possible outcomes correspond to the various components of the conflict. The drive derivatives may be expressed in a nonanalytic way; anxiety and depressive affect in the analyst may become overly strong; defenses may intervene in a way that interferes with analysis; self-punitive and/or self-injurious trends may intrude. For any combination of these reasons, to quote Reich (1951), an analyst's understanding or technique may be affected to the detriment of analysis. The nature of the disturbance will vary from case to case. An analyst may become angry or may gratify libidinal drive derivatives, overtly or in a disguised way; analytic work may become dull, uninteresting, or even repellent; the obvious meaning of some analytic material may be defensively ignored or obscured; an analyst may punish or injure himself or herself in a way that affects or interrupts analytic practice. Whatever the nature of the disturbance, however the details may vary from case to case, one can say in every instance that a countertransference which had formerly been a normal set of compromise formations, one which made analytic work fruitful and enjoyable, has, for some reason, been altered to a set of compromise formations which interferes with analytic work or makes it impossible altogether. Each of the clinical examples in the two papers which follow (by Drs. Silverman and Arlow) will bear out this assertion.

Such an alteration is therefore comparable to the onset of a neurosis in a patient. Instead of a normal compromise formation, a pathological one has appeared. Just as is true for neurotic symptomatology, so for pathological countertransference the best preventive is personal analysis. Without a satisfactory personal analysis, countertransference is only too often likely to prove an obstacle to one's analytic work. When countertransference does appear as a major obstacle, a return for more personal analysis is often indicated, just as it is when an expatient develops new symptoms, i.e., when pathological compromise formations appear in a patient who was successfully relieved of symptoms by an earlier analysis.

If a pathological compromise formation gives rise to countertransferential obstacles which are not too serious, self-analysis may be sufficient, all the more so if the analyst has already some familiarity with such conflicts from previous analysis (Kern 1978). If a pathological compromise formation is precipitated by an event not likely to recur, for example, a death in the analyst's family, or an acute illness, time alone may suffice to relieve the problem. In short, what remedies are indicated can be decided only when one knows all the relevant facts about the case in hand. In every case the psychological factors which brought about the change in the analyst's compromise formations from normal to pathological will be unique; that is, the precipitating factors will never be the same for any two cases, nor will one be able to identify the precipitating factors with certainty if one does not have access to all the relevant facts of the case.

To summarize, countertransference is ubiquitous, it is a set of compromise formations, it is what makes analyzing worthwhile for the analyst. It is also what makes personal analysis an essential part of one's analytic training. Like all compromise formations, the ones that we call countertransference can shift. The new or altered compromise formations can facilitate or impede analytic work. The shifts that impede it are the ones we will hear about in some of the following papers.

REFERENCES

Brenner, C. (1976). *Psychoanalytic Technique and Psychic Conflict*. New York: Int. Univ. Press.

Freud, S. (1915). Observations on transference-love (further recommendations on the technique of psycho-analysis III). *Standard Edition,* 12.

Heimann, P. (1977). Further observations on the analyst's cognitive process. *Journal of the American Psychoanalytic Association* 25:313–333.

Kern, J. W. (1978). Countertransference and spontaneous screens: an analyst studies his own visual images. *Journal of the American Psychoanalytic Association* 26:21–47.

McLaughlin, J. T. (1981). Transference, psychic reality, and countertransference. *Psychoanalytic Quarterly* 50:639–664.

Reich, A. (1951). On counter-transference. *International Journal of Psycho-Analysis* 32:25–31.

Chapter 4

Countertransference and the Myth of the Perfectly Analyzed Analyst

Martin Silverman, M.D.

The emphasis of my remarks will be upon the inevitability of countertransference in psychoanalytic work and upon the need for psychoanalysts to be ever vigilant to its emergence. Although some analysts have viewed countertransference as a necessary and desirable source of information about what is going on in the patient, it is my firm impression that it always signifies that something has gone awry in the analyst's use of himself as an analyzing instrument.

When a psychoanalyst is working effectively, he makes use of a combination of empathic, emotional receptivity and cognitive

Presented at the Regional Conference of Psychoanalytic Societies of Greater New York at Princeton, New Jersey, June 8–10, 1984, as part of a panel discussion chaired by Dr. Edmund Slakter. It also appeared as an article in the *Psychoanalytic Quarterly,* 1985, 54(2):175–199.

validation that permits him to read the unconscious messages which underlie the analysand's conscious communications—in part directly and in part by understanding their effects upon his own psychological sensors. He does this by permitting himself, in a special manner that is under more or less continuous ego control, to respond emotionally to the patient's communications in small ways that can be detected as signals of the unconscious emanations from the patient. Knowledge of his own self and control over his own inclinations to seek gratification of his instinctual urges through interactions with others, gained during his training analysis, protect him against the danger of misreading his reactions and succumbing to the temptation to use the patient as an object of his own instinctual wishes.

It is not possible, however, for a psychoanalyst to maintain this optimal analytic stance indefinitely. Psychoanalysis can only be carried out by two human beings, the analyst being no less human than the analysand. An analyst is able to tolerate the strains, frustrations, importunate demands, and emotional assaults that are so much a part of his daily experience not only because of his professional understanding of their necessity but also because of his human and humane interest in facilitating his patient's achievement of improved emotional well-being. As Jacob Arlow once put it to me, a psychoanalyst needs to be soft-hearted as well as hard-headed.

Anna Freud (1954) stated that a psychoanalyst ideally should be no more than a blank screen reflecting back to the analysand what is being projected onto him, without introducing anything from his own feelings and attitudes, but, of course, she stated, none of us can do that. An analyst cannot be guided primarily by self-interest, but must have feelings for his patient as a troubled, struggling, fellow human being. The danger is ever present, however, as Anna Freud emphasized, for him to be drawn into complicity with the patient in a surreptitious, joint acting out of the wish to obtain gratification of each other's repressed infantile wishes. If the analyst is indeed immersed in the intense emotional interchange that the analytic situation is designed to provoke, he is subjected to powerful pressures to abandon his analytic neutrality. He is bombarded by a stream of complaints, supplications, subtle seductions, bitter accusations, and ingenious bits of blackmail from his patients. He is also subjected to an intense pull from within his own being to ease his burden by obtaining some measure of instinctual gratification from the analytic experience to make up for the deprivation and abuse to which he has given himself up. The analyst is continually drawn to do more than analyze, and his very humanness makes it difficult for him to invariably resist all the temptations.

The very nature of the psychoanalytic task makes it impossible to avoid the periodic emergence of countertransference reactions in the place of analytic empathy if the analyst truly is doing his job. It is of fundamental importance that the analyst be ready to recognize that this is taking place and to overcome it so that analytic empathy can be restored. Most of the time, when things are going well, this can be carried out quickly and smoothly. There are other times, however, when self-analysis needs to be carried out to correct a situation in the analyst that is interfering with his ability to do his work effectively. If countertransference reactions arise that transcend his ability to eliminate them via self-analysis, then a period of reanalysis with another psychoanalyst will be necessary.

For reasons that are intrinsic to the psychoanalytic method, no analyst can be entirely free of the tendency to develop counter-transference reactions. The psychoanalyst who believes himself to be so "well analyzed" that he is immune to countertransference reactions as he undergoes the emotional dislocations required of him in the almost "impossible profession" of psychoanalysis may be the most vulnerable of all to their development. Such an analyst is at serious risk of developing well-disguised, well-rationalized, subtle countertransference reactions that will limit or destroy his efforts to help his patients overcome the neurotic problems that are preventing them from realizing their potential in life.

THE ANALYTIC SITUATION

Psychoanalysis is a two-person enterprise that aims at gaining access to the unconscious conflicts that generate neurotic behavior. One participant, the analysand, is encouraged to give himself over to the free verbal expression of associatively linked derivatives of unconscious emotional strivings, but this is countered by unconscious defensive maneuvers that underlie his neurotic symptoms and character traits. The other participant, the analyst, strives to adopt a freely hovering attentive state in which he is receptive, emotionally and intellectually, to the analysand's utterances, gestures, and postural expressions in such a way that he is free to grasp their unconscious as well as conscious import without filtering, disguising, rejecting, or utilizing them for his own personal gains.

The analysand's attempt to restrict himself to verbal free association inevitably is outweighed by the inclination to direct his repressed instinctual wishes toward the person of the analyst in the hope of gratifying them. The analytic setting, by fostering regression and making the analyst available as a kindly, helpful, attentive, accepting object of the patient's drives, encourages the transference of unrequited infantile longings, libidinal as well as hostile, onto the analyst in place of the representationally internalized, original objects of their expression. The central course of psychoanalytic work consists in the analyst's painstaking, interpretative delineation of the analysand's transference resistance to free association. The patient, in other words, is drawn inevitably toward insisting that the analyst gratify his neurotic wishes (Calef and Weinshel 1983), while the analyst holds him to his agreement to gain understanding of the infantile roots of his demands by interpreting them as regressive transference resistances.

The analyst, being no less human than the analysand, is also inclined toward the utilization of an available object for the discharge of repressed infantile longings. The counterpart of the analysand's tendency to shift from free association of derivatives of unconscious neurotic strivings to acting them out in the transference is the analyst's tendency to slip from analytic empathy to countertransferential (including counteridentificatory) acting out of his own unconscious neurotic strivings with the patient. In two early papers, Freud (1910, 1912) cautioned that the only way for a psychoanalyst to avoid or to minimize the latter danger is to protect himself by undergoing analysis of his own neurotic tendencies. His first recommendation (1910) was for erstwhile analysts to undergo self-analysis, as he himself had done (Freud 1900, 1954). Later he recommended that the would-be analyst undergo a training analysis so that he might resolve his resistances and thus "become aware of those complexes of his own which would be apt to interfere with his grasp of what the patient tells him" (Freud 1912, p. 116).

In "Analysis Terminable and Interminable" (1937), however, Freud expressed serious reservations about the ability of anyone, including a future psychoanalyst, to so thoroughly analyze all the neurotic propensities within him in the course of an analysis that he could completely eliminate them. He concluded that one of the main functions of a psychoanalyst's own analysis is to prepare him for the ongoing self-analysis that must be a central part of his work throughout his career. He further advised that every psychoanalyst be prepared, if necessary, to undergo periodic reanalysis with another psychoanalyst, without shame and without regret. Beiser (1984), in a recent communication, described an experience of resolution of a countertransference blind spot via successful self-analysis, in the course of which she discovered that her own analyst had possessed a blind spot similar to the one which she later had to overcome herself.

As the analyst permits himself to drift freely in response to the patient's free associations, he allows himself to undergo a regressive emotional reaction. This produces, via the controlled utilization of introjective and projective processes, a trial identification (Fliess 1942) with the patient and a limited emotional response to the patient's expressions in the interest of grasping what is going on within the patient. As the analyst permits his intuitive and empathic abilities to bring him into resonance with derivatives of the analysand's powerful unconscious passions and desires, he is inevitably carried to the very line that lies between apperception of what is emanating from the patient and the evocation of his own latent passions and desires. The latter are ready to take advantage of the analysand's availability (either directly or vicariously, through identification) as an object of their expression and fulfillment. When the analyst's cognitive abilities are brought to bear upon the emotional stirrings within him, as must be done for empathy to be *analytic empathy* (Beres and Arlow 1974), it is only too easy for him to rationalize indications of his own pursuit of drive gratification or of defense against it (acting out with the patient or defensive blind spots) by formulating what he observes in terms of emotional reactions within the patient rather than recognizing his own countertransference. The working analyst repeatedly hovers between apperception and misperception. Therefore, he needs to be continuously vigilant to that which emanates from him rather than from the patient.

A dimension of the analytic situation that has received insufficient attention is that the analyst is not the only one who uses his empathic sensitivities to perceive derivatives of unconscious neurotic conflicts in the other participant. The analysand, too, uses his intuitive and empathic abilities to detect evidence of emotional conflicts in the analyst that can be played upon in the attempt to obtain transference gratifications. Patients are quick to recognize and to utilize the analyst's vulnerabilities in their efforts to obtain gratification rather than understanding of their unconscious desires, or in their efforts to externalize and ward off disturbing unconscious contents rather than gaining insight into their defensive operations. It is sometimes difficult for the analyst to be certain that he is accurately perceiving the unconscious meaning of what is being conveyed to him. He may instead be falling prey to the implantation of misleading views by an analysand who is playing upon the analyst's biases and personal inclinations to lead him astray. The ability of certain patients to subtly but skillfully produce desired feelings in and reactive responses by their analysts can be impressive. It seems to me likely that this has contributed significantly to the Kleinian concept of projective identification, to the tendency of some analysts (including Freud) to give credence to extrasensory perception and thought transmission, and to the tendency among followers of Kohut's later concepts to abandon defense analysis in favor of "empathic" kindness and acceptance of their patients' projective attribution of total responsibility for their neurotic disturbances to parental abuse and failure.

CLINICAL ILLUSTRATIONS OF COUNTERTRANSFERENCE PROBLEMS

It is well known that the presence of countertransference reactions can be signaled by the appearance in the analyst of boredom, sleepiness, vague malaise, irritability, excessively positive or negative feelings toward the patient (or toward the patient's past and present objects [Jacobs 1983]), difficulty in grasping the meaning of the analysand's communications, dreams about a patient, parapraxes, and various forms of acting out of neurotic inclinations with the patient. A less obvious sign of countertransference interference can be the failure of the analysis to progress satisfactorily despite seemingly proper technique and seemingly accurate understanding of the analysand's communications. The following is offered as an illustration of such a situation.

A woman in her early forties came for reanalysis after her first analysis of seven years' duration had come to an end when the analyst retired from practice. The picture she painted of her first analysis was curiously replete with internal contradictions. On the one hand, she described her first analyst as hardworking, essentially on target in his interventions, and genuinely interested in helping her overcome the frigidity (which began immediately after her marriage to a man with whom she had been very enjoyably orgastic until then), the work inhibitions, and the recurrent, severe premenstrual depression for which she had entered analysis. On the other hand, she stated that she never had felt at ease with him, never had felt that he empathized with her, and never had felt that they had gotten anywhere. Although she had "followed the rules," had worked hard, and had learned a good deal about herself, her symptoms had not changed in any way, and she felt that she had not made any fundamental changes in herself. She was astonished, in fact, that she had stayed in analysis with him for so long, since she had not achieved any meaningful analytic gains. Despite her pain, sadness, anger, and intense disappointment over what she considered an unsuccessful, long first analysis, she expressed a great deal of thinly veiled excitement when she spoke of her first analyst. She began her second analysis with clear allusions to hurt and puzzled disbelief that he had left her without having provided the love, adoration, baby, and penis she somehow had excitedly felt he had promised her if only she were an obedient, hardworking, pleasing analysand. Her first analysis, she indicated, had centered on the themes of penis envy, envy of her brother who was favored by her father, and her reactions to having grown up with an exciting, unpredictable, irascible father who had alternated between being physically and emotionally overstimulating (libidinally as well as aggressively) and being remarkably disappointing, frustrating, and infuriating. He also had presented her with a model of intermittent dishonesty and exploitation in his business practices.

Analysis of the residual transference to the first analyst, which, although quite ambivalent, appeared to center on a longing for him as a well-meaning, exciting doctor who helped her by performing painful operations on her (a recurrent dream representation of him), gradually became intertwined in the second analysis with a slowly evolving but then persistent theme that preoccupied her frequently. She became agitated and anxious when her husband requested that she change an analytic appointment to attend a function with him to which he very much wanted her to go and which she herself would have enjoyed attending. When she summoned up the courage to speak with me about the possibility of changing the appointment, she was astonished that I responded by granting her request. Her first analyst had impressed upon her the importance of adhering to the schedule of their appointments and had refused to make a change the few times she had requested it early in her analysis.

As the first winter approached since the beginning of her second analysis, she wondered repeatedly whether she would be charged for sessions she might miss when severe winter weather might prevent her from driving to my home office. Her first analyst, whose office was also in his home, had "rigidly" charged her for every missed session, even when heavy snowfalls or ice storms had made the roads virtually impassable. She literally had risked life and limb to drive to his office on occasions when prudence clearly had dictated that she stay off the streets. She finally had refused to pay for a session that she missed on a day when the roads were absolutely closed to all vehicles. She was surprised that my policy was to hold her responsible for missed sessions in general, but not to hold her financially liable on occasions when weather conditions were such that no one could be expected to drive to my office.

She expressed surprise, in fact, that my policy, which I described to her when we started our work together, was to make reasonable appointment changes when possible and to free her from financial responsibility when I could make alternative use of canceled time, although it was in her interest to miss as few sessions as possible. Her first analyst had never made an effort to reschedule or to make other use of the sessions she had (infrequently) missed. He always had charged her for them, explaining that it was in her interest to be held strictly accountable for the arrangements upon which they had agreed and to analyze her feelings about his charging her for the missed sessions. She also spoke about other differences in the way he and I seemed to work. She always had bridled at his opening the waiting room door, turning on his heels, and "marching" back to the consulting room, leaving her to follow him and to close the doors behind her along the way. I let her close the waiting room door behind her, but I held the door open for her and *followed her* into the consulting room. I raised no objection to her opening my morning newspaper and reading it, while he had objected to her looking through the books and records in the den that also had served as his waiting room. She was surprised when I questioned her fearful, apologetic tone as she spoke of something she had read in *The New York Times* about feminist psychologists who had expressed some new ideas about female development that were at variance with "classical" psychoanalytic theory. Her former analyst had instructed her not to read psychoanalytic literature, lest she use what she had read as an intellectual resistance to searching within herself. They had spoken about her resistances a good deal; although she felt that her analyst sincerely wanted her to make progress, she always felt guilty about "resisting" and always felt somehow that he wanted her to overcome her resistances so that she would do a better job and be a more satisfactory patient for him. While she felt that I was incisive, hard-headed, and took pride in my work, she had a somewhat different feeling about my aims and purposes. She felt that I was there as her assistant, to help her carry out whatever *she* wanted to accomplish, whereas with her former analyst she always had felt that she had to carry out the tasks *he* expected of her.

As we were exploring these matters, she associated them with her childhood fear of her father's explosive temper and her anger at him for repeatedly frustrating and controlling her by never being on time for her. She recalled many incidents of falling and ending up with splinters in her buttocks. These memories led her first to recall of the repeated enemas her mother had given her and then to other recollections: her mother holding her down, kicking and screaming, while the doctor gave her a penicillin shot in her behind; her father spanking her on her bare bottom; her mother terrifying her with stories of spiders coming out of the faucets as she ran her bath water; her father holding her nose so that she would have to open her mouth and let her mother put food into it, etc. The last few items, she indicated, she either never had shared with her first analyst or had mentioned tangentially on a single occasion, after which she had never returned to them.

At one point in this phase of the analysis, I commented to her that if she wanted to get at and resolve the matters within her that contributed to her problems, she would have to be willing to feel uncomfortable along the way. "You make it sound like an enema," was her reply. The realization that I had indeed permitted myself to be seduced into a countertransferential identification with her at times intrusive and assaultive parents helped me both to return to my stance as "the observing, evaluating, analyzing outsider" (Reich 1966, p. 347) and to understand better what had happened during my patient's first analysis. It seemed evident that her former analyst had succumbed to the invitation to engage in a covert, permanent transference-countertransference interaction with her. They talked about the right things, but on an emotional level they carried out an ongoing sadomasochistic interaction. This was probably well rationalized by the analyst as adherence to "classical" psychoanalytic technique, but he seems to have been satisfying her wishes for neurotic gratification on a regressed sadistic-anal level, rather than empathically perceiving the meaning of what was taking place and analyzing it. In the second analysis, when the countertransference tendencies the patient sought to elicit could be restricted to a signal level that permitted them to be recognized, understood, and overcome, the transference resistances could be analyzed and the psychoanalytic process could lead the patient into a transference neurosis that could be analyzed and resolved.

Psychoanalysis can aptly be characterized as a venture in which the patient goes to a doctor to be cured of a distressing illness and then fights tooth and nail against being cured. In the course of this, the patient utilizes every opportunity and every tool to defeat the doctor's curative intent. This includes (perhaps especially so) making use of the doctor's very techniques and approaches. A number of years ago, I heard Peter Neubauer say that "it is a parent's solemn responsibility to set rules and to enforce them, and it is a child's solemn responsibility to break them; development takes place in defiance, not in compliance." The analytic corollary of this is that it is a psychoanalyst's responsibility to provide analytic arrangements (not "rules") that promote analysis of, rather than acting out of, the analysand's unconscious neurotic conflicts. It is inevitable that the analysand will struggle against that intent and will use those very analytic arrangements in the effort. The analyst will be able to adhere to the analytic task only if he is continuously vigilant to the analysand's need to do this. He must also be alert to the patient's tendency to sound out the analyst's human weak spots in order to induce him to abandon his posture of analytic empathy in favor of subtle countertransference that will dovetail with the patient's transference wishes and unobtrusively gratify them. To expect that the analyst will always be entirely immune to this process is to misunderstand what psychoanalysis is all about.

Fortunately, the most common countertransference reactions are not of the permanent, ongoing type that posed such a problem in the case described above. They tend rather to be temporary and reversible, as exemplified in the vignette that follows.

A man in his early twenties was referred because of depression, anxiety, and masochistic trends that had so interfered with his functioning that, despite superior intelligence, he had had to withdraw from college with failing grades. Although his well-to-do father had offered him a place in the family business, he had spurned the offer and had pointedly renounced his father's affluent way of life in favor of a simple life in service to others. In keeping with this, he worked at menial, semi-rural jobs through which he supplemented the small salary his wife earned. After an extended consultation, he decided to enter analysis. Since he was adamant in his determination to pay for his treatment through savings and his own earnings rather than accepting money from his father, the analysis had to begin at a considerably reduced fee. He entered a local college and eventually graduated with high honors. He took a series of jobs that more appropriately suited his talents, did very well in them, and advanced rapidly each time.

When he felt that he had proved himself on his own, he returned to the family business, although not without trepidation. There, he took on increasing responsibility and contributed in a significant way to the company's rapid growth.

Analysis of his preoedipal and positive and negative oedipal conflicts enabled him to increasingly overcome the passive-dependent and passive-aggressive attitudes that had been inhibiting him from assertively pursuing his personal goals. His wife gave up her job. They bought a house (despite his father's strong objections) and started a family. He gradually recognized that he had adopted a passive-feminine, outwardly submissive but actually provocative, passive-aggressive, ambivalent attachment to his father in order to ward off his anxieties and accomplish certain neurotic aims. He worked hard to analyze this so that he might overcome it.

By the time the patient entered his sixth year of analysis, he had become a respected, self-respecting, outwardly successful young man. He liked the results of the redecoration my office had just undergone, but found himself tense and anxious as he worried about what it had cost me, and he was concerned that the redecoration must have interfered with my August vacation. In association, he thought of his envy of his parents for lavishly redecorating their home. He reported that his competitive anxieties had grown more intense, and he puzzled over his conflicted attitudes toward money. He was plagued with thoughts of being attacked, robbed of all he had, and left to starve. With embarrassment, he confessed to thinking, despite all his previous egalitarian assertions to the contrary, that a man is measured by the amount of money he has and makes. He worried about the stock market and thought about the invitation he once had extended to me to join him in buying stock in a company he knew about through his work. I had refrained from doing so, of course, in the knowledge that it could only have led to significant problems in the analysis whether I made or lost money in the venture. The stock had gone on to be the leading gainer on the New York Stock Exchange for that year, and my patient made enough money to buy two horses and to cover the costs of their keep for several years to come. He now reflected on his reasons for having given me the stock tip and concluded that he had wanted us to be "in the same bed" together, either making money together (although he was afraid that I might make more than he) or sharing the pain of loss together.

When his sister's stormy marriage finally dissolved and she entered the family business, he reacted with a series of dreams and fantasies either of being pursued and devoured or of being a predator chasing and devouring his prey. He wrestled with thinly disguised, murderous fantasies toward his father and siblings, aimed at eliminating the rivals who prevented him from being "king of the hill," only to retreat from them to bitter envy of his sister for being "kept" and lovingly provided for by his father without working for what she got. He was outraged that she actually put in very little work for the enviable salary she received.

In the midst of all this, he let me know that he had become bold enough to set plans in motion to buy a new house that undoubtedly was a good deal more expensive than mine. He was obtaining this house for himself at the very same age—in fact, a year earlier—at which his father had bought his own "big house." He gradually permitted me to discover the full range of details connected with his purchase. He did this with a subtle talent (that I had had no inkling he possessed) for deftly building the effect via small, understated, and therefore dramatically incisive, well-timed increments. He not only had raised his income far beyond the minimal subsistence level at which it had been when he first came to me for treatment; he was now so successful in the business I had helped him enter and build that he was making much more money than I was, with every expectation of making a great deal more in years to come. The house he was buying at an excellent price (which was five times more than I had paid for mine) and at an excellent mortgage rate stood on the top of a mountain on several lush acres, with a swimming pool, a tennis court, and a barn for his horses. He told me little stories about the wildlife and the bird feeders he installed, since he believed (correctly) that I loved such things and he wanted to "share his pleasure" with me. He toyed excitedly with the idea of bringing me a striking aerial photograph of his house and had repeated fantasies of inviting me to share his enjoyment of his wonderful new house and to play tennis with him on his new tennis court. The last reminded him of previous fantasies of playing tennis with me, which had turned out to be quite ambivalent, and he wondered if he didn't also want to beat me. He was able to see that alongside his gratitude toward me for helping him obtain so many enjoyable things was also the transference wish to outdo and humiliate me as he had wanted to do to his father all the time he was growing up. He expected me to react, he realized, like a fire-breathing dragon, the way his father always seemed to react to any forward step he dared to take.

He became aware that behind his wishes to share his good fortune with me and even to "feed" and take care of me was the wish to get rid of me so that he could have the money he paid me to use toward the house and land he was buying. He reacted by pulling back cautiously. When his fear of getting close to me was called to his attention, he expressed the fantasy that if he let himself get too close to me, he would kill me. He associated his childhood wishes to get rid of his father and siblings in order to have everything—money, power, and his mother—to himself. A fantasy of murdering his father terrified him. He could not imagine how anyone could get close without envy, jealousy, and fighting. He feared becoming ruthless, vicious, and rapacious like his father, though he began to wonder to what extent he had projected his own tendencies into his perceptions of his parents. He became increasingly teasing with me by continually hinting at being on the verge of sharing important, exciting things that never quite materialized. He would hint at wonderful money-making opportunities he could tell me about but never did and would sporadically mention that it probably was in order to consider raising the fee he paid me, only to quickly drop the idea and change the subject each time.

As I sat and listened to all this, I at first found it fascinating and felt pleased with all the signs of analytic progress and with the productive way my patient was working and we were working together. Gradually, however, I found myself growing irritable, impatient with the "repetitiveness" of the working through process I was observing, and tired of the "slow pace" into which my patient had settled after his initial flurry of rapidly productive hard work. I found it increasingly difficult to get up for our very early morning sessions and noticed that I was beginning, for one seemingly plausible reason or another, to keep him waiting for a few minutes before we started.

It did not take a great deal of self-scrutiny for me to realize that I resented my patient's teasing me by dangling offers to reward me for my labors, which indeed had been of enormous assistance to him, but then pulling back short of fulfilling them. He had been teasing me by accelerating his progress toward a good analytic result and by hinting at using some of the greatly expanded income I had helped him obtain, via an analysis that had proceeded for a long time at a low fee, to pay me more money, only to put the brakes on each time I became interested.

I thought of my own childhood, with its extremely modest financial circumstances, and of all the years of near poverty and accumulating debts as I went through college, medical school, psychiatric residency, and psychoanalytic training. And I thought about having treated this wealthy young man at a reduced fee because he had preferred not to avail himself of the plentiful funds that always had been there for him. But I was far from starving, I thought. I was not rich, but I was earning a good income. And although the fee had been low for a long time, it was quite acceptable now, though a little below my current minimal fee. I had not made all the money I would have made had I followed up on that stock tip, but after all, I knew about the rigors involved in being a psychoanalyst when I chose the profession, and I loved doing psychoanalytic work. Anyway, I was not interested in owning horses or even in riding them. Still, it was ironic that I had agreed to reduce my fee considerably for a long period of time to help someone overcome an inhibition against accepting from *his* father what I always had wished I had had an opportunity to receive from mine.

My thoughts led from here to a number of details involving my actual and fantasied relationship with my father, in the present as well as in the past. As a result of these self-analytic conversations with myself, which stretched over a number of weeks (and then, intermittently, over several more months), I realized that much more was involved than money and the provision of material things. My inability to deal quickly and easily with certain aspects of my emotional involvement with my father, which had been stirred by the analysis I was conducting, had been blocking me from sustaining the consistent, empathic, insightful attention to my patient's communications, of which I had been capable until then. It became clear to me that my patient's tantalizing provocations represented a seductive invitation for me to act out a negative oedipal fantasy with him by attacking him "from behind."

This was clearly discernible in the communications that were emanating from the analysand. For example, after several weeks of expressing obsessive fears of getting mud on my new couch, he finally managed to splatter it with mud. I interpreted this as a warning to me that he could play dirty. He admitted at first only to wanting to "make his mark" and projected his competitive, murderous rage onto me by perceiving me as a "butcher": I had replaced my benign desk with a "butcher block" table along the wall. He accused me the next day of eliminating the stains he had left on the couch in order to "obliterate his individuality." He was wheezing and coughing as our next session began. He said that he wished I could "surgically remove the organs" that made trouble for him. "I want you to make me a eunuch . . . masculine ambitions are dangerous." He reported that he coveted the twenty acres of beautiful land available behind his new house and had said to his wife, "If my father died and I had his inheritance, I could buy all of this." He recognized that this had not been his adult self speaking, but had been a residuum of something he had felt "way back" when, as a little boy, he had wanted his father out of the way so that he could "take over his business and his wife, control the babies, everything!" He went on: "He was an ogre. I was afraid of him, afraid if he knew what I thought and felt . . . he'd kill me. He was power hungry and didn't want to share or make concessions. It's better to surgically remove what gets you into trouble. Hmmmm! The concession I have to make here is to share everything with you. It makes me mad. I don't want to share with you! I want it all! Sharing is giving away, ending up with less." He contemplated his rage at his father and his wish "to be the young Turk, the tough one, instead of the turkey my father wanted to pluck!" As I noted before he left, his wheezing had disappeared in the course of his emotional outburst.

He sold his old house (at a considerable profit) and closed on the new one, which cost him the same amount that his father's house was valued at for tax purposes. He paid me promptly, as usual, and thought about paying me "month after month after month." "Protection money," I said. He vociferously agreed. He was terrified that his inclination to be ruthless and destructive would put him and others in danger, and he expressed a wish for me to keep him a "castrated, safe, controlled eunuch." He expressed fear of his envy of his father, whom as a boy he had perceived as a cruel, tough lord and master over his mother and over everyone else. He was afraid of his voracious wish to have "unlimited power and all that goes with it." He stated, "I'm afraid that buying that estate is setting in motion the vicious pursuit of the realization of all my dangerous fantasies!"

He continued to analyze and work through his oedipal conflicts, in the course of which he excitedly but anxiously perceived himself as moving toward symbolically "castrating" his father by taking over the business and drawing more money that he did (as his father had actually done with his own father), with fear of retaliation. He became excited when he saw a television show about whales and discovered that, so very different from humans, two males court one female and then it doesn't seem to matter to them which one impregnates her. He ruminated unhappily about being (a bit) overweight and made a parapraxis in which he meant to say that killer whales pose a danger to whales but instead said that they were dangerous to humans. He became confused, thinking that he may have underpaid me the previous month, to which he associated having gone from paying me a reduced fee for a long time because his income had been so small to reaching a point, with my help, at which he earned more than I did and expected to earn more and more. He anxiously mentioned the possibility of raising the fee he paid me, but quickly recanted. He expressed highly conflicted attitudes, ranging from wanting to provide for and take care of me, with affection and gratitude for my having helped him become a much happier person, to wanting to outdo and humiliate me and leave me to starve. He was as fearful of exposing tender, affectionate feelings toward me as he was of revealing fantasies of robbing and killing me.

He realized that he fantasized having obtained what he had by "stealing" from me. He was flourishing as the result of an analysis that had begun with a low fee and in which he had tried to get results passively, as gifts, rather than working for them. He expressed gratitude to me for "standing firm" and "patiently" waiting for *him* to obtain results from the analysis through his own efforts. "I'm no longer inhibited and noncompetitive," he said. "I've gotten balls, masculinity, from you. Or did I have them all the time? I watched you and tried to find out how *you* did things, and be like you. But you're smarter than I am. You wouldn't show me, and you wouldn't fight with me. You decided you'd rather wait ten years if necessary for *me* to find it in myself. I always used to fake it. I never believed I had the balls. I always thought I had to get them or imitate someone who did. I didn't really get my balls from you. I had them all the time. But I was afraid someone would take them from me, the way I wanted to take them from everyone who looked like a big man with big balls . . . I don't *need* to sulk and act like a little boy—which always enraged my father—and I can use my balls with a woman. You're not jumping and screaming and angry. And I bet you don't feel I've taken anything away from you! And don't think I haven't wanted to! I wanted your balls! But I don't need your balls. Where would I be if I had *your* balls? Back where I was ten years ago: hiding my balls and wanting to get yours so I wouldn't lose my own. I'm nervous . . . I'm a bit scared."

After the patient closed on his new house, he became more and more aggressive and assertive in his daily life. But he still suffered from anxiety lest he become a "destructive monster," a "prick," like his image of his father. And he still envied his "masochistic" sister for being female, having a baby, and being "kept" by his father. He made effective use of free association, which permitted him to gain insight into his envy of women: their breasts, an enviable source of "supply," and their mouthlike vaginas give them the means, he felt, to get loved and to be given sexual pleasure and babies. He came to see that in a childish way he wanted to have "it all, to have what father gets and what mother gets, to be male and female both. I couldn't compete with my father as a boy, but I couldn't hold a candle to my mother!" To candle, he associated flame, passion, and penis. If he couldn't have his mother one way (sexually, as a man), he realized, he would have her another way (identify with her as a woman, an identification modeled in part on the observation that his father dominated her as well as the children). He recalled my periodically confronting him about his insistence upon feeling miserable and feeling that he did not have enough no matter how much he had.

He said: "What am I so unhappy about? That I can't have a baby? That I can't measure up to my mother? To my father? That I can't be a woman? So absurd!"

In the weeks that followed, this theme was worked through intensively, mainly within the setting of the transference. He gradually came to see that as frightening to him as it was to think of violent, bloody battles between us, it was just as frightening to find that he wanted me to love and protect him. He recalled that as a boy he had furtively stolen money from his father's pocket. He had done this not only out of competition and anger but also as a derivative of his wish for his father's love. He felt that he was repeating this by paying me less than he could. But he avoided any discussion of increasing the fee. It gradually became clear, via dreams and other forms of expression, that he was afraid I would not simply ask for more money, but would "gouge" him and "take away everything." I noted his dangling the money before me tantalizingly, *inviting* me to attack him and take it away. "It is a fear and also a wish," he replied. His next thought was that he had heard about a man who had gone into his son's room to investigate a noise, only to have his son shoot him in the belief that he was a burglar. When I connected this with his provoking me to go after him for his money, he recalled his resentment of his father's intrusions into his bedroom when he had been growing up and his repeated fantasy of blowing his father's head off with a shotgun.

At this point in the analysis the patient began to withhold not only money but his thoughts as well. His free associations dried up and were replaced by a dreary, repetitive, staccato recital of complaints about the slow progress of his treatment. He wheezed a bit as he related his difficulty in speaking freely to the fear that what he shared with me was lost to him. He challenged me to come after him and "dig" the thoughts and feelings out of him.

He continued to subtly encourage me to lose my patience and demand more money from him. He didn't like to see me incurring the expense of repairing the sidewalk in front of my office, for example. The money he gave me should go for food only and nothing more, he said. He deftly contrasted this with his own ambitions. In business, he said guiltily, he presented himself as a plodding, soft-spoken, scrupulously fair and honest man who impressed everyone with what a good loser he could be as he trudged along unaggressively, yet he "somehow" landed most of the lucrative contracts he pursued in competition with rival companies. He was on the brink, in fact, of obtaining exclusive rights to a product that could give him an edge over his competitors, which would cut them out of the market altogether. And this was in a branch of the business that he had just developed into something very profitable, much to his father's surprise.

He connected all this with his feelings about the analytic fee. He probably should pay me more, he said, but he wasn't about to offer it himself. He couldn't understand why I didn't insist on a fee increase, though he expected that he would be very angry if I did. He fantasied my attacking him, "beating the shit out of him," and "dumping him, bleeding, on the doorstep," although somehow he would end up the victor rather than the vanquished. He was not sure how, but he felt this was connected in some way with his childhood wish to have his mother to himself. I called attention to his allusion to the idea of provoking me into raping him anally and making him bleed like a menstruating woman; although outwardly he was picturing himself as being treated like a woman, his plan was to come out of it a masculine winner rather than a loser. In subsequent sessions, he confirmed this, via multiple corroboratory fantasies and lines of thought, and he struggled to understand it.

He pondered over his conflicted attitudes about paying me, in the course of which I called attention not only to his wish for me to castrate him and take everything away from him but also to his wish to be freed of his neurotic anxieties "at no cost," i.e., without having to give up the infantile strivings that underlay them. Mindful of what he had teasingly attempted to provoke me to do, I interpreted his behavior with me in terms of the attempt to buy me off: he wished to get me to accept money from him in lieu of analytic work through which he would lose not only his neurotic anxieties and inhibitions but his neurotic sources of infantile gratification as well. This led to very fruitful work, in which we came to understand the transference–countertransference transactions in terms of his wish to act out exciting but terrifying primal scene fantasies (with both positive and negative oedipal identifications) with me instead of analyzing them. It was only after we had accomplished this, nearly a year after he first mentioned the idea of a larger free in accordance with his greatly improved financial circumstances, that we finally increased the fee. Had I been unable to recognize the countertransference traps into which I had been so cleverly led and had permitted myself to press him quickly for a fee increase rather than holding firm to the analytic goal of working with him first to understand what was involved, we would have acted out his neurotic conflicts together instead of analyzing them.

CONCLUSION

I have attempted to explicate the impression that countertransference is an inevitable feature of every psychoanalysis. I see it as inevitable because of the very nature of the psychoanalytic process and because of the impossibility of any analyst's gaining so thorough an understanding of and control over his own unconscious inclinations from his training analysis that he will be completely impervious to the skillful efforts of his analysands to draw him into acting out their neurotic conflicts with them rather than analyzing them. Two clinical examples have been presented. In both, the very arrangements and "rules" of analysis were implicated in the transition from understanding to enacting the unconscious inclinations.

Annie Reich (1951, 1960, 1966) addressed herself cogently to this aspect of psychoanalysis. As she pointed out, countertransference always represents an interference with analytic progress, just as the analysand's transference always represents a resistance to it. The analyst's ability to recognize, analyze, and learn from it, so that he can return to analytic empathy and cognitive understanding, is as necessary as is analysis of the patient's transference to the analyst of his neurotic inclinations. A psychoanalyst needs to be vigilant to the emergence of countertransference reactions so that he can become aware of them, without shame and without feelings of inadequacy or failure. He can then employ self-analysis (or a period of reanalysis with another analyst if necessary) to understand and overcome them. As Annie Reich put it at the end of her last paper (1966) on the subject, "The possibility of gliding from a controlled, aimdirected use of one's unconscious into being run by it, is always there. Who is so free of guilt that he may throw the first stone?" (p. 360).

The importance of self-analysis in the work of the psychoanalyst has been given increasing recognition (e.g., Baum 1977 [and in Panel 1974], Beiser 1984, Calder 1980, Fleming 1971, Gardner 1983). It is only one avenue, however, of several that are available to help psychoanalysts remain alert to their countertransference inclinations so that they can maintain control over them. Another is an ongoing communication with their analytic colleagues, who also are struggling with this difficult dimension of psychoanalytic work, a communication that is afforded by involving themselves in study groups and by teaching, writing scientific papers, and participating in panels such as this one.

REFERENCES

Buan, O. E. (1977). Countertransference and the vicissitudes in an analyst's development. *Psychoanalytic Review* 64:539–550.

Beiser, H. R. (1984). An example of self-analysis. *Journal of the American Psychoanalytic Association* 32:3–12.

Beres, D. & Arlow, J. A. (1974). Fantasy and identification in empathy. *Psychoanalytic Quarterly* 43:26–50.

Calder, K. T. (1980). An analyst's self-analysis. *Journal of the American Psychoanalytic Association* 28:5–20.

Calef, V. & Weinshel, E. M. (1983). A note on consummation and termination. *Journal of the American Psychoanalytic Association* 31:643–650.

Fleming, J. (1971). Freud's concept of self-analysis. In *Currents in Psychoanalysis,* ed. I. M. Marcus. New York: Int. Univ. Press, pp. 14–47.

Fliess, R. (1942). The metapsychology of the analyst. *Psychoanalytic Quarterly* 11:211–227.

Freud, A. (1954). Problems of technique in adult analysis. In *The Writings of Anna Freud, Vol. 4. Indications for Child Analysis and Other Papers, 1945–1956.* New York: Int. Univ. Press, 1968. pp. 377–406.

Freud, S. (1887–1902). *The Origins of Psycho-Analysis. Letters to Wilhelm Fliess, Drafts and Notes: 1887–1902.* New York: Basic Books, 1954.

_____ (1900). The interpretation of dreams. *Standard Edition 4/5.*

_____ (1910). The future prospects of psycho-analytic therapy. *Standard Edition* 11.

_____ (1912). Recommendations to physicians practicing psycho-analyis. *Standard Edition* 12.

_____ (1937). Analysis terminable and interminable. *Standard Edition* 23.

Gardner, M. R. (1983). *Self Inquiry.* Boston, Toronto: Little, Brown & Co.

Jacobs, T. J. (1983). The analyst and the patient's object world; notes on an aspect of countertransference. *Journal of the American Psychoanalytic Association* 31:619–642.

Panel (1974). The analyst's emotional life during work. R. Aaron, Reporter. *Journal of the American Psychoanalytic Association* 22:160–169.

Reich, A. (1951). On counter-transference. *International Journal of Psycho-Analysis* 32:25–31.

_____ (1960). Further remarks on counter-transference. *International Journal of Psycho-Analysis* 41:389–395.

_____ (1966). Empathy and countertransference. In *Annie Reich: Psychoanalytic Contributions*. New York. Int. Univ. Press, 1973, pp. 344–360.

Chapter 5

Some Technical Problems of Countertransference

Jacob Arlow, M.D.

There is a considerable difference of opinion as to what should be included under the heading of countertransference. My own views are closest to those expressed by Annie Reich (1951):

> Counter-transference . . . comprises the effects of the analyst's own unconscious needs and conflicts on his understanding or technique. In such cases the patient represents for the analyst an object of the past on to whom past feelings and wishes are projected, just as it happens in the patient's transference situation with the analyst. The provoking factor for such an occurrence may be something in the

Presented at the Regional Conference of Psychoanalytic Societies of Greater New York at Princeton, New Jersey, June 8–10, 1984, as part of a panel discussion chaired by Dr. Edmund Slakter. It also appeared as an article in the *Psychoanalytic Quarterly*, 1985, 54(2):164–174.

patient's personality or material or something in the analytic situation as such. [p. 26]

This definition describes countertransference in the narrow sense. On another occasion (1960), Annie Reich said:

> One of the prevailing misconceptions is the equation of counter-transference with the analyst's total response to the patient, using the term to include all conscious reactions, responses and ways of behaviour. This is as incorrect as to call transference everything that emerges in the patient in relation to the analyst during analysis, and not to distinguish between the manifestations of unconscious strivings and reality-adapted, conscious behavior or observations. The analyst is for the patient, and the patient for the analyst, also a reality object and not only a transference or counter-transference object. There has to be in the analyst some (aim-inhibited) object-libidinous interest in the patient, which is a prerequisite for empathy. Conscious responses should be regarded as countertransference only if they reach an inordinate intensity or are strongly tainted by inappropriate sexual or aggressive feelings, thus revealing themselves to be determined by unconscious infantile strivings. [pp. 389–390]

Since our main interest is in discussing clinical material, I will restrict the presentation of my general comments to a number of seemingly dogmatic statements. There are several situations in the psychoanalytic interaction that foster the emergence of counter-transference in individuals who are so disposed. The first occurs when the analyst identifies with the patient, in the sense that the patient's unconscious fantasies and wishes correspond to persistent unconscious fantasies and wishes of the analyst. Here it becomes necessary to distinguish between empathy and counter-transference (Beres and Arlow 1974). In both empathy and countertransference an identification is effected with the patient. In empathy the identification is transient, a temporary sharing of derivative expressions of the patient's unconscious fantasies and wishes. In the usual course of events, this is followed by a breaking-off of the identification, a separation from the patient. The experience of sharing the patient's unconscious fantasy derivatives serves as a clue to the understanding of the patient's conflicts (Arlow 1979). In the case of countertransference, however, the analyst remains fixed at the point of identification with the patient. He is caught up in conflicts identical to those of the patient. Accordingly, the analyst becomes prone to the vicissitudes of these conflicts, and he may tend to act out or to respond defensively. Many people fail to make an adequate distinction between the transient identification that is characteristic of empathy and the persistent identification that leads to countertransference. It was an awareness of this confusion which led me to say that one man's empathy is another man's countertransference.

The effects of persistent countertransference identification are varied. The classic blind spot, i.e., the "refusal" or inability to "see" what the material is about, is only one form of response, and in my experience by no means the most common one. Actually, what is happening is that the analyst does not want the patient's material to remind him of his own unconscious conflicts. Therefore, he misses the interpretation or fails to give it, justifying his reluctance through various rationalizations. Additionally, there is a tendency to divert the patient from continuing the pursuit of derivatives of his unconscious conflict by some intervention which directs attention to other elements in the material, and also to assume a moralistic stance and to condemn in the patient what the analyst cannot stand in himself.

A second form of countertransference disturbance arises from the nature of the material that the patient presents. This may evoke fantasy wishes in the analyst not necessarily identical with the unconscious wishes of the patient. They may be complementary, as in the case of the patient's wish to be rescued and the wish of the analyst to rescue. In instances where there is a strong unresolved conflict operative in the analyst, material quite peripheral to the patient's central conflicts may nonetheless have an evocative effect upon the analyst's potential for countertransference.

And third, there are those instances in which something in the psychoanalytic situation as such is evocative of the analyst's conflicts. The wish to rescue has already been referred to. The analytic setting may represent a theater where the analyst may play out some unconscious role of being the central performer to an admiring audience — an opportunity to display his cleverness or to use the analytic situation as a testing ground for his capacities. On the other hand, he may assume the role of the admiring auditor, unconsciously identifying with the patient. The physical conditions of the analytic situation, the patient supine, the analyst and/or the patient passive, may be read by the analyst in terms that stimulate unconscious wishes connected with passivity, masochism, etc.

In my experience, instances of the first category of factors predisposing to countertransference—i.e., persistent countertransference identification—are the most numerous. To illustrate this process, let me cite an example that I have published previously (Arlow 1963). This material comes from the supervision of a candidate whose patient was a young, male, homosexual alcoholic. It was characteristic of the patient's behavior to ingratiate himself in a submissive way with strong men whom he admired and whose prowess he wished to grasp for himself during the act of fellatio. He corresponded to the type of homosexual patient described by Nunberg (1938) and by Anna Freud (1952), namely, the type of individual who submits his penis to be sucked, but who in fantasy identifies himself with the person sucking in an act of castrating the powerful man. Conflict over these wishes had resulted in many crippling inhibitions. The mechanism underlying the patient's perverse trends became understandable in a dream which the therapist reported during a supervisory session. In the dream the patient is lying on the couch. He turns around to offer the therapist a cigarette. The therapist had been having difficulties with this patient and had been nonplussed by this particular dream. At the point when he reported to me that the patient in the dream had turned around to offer him a cigarette, the candidate took one for himself, and, although he knew very well that I do not smoke, extended the pack to me and asked, "Do you want a cigarette?"

The reason for the candidate's difficulty with this particular dream and with the patient could be understood by this bit of acting out. He had identified with the patient and, through his identification, had demonstrated a very probable source of countertransference difficulty, namely, the possibility that he and the patient had similar problems.

The second illustration is from the experience of a female therapist. The patient was a young professional woman, whose main difficulty related to her unhappy experiences with men. She had been married and divorced, had a number of stormy sado-masochistic relations with several men, one of two of whom were definitely criminal types, and presently was trying to get herself married to a man who had assured her from the very beginning that he had no intention of marrying her.

At this point in the treatment, the patient's conflicts concerning her younger brother had come to the fore. Interpretations had been based primarily upon sibling rivalry, growing out of competition for the mother's love and attention. Finally, the material demonstrated that there were other dimensions to the anger, in addition to the thought of having been displaced in the affections and attention of the mother. The associations revealed envy of the brother because he was a boy and resentment that she, the patient, had not been given a penis. In this context, there appeared hitherto unreported memories of trying to harm the brother while he was in the patient's charge. When he was young, she would pinch him when no one was looking. Later, she would twist his arm and threaten him if he reported these acts to their parents. Several dreams were reported, of which this one is typical. The patient is taking care of her brother at the seaside, and they are walking near the surf. Suddenly a shark comes out and bites his leg, but also bites the patient's arm. Among her other symptoms, this patient complained of a fear of mice and insects. She was afraid of being bitten. This material, as well as other associations, made possible the interpretation of a hostile impulse directed toward the brother's genitals. The patient responded with a memory of reaching into her brother's diaper with the intention of feeling his genitals, but the therapist did not carry the interpretation of the material any further. She did not point out the wish to grab the genitals and to eat them, although she was well aware of the nature of the patient's unconscious wish (*cf.*, Arlow 1963).

Earlier, the therapist had permitted the patient to rationalize the anger and envy of the brother in terms of dependency, frustration, and sibling rivalry for the mother's care. At this point, she rationalized her withholding the "deeper" interpretation in terms of waiting for the patient to state the wish herself in more explicit terms. When the handling of this problem was discussed with the therapist, she mentioned that she had a similar problem with a younger brother of her own, which apparently she had not fully explored or worked through in her own treatment. She was very appreciative of the insight that she got into the countertransference and was determined to handle the matter more directly.

What happened was striking. She pursued the subject, but in an aggressive, accusatory fashion. She was not satisfied that the patient could accept her interpretation of her wish to castrate her brother. Unwittingly, she was insisting that the patient actually try to recollect the wish to bite and to eat the genitals. She was treating the patient as if she were a sinner who could not be forgiven until the crime had been fully confessed. Accordingly, in the first stage of her problem, she was defensively fending off being reminded by the patient's material of her own impulses toward her younger brother. In the second part of her activity, having become aware of her identification with the patient, she was trying to make her feel guilty and remorseful for those wishes, as she herself must have felt at some earlier period. The discussion of this second phase of her countertransference response proved very effective. Once she dropped her accusatory stance (which had not escaped the patient at all), new and very important material began to appear. This material concerned memories of being in the parental bedroom and of observing the primal scene. The material indicated that the patient wished to be in her father's position, having relations with the mother, and that she fantasied acquiring his phallus by eating it, in order to make it possible for her to fulfill the father's role in intercourse with the mother.

The third example concerns the supervision of a patient, a young physician who was struggling with his sexual role. He had powerful conscious homosexual impulses, which he could not accept. At the same time, he was extremely fearful of women and terrified of being trapped in any relationship with them. Supervision began five months after the patient had been taken into treatment, yet from the way the male therapist presented the material to me, it sounded as if treatment had only just begun. The preliminary material afforded some insight into the nature of the patient's difficulty. The patient spoke mainly of his mother, who was pictured as a cold, inhibiting, threatening woman. Metaphors revealing a fantasy of being sucked up and swallowed by machines gave us some insight into the nature of his unconscious fears. In addition, it was plain to see that the patient had a great fear of being trapped and a need to submit masochistically to men.

The first transference problem took the form of behavior concerning appointments. The patient kept trying to control the analysis by creating situations that would make it necessary for him to cancel sessions. Some of these could be rationalized in terms of his professional responsibilities, but other excuses seemed trivial, e.g., canceling his session so that he could give a party for his friends to watch a special television program, or taking long weekends or informing the analyst that he was going on vacation at a time other than the analyst's vacation, without discussing it in advance or seeing if he could rearrange his schedule. The candidate did not deal with this behavior as a problem, and when it was called to his attention, he seemed unable to call it to the patient's attention. Instead, he lapsed into a confused, helpless attitude, as if he were afraid to confront the patient. The patient responded by cutting more sessions for various reasons, until it reached the point where little analytic work could be accomplished.

I pointed out to the candidate that such behavior was incompatible with the pursuit of an analysis and also contrary to the analytic agreement. It was necessary to indicate this to the patient. This belated interpretation promptly revealed the nature of the patient's underlying motivation. His behavior was intended to provoke the analyst, part of his deep-seated masochistic problem. In the following weeks, the patient kept repeating his provocative behavior in the form of bafflement, saying that he was not clear about the nature of the analytic arrangement, and would the analyst please explain it to him once again. He accused the analyst of treating him unfairly, even though nothing had been done. He kept misinterpreting the candidate's remarks. For example, when the candidate suggested that perhaps the patient could arrange for a change of schedule that would make it possible for him to take his vacation at the same time as the analyst, the patient reacted with the thought that when he came back from his vacation, the analyst would have terminated the treatment. In every way, in the patient's eyes, he was being threatened, accused, demeaned, and mistreated.

Instead of interpreting the misinterpretation of the interaction in terms of the patient's masochistic needs, the candidate kept trying to straighten out the "reality" of his statements and their interaction, without, however, stating explicitly what the psychoanalytic contract requires.

I tried to explore with the candidate why he had not pointed out to the patient how he was consistently recasting everything in terms of a fantasy of being assaulted or demeaned, as we had been discussing during supervision. He replied that the patient was not clear about the responsibilities regarding time and that he was trying to explain it to the patient. Since I had not been present at the initiation of treatment, I asked him how he had set the terms of the analytic contract with the patient, and why he had not reminded the patient of those terms. What followed was a dramatic re-enactment in the supervisory situation of what had been taking place in the analytic situation. The candidate kept asking me for clarification as to what I wanted. He wanted amplification of the technical maneuvers, etc. I found myself repeating what I had told him in several different ways, until I pointed out to him that he was recapitulating with me in the supervision what the patient had been doing with him in the analysis. He recognized this immediately. It was clear to him that he had been identifying with the patient's masochistic, provocative behavior, and was trying to get me to be angry and abusive toward him, very much as the patient was trying to get him to scold him and to throw him out of treatment. Once he stopped reacting to the patient, the nature of the material changed dramatically, and what emerged were associations concerning passive sexual wishes, first displaced onto a substitute transference object and then subsequently clearly directed toward the therapist.

In conclusion, I should like to make a few observations. First, much as we observe and study the patients, the patients do the same to us. They observe our reactions, often in order to ascertain what they can do to provoke gratification of their infantile strivings. The repertoire of behavior available to the patient for this purpose is enormous, but I would like to emphasize the role of silence (Arlow 1961). By placing the burden of intervention on the therapist, the patient is able to get a good sampling of the spontaneous productions that the silence occasions in the analyst. Silence is one of the most effective instruments for stimulating countertransference responses in the analyst.

Secondly, I would like to point out that countertransference reactions and defenses on the part of the analyst are very often borrowed from the patient. Thus, there is possible a community not only of unconscious wishes between patient and analyst, but also of defenses against those wishes. In supervision, when some countertransference interference in technique is pointed out to the analyst, one can observe quite frequently how the analyst reacts defensively to the supervisor's observations in the same way as the patient had responded to the analyst's interpretations.

My final point is the importance of recognizing in ourselves indicators of countertransference reactions. Their manifestations are protean. Essentially, they all fall under the heading of loss of analytic stance. Most commonly discussed are the so-called "blind spots" that are picked up in supervision, feelings of confusion that persist when the analyst is unable to grasp the flow of associations, that is, a sense that he has lost his empathic contact with the patient. More dramatic and often more discussed are those examples of excessive emotion, loss of control, irritability, sleepiness, or boredom. Equally important are a number of indicators outside of the analytic situation that the analyst would do well to consider as evidence of possible countertransference involvement. Recurrent thoughts about the patient outside of working hours, especially those characterized by mood changes, such as depression, usually indicate the probability of some countertransference disturbance. The same is true if the patient appears in the manifest content of the analyst's dreams or if there are intrusive fantasies centering on the patient. More subtle, but perhaps equally significant, is the tendency to recount events of the analysis or to talk to others about the nature of the patient's problems, even when professional confidence is not breached. Finally, there are the well-known slips of the tongue and parapraxes that occur in connection with the patient, particularly in scheduling, lateness, and forgetting of appointments. In general, the range of countertransference reactions is almost as wide and as varied as the transference reactions of the patients. The difference resides in the fact that much more attention is paid to the latter than to the former.

REFERENCES

Arlow, J. A. (1961). Silence and the theory of technique. *Journal of the American Psychoanalytic Association* 9:44–55.
_____ (1963). The supervisory situation. *Journal of the American Psychoanalytic Association* 11:576–594.
_____ (1979). The genesis of interpretation. *Journal of the American Psychoanalytic Association* Suppl. 27:193–206.
Beres, D. & Arlow, J. A. (1974). Fantasy and identification in empathy. *Psychoanalytic Quarterly* 43:26–50.
Freud, A. (1952). Studies in passivity. In *The Writings of Anna Freud,* Vol. 4. *Indications for Child Analysis and Other Papers,* 1945–1956. New York: Int. Univ. Press, 1968, pp. 245–259.
Nunberg, H. (1938). Homosexuality, magic and aggression. *International Journal of Psycho-Analysis* 19:1–16.
Reich, A. (1951). On counter-transference. *International Journal of Psycho-Analysis* 32:25–31.
_____ (1960). Further remarks on counter-transference. *International Journal of Psycho-Analysis* 41:389–395.

Chapter 6
Countertransference: Concepts and Controversies

Harold Blum, M.D.

Interest in the topic of countertransference occurs at a time of special interest in the inner life of the analyst. I refer to the analyst at work in the psychoanalytic situation and to renewed interest in the analyzing instrument, the analyzing functions, the work ego, empathy, the formulation of interpretations, and so on. How does the analyst observe and infer, listen, learn, and intervene? What is the analyst thinking and feeling during the analytic hour, and what is his contribution to the analytic situation and process? There has been a noticeable shift in recent years away from singular concentration on the intrapsychic processes of the patient and the

Presented at the Regional Conference of Psychoanalytic Societies of Greater New York at Princeton, New Jersey, June 8–10, 1984, as part of a panel discussion chaired by Dr. Edmund Slakter. It also appeared as a chapter in *Psychoanalysis: The Science of Mental Conflict: Essays in Honor of Charles Brenner.* Analytic Press, 1986.

patient's response to interpretation and other interventions to the thoughts, feelings, attitudes, values, etc. of the analyst; the analyst's input and influence upon the patient's associations, and the patient's overall adaptation to the analysis. Earlier psychoanalytic concerns about suggestion, education, manipulation of the patient, and later, about the introduction of parameters have now focused upon the personality of the analyst and the patient's reactions to the analyst's actual personality. This present-day interest in a two-person analytic field of forces and the analyst as participant/observer has many ramifications. For some, who the analyst is, becomes as or more important than what he does. In some quarters, attention to the real relationship and to the analyst's actual personality and influence has tended to cast the transference of the patient in a new light. The analyst is seen not only as the classical object of transference, but is so evoking and provoking of particular transference responses that the transference becomes more allied to the present situation than, first and foremost, a repetition of the infantile past. In a different direction, study of the analyst's own reactions and responses has intensified interest in that area of analyst reaction denoted by the term "countertransference." Countertransference is not a term that is easily defined but it has always classically dealt with impediments and interferences with the analyst's neutrality, empathy, and interpretations in the analytic process.

Freud introduced countertransference as a concept in 1910 after he already formulated transference. Countertransference has also been relegated to lesser and later studies when compared to other aspects of the theory of psychoanalytic technique. It is not hard to understand, that beginning with Freud, there would be reluctance and reticence, issues of discretion and confession for analysts to divulge in depth, their countertransference difficulties. I emphasize the difficulty and impediment side of countertransference in contrast to the more recent literature on the beneficial uses of countertransference,a point to which I shall return. It is difficult to do analysis, a very complex intimate profession with many occupational hazards. Unlike other forms of medical and therapeutic endeavors, psychoanalysis involves much more than special knowledge, skill, and experience. It involves the personality of the analyst, his work ego and inner resources, his capacity for reversible regression and progressive reorganization, for maintaining neutrality and objectivity in the face of emotional storms. The analyst's exposure of his technique, of his technical difficulties or errors, becomes, in part, a self-revealing exhibition of his inner life and, particularly, of his own unresolved conflicts and problems. Attempts at open discussion of countertransference too often meet with an embarrassed silence. The analyst's discretion and his defenses are both reasons why it is so difficult to obtain clinical material illustrative of countertransference reactions. Anyone who has experienced and observed supervision knows the problems engendered when countertransference comes to the fore. And yet, it is from supervision that we can glean and discuss some outstanding examples of countertransference without presenting our own countertransferences which may make us so uneasy. We may recognize the countertransference of colleagues in other situations, such as in reanalysis, training analysis, the treatment of psychiatrists, etc., not all of which are equally adapted to analytic neutrality, confidentiality, and comfort.

How the analyst handles the countertransference once it is recognized is another matter. The time-honored prescriptions have been more work in the training analysis, in the case of candidates; self-analysis; return to analysis (once recommended by Freud every five years); and consultation. The difficulty with the conscious recommendations is that countertransference is not always recognized in full awareness, is not always fully accepted after it is recognized, and the response of the analyst to becoming aware of the countertransference is highly variable. All of the proposed solutions have their own advantages and side affects. In the day-to-day ongoing work of psychoanalysis, we depend upon self-analytic abilities to deal with countertransference issues. Analysts are vulnerable to all human frailties, to conflict and regression. Where self-analysis does not succeed in resolving countertransference, return to analysis or reanalysis may be indicated. The point I wish to stress here is that every analyst should have a capacity for self-analysis and that for the candidate as opposed to other patients, I would regard evidence of self-initiated progress in the analytic work and the manifestations of self-analytic initiatives as a requirement for termination. I myself do not hold to termination and post-termination self-analytic capacities for any other group of patients except candidates, and I rather think that apart from analysts, most patients do not lead self-analytic lives. Moreover, our ordinary patients are not later immersed in an analytic process to help others and thereby exposed to stimulation, activation, and provocation of their own unconscious conflicts as occurs in the daily life of the psychoanalyst.

The analytic countertransference may be defined as a counter-reaction to the patient's transference which is unconscious and indicative of the analyst's own unresolved intrapsychic conflicts. In defining the countertransference in essentially this form, Freud (1910) observed, "No psychoanalyst goes further than his own complexes and internal resistances permit; and we consequently require that he shall begin his activity with a self-analysis and continually carry it deeper while he is making his observations on his patients" (p. 145). There are many variations on the definition of the countertransference as counter to the particular patient's transference. A closely related concept involves the analyst's transferences which are ready to attach themselves to a particular patient, his character or transferences, and are often activated by something within the patient which touches on the analyst's infantile unconscious conflicts. The analyst may have neurotic reactions to any aspect of the patient and not only to the transference. In actuality, transference and countertransference are intertwined elements of the same analytic process, but it may add to clarification, rather than confusion, to theoretically distinguish between the analyst's transferences to patients and his countertransference to the transference of the particular patient. The distinction which sounds impossible, and often is in many cases, might be clinically useful, e.g., in concerning an analyst's reaction to a pregnant patient because of her pregnancy and not because of her own individual transference neurosis.

The analyst's transference reaction to the patient as a pregnant woman may not be identical to his countertransference to her transference. The term countertransference implicitly stresses what is evoked by the patient's transference, and in less precise definition, by the patient's psychopathology. The analyst may respond irrationally to a patient's presenting symptoms or to an aspect of his history, e.g., perverse tendencies. The patient's psychopathology is related to the analyst's countertransference but not necessarily to the analyst's use of the patient as a transference object. In this theoretical distinction the analyst may have a transference reaction to the patient at the point of referral before the analyst has a countertransference to the patient's analytic transference reactions. The analyst's transferences may be displaced from other patients, as though still consciously or unconsciously preoccupied with another patient. His own personal life may be associated with his vulnerability to countertransference reactions and/or the extension of his personal problems into his professional work. His own "agenda" may then interfere with the patient's free association, although not necessarily an agenda directly evoked by the patient's psychopathology.

In actual analytic work, the analyst's countertransference and spontaneous transference to the patient tend to merge and are usually inseparable. Countertransference is based upon the ubiquity of transference reactions (Brenner 1982) and cannot be understood apart from the analytic transference. A circular process may also occur, so that in the case of unanalyzed interfering countertransference reactions, the analyst has a countertransference to the patient's transference, and the patient, in turn, responds to the analyst's countertransference with the development of a so-called transference-countertransference bind or unconscious transference-countertransference collusion. Some types of analytic stalemates, psychotherapy on the couch and wild analysis, have dimensions of such a bind and bilateral neurotic enmeshment. The patient may masochistically adapt, for example, to persistent countertransference contempt. In extreme forms, the therapeutic relationship regresses to a pathological relationship and to a form of *folie à deux*.

Interestingly enough, many of the reports of colleagues of countertransference reactions are indicative of conscious awareness of the disturbance. The source of the disturbance of analytic function lies, at least temporarily, outside of the analyst's awareness. The analyst may become aware of his countertransference in innumerable fashions ranging from loss of attention and attunement to symptoms, to inappropriate responses and interventions, parapraxes, fantasies, dreams, violations of the framework with irregularities in the handling of time, schedule, and fees. The desire to help may be subverted with too much therapeutic zeal and rescue fantasies, or loss of therapeutic interest and concern with boredom, or subtle devaluation of the patient's efforts at mastery. Any aspect of the analytic relationship and analytic work may be compromised. It may be evident in silence or in speech as in changes of pitch, pressure, syntax, etc. Countertransference always involves some move by the analyst away from an analytic attitude and neutrality. Patients invariably have transference reactions to the countertransference (Little 1951, Gill 1982) as well as to the analyst's character, style, interventions, and the analytic setting. It may be inferred that analogous reactions occur in life between any two people who have repetitive, prolonged intimate contact, though the transferences of everyday experience are not analyzable. It is certainly of importance whether countertransference occurs with a particular patient or with most or all patients, whether it is part of a general tendency or specific to a case with which the analyst finds himself in difficulty, whether it is acute or chronic, whether it is always there like the transference, and whether it is symmetrical to the transference so that one could talk at times of the countertransference neurosis (Racker 1968). To my mind, the latter would be such an extreme form of interference in the analytic work that analytic progress would be impossible. A. Reich (1960) wrote of permanent countertransference which is doubtless related to the analyst's chronic neurotic symptoms and inhibitions and to character disorder. If the analyst is angry with all of his patients and is chronically angry, is that angry analyst embroiled in countertransference? These reactions would not be counter to the transference as defined by Freud, but even here, close observation shows the nuances and variations on the theme with each case and how often the analyst's character disorder is interwoven with his transference and resistance tendencies toward his patients. The chronically angry analyst will be prone to acute and specific negative countertransference.

Before illustrating some of these problems of countertransference, I would like to indicate changes in the way some analysts define the term and utilize the concept. These analysts use a much broader concept of countertransference. In addition, some analysts also have a much more positive view of the contribution of countertransference to the patient's analysis, seriously regarding it as diagnostic, useful, valuable, or even indispensible. Sublimations of voyeurism and parental authority may enhance the analyst's professional gratifications in analytic work, but these aim-inhibited, sublimated countertransference contributions to analytic work are quite remote from the interference of countertransference seduction or dogmatic interpretation. (I am dubious that countertransference is a prerequisite of analysis rather than an impediment, and that as A. Reich (1951) proposed, without it the necessary talent and interest are absent.)

The analysts who take the so-called totalistic as opposed to the classical position (Kernberg 1965) regard the countertransference as the total emotional reaction of the analyst to the patient. Going beyond conscious and unconscious reactions to the patient's transference, an interfering reaction of the analyst to work with the patient may be then subsumed under countertransference. The boundaries between these different reactions may not always be easy to evaluate, but the totalistic reaction becomes quite diffuse and may confuse efforts to delineate the countertransference in terms of the analyst's narrower internal reactions to the patient's neurotic transferences and psychopathology. Definitions and concepts may be furthter complicated by confusing countertransference and diagnostic assessment so that diagnosis and assessment of analyzability may depend, to an unusual degree, upon countertransference reactions to the potential patient rather than upon primary observation and evaluation of the patient. There are, of course, countertransference reactions at the very inception of treatment so often seen with the student analyst and the low fee or clinic patient. Countertransference reactions to termination are common, e.g., when the analyst may also find that old problems of separation and loss have resurfaced within himself.

The analyst's struggle to maintain neutrality appears related to controversies concerning the meaning of neutrality. For Freud (1914, p. 164) neutrality was maintained "through keeping the countertransference in check." Freud (1913) indicated that neutrality did not mean cold indifference or loss of spontaneity and even recommended an attitude of "sympathetic understanding" (p. 140). At times, other analysts have gone much further away from the neutrality recommended by Freud or contemporary "benevolent neutrality" in the direction of conveying positive interest and support. The anaclitic needs of the patient were to be met by a diatrophic attitude of the analyst (Gitelson 1952) and this, in turn, was to have a favorable effect in catalyzing the patient's capacity for developmental thrust and for participation in the analytic process. In brief, a positive countertransference was advocated and controversy immediately arose concerning whether the diatrophic attitude was really an abandonment of the analytic attitude and a substitution of preliminary supportive psychotherapy.

Two other controversies should be noted. The first concerns a point mentioned before—the beneficial utilization of countertransference to promote the analytic process. In this viewpoint, the countertransference, first seen as a resistance, almost becomes the carrying vehicle of the treatment, analogous to changing views of the role of transference in analysis (Tyson 1984). While recognition of countertransference and overcoming the countertransference as Freud recommended is beneficial and often essential, it does not follow that unrecognized and unanalyzed countertransference is an asset rather than a liability in analytic work. The patient and his conflicts should not be confused with the analyst and the analyst's own conflicts. It does not follow analytically and logically that analysis of the patient can be accomplished by the analyst's self-analysis. If the analyst were to assume that his reactions were identical to those of the patient or to those of significant objects in the patient's life, this would be unanalyzed complementary and concordant identification, a form of counteridentification (Racker 1968).

Following Racker, indirect countertransference has been described toward objects in the patient's life, e.g., in relation to the parent in adult analysis (Jacobs 1983) and in child analysis (Bernstein and Glenn 1978). The analyst might identify with a patient's irrational blame and reproach of his mother for her purported inadequacies and pathogenic influence. The analyst's use of trial identification, a vital component of empathy, would be radically altered in the direction of persistent overidentification.

Fliess (1953) described both the analyst's transient trial identification and the analyst's more enduring identification with the patient. The analyst's uncontrolled regressive identification with the patient is a major dimension of countertransference, "counter-

identification." The patient and analyst may have similar conflicts, complementary conflicts, or the analyst may unconsciously
identify with a peripheral feature of the patient or situation which
relates to his own conflicts (Arlow 1985). Neither the process nor
the products of such identification would be available for analytic
scrutiny and judgment in the form of trial identification, of
empathy, and secondarily processed in gaining analytic understanding of the patient (Beres and Arlow 1974). Countertransference confuses and should not be confused with empathy. The
analyst is not immune from subjectivity and countertransference
precisely because of his own unresolved unconscious conflicts.
The analyst's own infantile conflicts and attitudes cannot be
regarded as a replication of the patient's psychic reality. It is one
thing for the patient to elicit and evoke countertransference
reactions; it is quite another to assume that the patient places
reactions inside the analyst and that the countertransference can
be used to replace rather than to refine analytic empathy and
understanding (Fliess 1953, Blum 1984).

Heimann (1950) emphasized the value of the analyst's countertransference for comprehending the patient's transference; assuming the countertransference is correctly understood by the analyst,
it became, for her, a major pathway in the formulation of
interpretation. Little (1951) went a step further proposing that
countertransference assume even greater importance in the treatment of very disturbed and psychotic patients. Under these
circumstances, the lion's share of the analytic work would derive
from countertransference data. Some analysts proposed that the
countertransference-transference relationships might recapitulate
the infantile object relationships of the patient in a manner that
was more complete and convincing than transference analysis
alone. If the patient were seductive and the analyst responded with
his own erotic fantasies, then this might better indicate the
repetition of the past object relations than transference considerations alone in the case of a patient with a history of primal scene
exposure.

The patient's efforts to evoke, extract, or manipulate analytic
response are part of the analytic transference relationship. For
some analysts (Grinberg 1962), the projection of omnipotent
fantasy onto the analyst emotionally influences the analyst, and

the patient attempts to control the analyst who embodies the forbidden fantasy. This process has been called "projective identification," a complex term with imprecise, ambiguous meaning (Meissner 1980). The analyst who is subject to the patient's communications and cueing may identify with what the patient attributes to him, then conforming to the patient's fantasy expectations. This analytic reaction has been called "projective counteridentification," and implies the analyst's passive submission to the patient's projective attribution. The analyst would feel and act out of character, ostensibly based upon the patient's conflicts more than his own neurotic reactions (similar to Heimann's [1950] regarding countertransference as a creation of the patient).

Discussion here is necessarily limited, but concepts of projective identification remain elusive, both intrapsychic and interpersonal processes. As an attempt to bridge the intrapsychic and interpersonal, the concepts call attention to introjective-projective processes in the transference-countertransference field, though other defense mechanisms are also important. If an object is marred to justify the subject's projection, as when a paranoid personality provokes the very hostility he expects from others, the behavioral communication and registrations inevitably involve a complexity that transcends projection and identification. Intrapsychic processes can only be inferred from their verbal and nonverbal behavioral derivatives.

Patients use highly variable strategies to induce and seduce the analytic response they expect or demand. Both analyst and patient may have shared fantasies, erotic, aggressive, narcissistic, etc., which may derive from similar shared fantasies of their childhood. Unanalyzed shared fantasies which had some reality validation in childhood often underlie persistent countertransference difficulty (as in childhood seduction or other traumatic experience).

In reviewing the problems of subjectivity, counteridentification, failure to reverse regression with a loss of boundaries between analyst and patient and defensive countertransference distortion of the analytic data, I do not wish to preclude the possible value of countertransference analysis for the cues and clues it may provide for an enriched understanding of the patient. Countertransference analysis may secondarily convert a hindrance to a help, adversity to advantage. If the patient doesn't meet our therapeutic expectations, if we are frustrated and disappointed with his progress, if we feel irrationally critical or angry at the patient, we are entitled to ask what the patient is doing to provoke us, and in what way our silence or speech, our interventions or failure to intervene appropriately are defended against, or are gratifying the patient's transference. We may find, at times, that the countertransference does duplicate or mirror, in some degrees, some of the transferences of the patient, but this cannot be taken as an assumption, and can only be understood through reciprocal illumination of the transference and countertransference. The emergence of insight in the analytic situation is neither symmetrical nor synchronous in the analyst and patient and depends upon many observing, cognitive, and interpretive functions as well as affective responses. Without analysis, the countertransference experience cannot reliably provide additional clues to the transference conflicts and tends to favor the analyst's own conjectures and distortions over his objective observations of the patient in the ordering of the analytic process (Blum 1982).

I shall turn now to some clinical examples of countertransference, highlighting the distorting influence upon the analytic process, but allowing for the potential usefulness of analyzed countertransference to learn about both the analyst and the patient. This potential was probably realized by the first analyst as he surveyed transference-countertransference reactions in Anna O's erotic feelings for her physician, Dr. Breuer, and Breuer's countertransference flight from the erotic transference. In the Irma Dream, Freud gives indications of his own countertransference toward his patient, his need to write the case up for his "supervisor" Breuer, and his particular efforts to deal with his guilt toward patients. Despite the lack of an initial categorization or designation of the concept, countertransference has been a significant issue in the inception and evolution of psychoanalytic thought. To repeat, there are countertransferences in every psychoanalytic treatment since the analyst has transference reactions to as well as realistic appraisals of the patient. Some countertransference reactions can be extremely subtle and others are quite gross, e.g., where the analyst falls asleep, calls the patient wrong name, or forgets his appointment, or can't wait for a particular patient session which "makes his day," etc.

The transference repetition and abreaction of traumatic experience may elicit intense countertransference reactions as in cases of child abuse or criminal assault. The pain, traumatic anxiety, grief, and guilt experienced by Holocaust victims do not fail to touch the inner life of the analyst or therapist. The analyst may avoid the issues altogether in silent collusion, may engage in shared fantasies of rescue and revenge, may focus upon Holocaust experience to the exclusion of other important material. Identification with the victim and the aggressor in the countertransference, taking on the patient's guilt and the guilt of those who hurt or failed to help the patient, are among many salient problems the analyst is likely to confront. "Horror stories" which were realities, and realities which were nightmares may lead the analyst to overprotect the patient or himself and depart from an analytic attitude in working with the patient.

Analysts are aware of the countertransference potential in cases of massive trauma and that the countertransference may be one of the limiting factors in working with such patients. Many borderline patients have been severely traumatized and, reciprocally, many therapists have been severely tested if not traumatized in work with severely disturbed and regressed patients. Analysts treating patients with suicidal tendencies or with malicious behavior toward others, e.g., the analyst, may all too readily find themselves enmeshed in transference-countertransference binds as well as in difficult treatment decisions. The introduction of parameters may be therapeutically indicated or unconsciously dictated by transference and countertransference reactions. Very ill patients with stormy, tormenting transferences stir up countertransference responses that are often easily recognized though initially unconscious. Analytic capacity to confront chaos and primitive affects may transcend specific countertransference (Kernberg 1965).

These rather dramatic instances of countertransference represent the more visible part of the countertransference spectrum. As a universal response, countertransference can always be found, however, in a minimal, subtle, signal form. Major countertransference is not limited to the severely disturbed patient and represents the unconscious unresolved conflicts of the analyst. If borderline and psychotic patients have stimulated interest in countertransference, it is an interest that has periodically surfaced in relation to all types of patients, whether hysterical and seductive or narcissistic and omnipotent.

The following clinical material has general application and is not restricted to seriously disturbed patients and therapists. Reciprocal and circular transference — countertransference influence — is illustrated. The examples I present are not limited to candidates in supervision or the serious errors or oversights and misunderstandings of other analysts but are graphic illustrations of ubiquitous problems that are only more likely to occur with the analytically inexperienced candidate who has yet to complete his own analytic training and often his own personal analysis. Moreover, analytic errors are not only or always due to countertransference.

The first example concerns a sadomasochistic patient who was frequently late, demanding, and complaining in the analysis. She tended to frustrate, annoy, and provoke her student analyst. There was no sign that he liked working with the patient, and it rather seemed as though he girded himself for a struggle and was disappointed with the failure of his interpretations to have any effect upon the patient's complaints or her tendencies to masochistically act out. (Some analysts may unconsciously instigate, encourage, or enjoy the patient's acting out tendencies, unwittingly contributing to complications if not impasse in the analytic process.) On two occasions, the analyst locked the patient out of the office, forgetting to unlock the waiting room door. One of these occasions was on the patient's birthday. In the next session, the patient spoke about an insolent waiter who kept the patient waiting unconscionably and who provided terrible service. The patient vowed never to return to the restaurant, but she did return to the analytic session. She did not refer directly to the lockout and was afraid of the intensity of her disappointment and rage which seemed to be outside of awareness. She could not discuss her thoughts of quitting or her fears of being thrown out by the analyst. The lock-out was also a message that she interpreted as "get lost" and an act of neglect and rejection.

Another patient might have reacted with overt outrage, might have been openly critical of the analyst, or might even have been gleeful over the analyst's egregious error. In this situation, this masochistic patient elicited a sadomasochistic countertransference. Her final quitting of treatment was overdetermined by her transference conflicts and by the influence of the analyst's countertransference. But it is entirely possible that the patient's departure from treatment included a determinant of acting out of the countertransference fantasy of the analyst, like a child who tends to act out the unconscious fantasies of the parents. I previously described this (Blum 1982) as a malignant cycle of unresolved transference-countertransference, distinguishing between the countertransference as an analytic reality to which the patient was reacting and the spontaneous, irrational, unconscious fantasies of the patient about the analyst. This brings me to a point emphasized by Little (1951) and since then by many others. The countertransference always has an impact upon the analytic process when the analyst's reaction is more than an internal signal. The patient was actually persistently reacting to the analyst's chronic countertransference rather than only to the episodic lock-outs. The candidate tended to be sleepy during the patient's sessions and was, in a sense, emotionally detached so that the patient felt tuned out rather than appropriate attunement. Her masochism was gratified in the passive/aggressive withdrawal of her analyst. A correct interpretation of the patient's masochistic transference fantasies would have to take into account the grain of truth of mistreatment and victimization within the fantasy and that the fantasy was anchored to a reality in the analytic situation. Some dimension of the mistreatment was not transference distortion but a correct perception of a rejecting analytic attitude of "lock out" to which the patient masochistically adapted. Here, interpretation and resolution of the countertransference would have been indispensable to a fuller understanding of the patient's tenacious masochistic transference onto the establishment of a progressive analytic process. The countertransference was a reciprocal rather than a mirror reflection of the patient's transference, and the neurotic conflicts of analyst and patient stem from both their individual pasts and were not created *de nouveau* in the analytic situation. It may be presumed that the patient's masochistic tendencies may not have been expressed, exploited, or gratified in the same form in other situations. The patient's fantasy memories of victimized rejection had a reality as well as a transference meaning.

Countertransference is often related both to the specific features of the patient's transference and to the analyst's character pathology. A very dependent and demanding patient with oedipal jealousy of the analyst, also expressing her possessiveness of the preoedipal mother, had a pattern of preweekend anxiety and anger. She resented the weekend separation and would entreat the analyst for extra time and attention; the patient would speak under pressure and with some agitation or she would withdraw into silence. The analyst would attempt to pacify her demands and complaints by talking more during the Friday session, then accompanying the patient to the door, and defended his behavior as therapeutically indicated. It turned out that if the patient did not respond to the analyst's intervention, he, too, would tend to withdraw into silence. The alternation of speech and silence during the hours was influenced not only by the proximity of the weekend but by the reciprocal response of both parties to each other, including their nonverbal, psychological contact or distance. The peculiar adaptation or subversion of the analytic process was further complicated by the supervisory relationship. The analyst might be much more talkative, ready to interpret after the supervisory session. Conversely, a disappointing supervisory session might result in increased silent detachment from the patient. The supervisor could be appeased or defied in the analyst's response to the patient.

Here the analyst's own preoccupation with frustration and gratification, reward or punishment, compliment or criticism, persistently intruded and distorted the analytic process. The patient identified with the analyst's style, and he demonstrated counteridentification with the patient and probably with the supervisor. The analyst's conflicts, particularly his overt narcissistic needs, interfered with analysis and with learning about his own problems. Attempts to distinguish his problems from those of the patient were partially perceived as supervisory complaint and criticism. The analyst did not recognize the many references in the patient's fantasies to his controlling and critical attitudes and to his inconsistent closeness and distance. She felt teased, had fantasies of seduction and abandonment, of sexual abuse and rejection by her father, of stimulation and withholding by big breasted women representing her mother. The analyst had difficulty recognizing and self-interpreting the patient's transference reactions to the countertransference and the transference-countertransference bind in which he and the patient were enmeshed. His narcissistic character problems, activated by her provocation, were still sufficiently ego-syntonic that the critical observations of patient and supervisor were disregarded. The countertransference itself, though characterological, also had defensive, aggressive, and libidinal dimensions and exemplified overdetermination and compromise formation (Brenner 1985).

The analyst's own preferential listening and intervening, his preference for particular patient associations or behaviors are bound to influence free association and analytic comprehension. Analysis of the analyst's intrusion of his own injunctions and ideals, avoidances and preferences, is essential for grasp of the countertransference. Patients will also identify with the attitudes and defenses of former analysts and therapists. Such similar defense is not necessarily typical of divergent and diverse countertransference defenses. The analyst may identify but also rely upon a whole gamut of defenses. The patient may deny signs of the analyst's ill feelings or illness while the analyst may isolate feelings, and only later discover repressed fantasies about the patient. Where identifications with each other's defenses have occurred, this may range from the silent pact to shared humor to projected common antagonism toward each other or a third party. Projective and introjective processes may be more or less important and are not necessarily predominant in any countertransference.

However clamorous the countertransference may be, its interpretation to the patient is generally silent. I do not advocate, and question conveying reports of the analyst's inner life to the patient. Historically, the more positive attitude toward countertransference interpretation to the patient probably derives from the group of papers by Winnicott (1949) and Little (1951). In particular, Winnicott (1949) advocated the expression of countertransference hate in work with psychopaths or psychotics because the patient might need to objectively experience evoked hatred and because the analyst might need to convey such controlled, clarified countertransference. Little (1951), however, generalized that the sources of analytic errors due to countertransference should be explained to the patient. The analyst would be recognized then as human, candid, and unafraid of his own conflicts.

To my mind, countertransference explanation too readily becomes exhibition and confession which only further "contaminates" the transference. The countertransference "contamination" or difficulty is then magnified by the analyst's self-revelation which is a real departure from analytic anonymity and neutrality. The patient is likely to be confused, seduced, or intimidated and hurt by the intrusion of the analyst's self-analysis. This does not mean that the analyst represents himself as omniscient or omnipotent and having flawless technique, but rather that he does not burden the patient with his own problems, with his own self-observations, and self-analysis. We may acknowledge to the patient that an error occurred, that our anxiety and anger were correctly perceived by the patient, etc. It is important for both analyst and patient to understand the effect the analyst's problems has had on the transference in the analytic process, to analyze rather than to simply acknowledge or apologize.

We have recently had reports of some of the subtle and difficult transference-countertransference problems encountered when the analyst becomes ill (Dewald 1982, Abend 1982) and many of the issues of whether and how much to tell the patient have applications to more general countertransference considerations. How much information is useful or detrimental for a particular patient? Finally, in self-analysis as a reanalysis, those areas insufficiently explored because of previous countertransference may be particularly problematic. If the trouble with self-analysis is countertransference, it may be one's own countertransference and the area of countertransference experienced (and not analyzed) in previous formal analysis. Certain forms of countertransference may be based on identification with the countertransference of the analyst's analyst, perpetuating particular areas of difficulty in the next generation of analysts.

REFERENCES

Abend, S. (1982). Serious illness in the analyst: countertransference considerations. *Journal of the American Psychoanalytic Association* 30:365–380.

Arlow, J. (1985). Some technical problems of countertransference. *Psychoanalytic Quarterly* 54:164–174.

Beres, D. & Arlow, J. (1974). Fantasy and identification in empathy. *Psychoanalytic Quarterly* 43:26–50.

Bernstein, I. & Glenn, J. (1978). The child analyst's emotional reactions to his patients. In: *Child Analysis and Therapy,* ed. J. Glenn. New York: Aronson, pp. 375–392.

Blum, H. (1982). The position and value of extratransference interpretation. *Journal of the American Psychoanalytic Association* 31:587–618.

_____ (1984). Countertransference and the theory of technique: discussion. *Journal of the American Psychoanalytic Association* publication pending.

Brenner, C. (1982). *The Mind in Conflict.* New York: Int. Univ. Press.

_____ (1985). Countertransference as compromise formation. *Psychoanalytic Quarterly* 54:155–163.

Dewald, P. (1982). Serious illness in the analyst: transference, countertransference, and reality responses. *Journal of the American Psychoanalytic Association* 30:347–364.

Fliess, R. (1953). Countertransference and counteridentification. *Journal of the American Psychoanalytic Association* 1:268–284.

Freud, S. (1910). The future prospects of psychoanalytic therapy. *Standard Edition,* 11.

_____ (1913). On beginning the treatment. *Standard Edition,* 12.

_____ (1914). Observations on transference love. *Standard Edition,* 12.

Gill, M. (1982). *Analysis of Transference.* Vol. 1. New York: Int. Univ. Press.

Gitelson, M. (1952). The emotional position of the analyst in the psychoanalytic situation. *International Journal of Psycho-Analysis* 33:1–10.

Grinberg, L. (1962). On a specific aspect of countertransference due to the patient's projective identification. *International Journal of Psycho-Analysis* 43:436–440.

Heimann, P. (1950). On countertransference. *International Journal of Psycho-Analysis* 31:81–84.

Jacobs, T. (1983). The analyst and the patient's object world: notes on an aspect of countertransference. *Journal of the American Psychoanalytic Association* 31:619–642.

Kernberg, O. (1965). Notes on countertransference. *Journal of the American Psychoanalytic Association* 13:38–56.

Little, M. (1951). Countertransference and the patient's response to it. *International Journal of Psycho-Analysis* 32:32–40.

Meissner, W. (1980). A note on projective identification. *Journal of the American Psychoanalytic Association* 28:43–68.

Racker, H. (1968). *Transference and Countertransference.* New York: Int. Univ. Press.

Reich, A. (1951). On countertransference. *International Journal of Psycho-Analysis* 32:25–31.

_____ (1960). Further remarks on countertransference. *International Journal of Psycho-Analysis* 41:389–395.

Tyson, R. (1984). Countertransference Panel, Chairperson's Introduction. *Journal of the American Psychoanalytic Association,* publication pending.

Winnicott, D. (1949). Hate in the countertransference. *International Journal of Psycho-Analysis* 30:69–75.

Chapter 7
Countertransference and Role-Responsiveness

Joseph Sandler, M.D.

As we know, the term "countertransference" has a great many meanings, just as the term "transference" has. Freud first saw countertransference as referring to the analyst's blind spots which presented an obstacle to the analysis. From the beginning, countertransference was consistently seen by Freud "as an obstruction to the freedom of the analyst's understanding of the patient." In this context Freud regarded the analyst's mind as an "instrument . . . its effective functioning in the analytic situation being impeded by counter-transference." Countertransference in the analyst was equated with the resistance in the patient (Sandler, Dare and Holder 1973).

As far as *transference* is concerned, it will be remembered that Freud saw it first as a hindrance, but later regarded it as an

---

Reprinted from the *International Review of Psychoanalysis,* 1976, 3:43–47.

indispensable vehicle for the analytic work. However, he did not take a similar step in regard to countertransference, but this inevitable step was taken after Freud. It was a crucial development in the psychoanalytic literature when the countertransference began to be seen as a phenomenon of importance in helping the analyst to understand the hidden meaning of material brought by the patient. The essential idea is that the analyst has elements of understanding and appreciation of the processes occurring in his patient, that these elements are not immediately conscious and that they can be discovered by the analyst if he monitors his own mental associations while listening to the patient (Sandler, Dare and Holder 1973). The first explicit statement of the *positive* value of countertransference was made by Paula Heimann (1950). Others have written on and developed the topic. However, the two papers by Paula Heimann (1950, 1960) have to be singled out as landmarks in the change of view of countertransference. She started by considering countertransference as referring to all the feelings which the analyst may experience towards his patient. Heimann remarks that the analyst has to be able to "*sustain* the feelings which are stirred up in him, as opposed to discharging them (as does the patient), in order to *subordinate* them to the analytic task in which he functions as the patient's mirror reflection." She assumes "that the analyst's unconscious understands that of his patient. This rapport on the deep level comes to the surface in the form of feelings which the analyst notices in response to his patient, in his 'countertransference' " (Heimann 1950).

I shall not mention the other important writings in this field, except to say that, of course, countertransference had been written about before Heimann's work and it had been pointed out that countertransference is a normal phenomenon. But what seems to have been stressed has been the differences between what one might call the "appropriate" and "useful" countertransference on the one hand and the "dangerous" or "undesirable" countertransference response on the other. Heimann's contribution was to show clearly that the reaction of the analyst may usefully be the first clue to what is going on in the patient.

In *The Patient and the Analyst* the literature on transference was discussed in some detail (Sandler, Dare and Holder 1973) and we concluded by commenting that, in our view,

> transference need not be restricted to the illusory apperception of another person . . ., but can be taken to include the unconscious (and often subtle) attempts to manipulate or to provoke situations with others which are a concealed repetition of earlier experiences and relationships. It has been pointed out previously that when such transference manipulations or provocations occur in ordinary life, the person towards whom they are directed may either show that he does not accept the role, or may, if he is unconsciously disposed in that direction, in fact accept it, and act accordingly. It is likely that such acceptance or rejection of a transference role is not based on a conscious awareness of what is happening, but rather on unconscious cues. Transference elements enter to a varying degree into all relationships, and these (e.g., choice of spouse or employer) are often determined by some characteristic of the other person who (consciously or unconsciously) represents some attribute of an important figure of the past.

In our conclusions about transference we took the step of extending the notion of the patient's *projection* or *externalization* of some aspect of the past or of a figure of the past, on to the person of the analyst, to *all* his attempts to manipulate or to provoke situations with the analyst. I believe such "manipulations" to be an important part of object relationships in general, and to enter in "trial" form into the "scanning" of objects in the process of object choice. In the transference, in many subtle ways, the patient attempts to prod the analyst into behaving in a particular way and unconsciously scans and adapts to his perception of the analyst's reaction. The analyst may be able to "hold" his response to this "prodding" in his consciousness as a reaction *of his own* which he perceives, and I would make the link between certain countertransference responses and transference via the behavioural (verbal and non-verbal) *interaction* between the patient and the analyst. Paula Heimann went as far as to point out that the analyst's response to the patient can be used as a basis for understanding the patient's material, often by something which he catches and holds in himself. I should like to try to take this a little further.

No one can doubt the value of the analyst's continuing analysis of his countertransference. We can, I believe, start by assuming that the understanding of countertransference *is* important. My own interest in the subject has, in recent years, run parallel with an interest in the psychoanalytic psychology of object relationships, and what I present in the following is based on the assumption that a relationship or, to say the least, an interaction, develops between the two parties to the analytic process. We are all aware of the special features of the analytic situation, with its capacity to induce the regressive revival of the past in the present, in a way which is usually entirely unconscious in or rationalized by the patient. On the other hand, we have the use made by the analyst of his special skills, including the employment by him of such capacities as that for free-floating attention, for self-analysis and for the maintenance of what Winnicott (1960) has called the "professional attitude." By free-floating attention I do not mean the "clearing of the mind" of thoughts or memories, but the capacity to allow all sorts of thoughts, day-dreams and associations to enter the analyst's consciousness while he is at the same time listening to and observing the patient.

I have mentioned the interaction between the patient and the analyst, and this is in large part (though, of course, not wholly) determined by what I shall refer to as the intrapsychic role-relationship which each party tries to impose on the other. One aspect of such a role-relationship can be appropriate to the task in hand, i.e., to the work of analysis. Certainly from the side of the *patient* we may see a whole variety of very specific role-relationships emerge. What I want to emphasize is that the role-relationship of the patient in analysis at any particular time consists of a role in which he casts himself, and a *complementary* role in which he casts the analyst at that particular time. The patient's transference would thus represent an attempt by him to impose an interaction, an interrelationship (in the broadest sense of the word) between himself and the analyst. Nowadays many analysts must have the conviction (or at least the uneasy feeling) that the conceptualization of transference as the patient's libidinal or aggressive energic cathexis of a past object being transferred to the image of the analyst in the present is woefully inadequate. The patient's unconscious wishes and mechanisms with which we are concerned in our work are expressed intrapsychically in (descriptively) unconscious images or fantasies, in which both self and object in interaction have come to be represented in particular roles. In a sense the patient, in the transference, attempts to *actualize these in a disguised way,* within the framework and limits of the analytic situation. (I want to use the term *actualization* in the dictionary sense of the word, not in the specific technical senses in which it has been used by certain writers. The *Oxford English Dictionary* defines *actualization* as "a making actual; a realization in action or fact," and *actualize* as "to make actual, to convert into an actual fact, to realize in action.") In doing so he resists becoming aware of any infantile relationship which he might be attempting to impose. I want to underline, at this point, the difference between the manifest content of what the patient brings and the latent unconscious content (in particular the infantile role-relationships which he seeks to express or enact, as well as the defensive role-relationships which he may have constructed). If the patient keeps to the rules he will report rather than enact, and our clues, as analysts, to the unconscious inner role-relationship which the patient is trying to impose, come to us via our perceptions and the application of our analytic tools.

One could regard even the simplest instinctual wish as, from early in life, a wish to impose and to experience a *role-relationship* as a vehicle of instinctual gratification. However, what I have to say here applies not only to unconscious instinctual wishes, but *to the whole gamut of unconscious (including preconscious) wishes related to all sorts of needs, gratifications and defences.*

Parallel to the "free-floating attention" of the analyst is what I should like to call his *free-floating responsiveness.* The analyst is, of course, not a machine in absolute self-control, only experiencing on the one hand, and delivering interpretations on the other, although much of the literature might seem to paint such a picture. Among many other things he talks, he greets the patient, he makes arrangements about practical matters, he may joke and, to some degree, allow his responses to depart from the classical psychoanalytic norm. My contention is that in the analyst's overt reactions to the patient as well as in his thoughts and feelings what can be called his "role-responsiveness" shows itself, not only in his feelings but also in his attitudes and behavior, as a crucial element in his "useful" countertransference.

Let me give one or two examples to illustrate what I mean.

1. This patient, aged 35, had not had any previous analysis and had very little knowledge of the analytic process. He was referred to me because of extreme anxiety about making public presentations of his work, although he felt absolutely competent and at ease in private and informal discussions. He had had a very narrow education, was the son of Eastern European immigrants, but because of his great financial and organizational skills had risen to a very high position and in an extremely large financial organization. In the initial interview I found that he responded extremely well to trial interpretations, and I felt that work with him was going to be rewarding and a pleasure. During the first week or two of his analysis I found that I was talking very much more than I usually do. I should say that I am not an unduly silent analyst. After a little while I felt that something was making me anxious in regard to this patient, and some self-analytic reflexion on my part showed me that I was afraid that he would leave, that I was anxious to keep him, to lower his anxiety level so that he would stay in analysis and that I was talking more than usual in order to avoid the aggressive side of his ambivalent feelings. When I saw this, I felt relieved and reverted to my more usual analytic behaviour. However, I noticed at once the urge to talk during the session and became aware that the patient, by a slight inflexion of his voice, succeeded in ending every sentence with an interrogation, although he did not usually formulate a direct question. This gave me the opportunity to point out to him what he was doing (he was quite unaware of it, just as I had been unaware of it in him) and to show him how much he needed to have me reassure him by talking. He then recalled how he would feel extremely anxious as a child when his father returned home from work, and would compulsively engage his father in conversation, asking him many questions in order to be reassured that his father was not angry with him. His father had been a professional fighter, was very violent, and the patient was terrified of him but needed his father's admiration and love, to be the preferred child. (Later in the analysis we were, as one might expect, to see his fear of his own

hostility to his father.) He told me that his father had the habit of not listening and not responding, and how frightening this was. The patient then realized that from early childhood onwards he had developed the trick of asking questions without directly asking them, and this had become part of his character, being intensified in situations where he feared disapproval and needed supplies of reassurance from authority figures.

The point I want to make here is that, apart from the "ordinary" elements in his analytic work, the analyst will often respond overtly to the patient in a way which he feels indicates *only* his own (the analyst's) problems, his own blind spots, and he may successfully resort to self-analysis in order to discover the pathology behind his particular response or attitude to the patient. However, I want to suggest that very often the irrational response of the analyst, which his professional conscience leads him to see entirely as a blind spot of his own, may sometimes be usefully regarded as a compromise-formation between his own tendencies and *his reflexive acceptance of the role which the patient is forcing on him.*

Naturally, some analysts will be more susceptible to certain roles than others, and also the proportion of the contribution from the side of the patient and from the side of the analyst will vary greatly from one instance to another. And, of course, not all the irrational actions and reactions of the analyst are reflexions of the role into which he is manoeuvred by the patient. What I wanted to show in this example was simply how the patient, by a rather subtle element in his behaviour, evoked an overt response from the analyst which, at first sight, seemed to be *only* irrational countertransference. Let me say emphatically that I am absolutely opposed to the idea that all countertransference responses of the analyst are due to what the patient has imposed on him.

Let me give a further example.

2. This refers to a patient in her late twenties and a schoolteacher. She came to treatment because of social and sexual difficulties, and after some time it became clear that she was terrified of her penis-envy and of her hostility towards her mother, had multiple phobic anxieties and needed, mainly through intellectualization and organizational control of others, including her teaching, to "structure" her world so that she always knew exactly "where she

was." Her need to do this emerged in the transference, and after some three years of analytic work her psychopathology had become very much clearer and she was much improved and happier. However, there was one strand of material which had remained rather obscure. From the beginning she had cried during each session, and I had routinely passed her the box of tissues whenever she began to cry. Now I did not know why I did this but, having begun the practice, I did not feel inclined to change it without some good reason. Without knowing why, I had not felt it appropriate to take up her failure to bring her own tissues or a handkerchief, although with other patients I would have done this. There were many determinants of her crying, including her mourning for the mother she wanted to kill, for the father she felt she had to give up, and so on. It transpired that when she was about two years old and a second child, a brother, had been born, she felt that she had lost her mother's attention, and remembered that at about two and a half years of age she was relegated to playing on her own in the back-yard while her brother was being washed and changed. At this time she had also been sent to a kindergarten, and she had the memory of being very withdrawn and climbing into the rabbit hutch at the nursery school and cuddling a white rabbit. She then told me that she had later learned that after a short while at this school she was diagnosed as "autistic" by the school psychologist, and was apparently very regressed and had uncontrollable rages and tantrums. By this point in her analysis we were able to get at the repetition in the present of her fear of soiling and disgracing herself, and her need to control her objects as she had to control her sphincters. However, there was clearly something which was an important unconscious fantasy for her and which had not been elicited. I had the feeling that we were somewhat "stuck" in the analytic work. One day something rather unusual happened in the analysis. She had begun to cry silently but this time I failed to respond, and she suddenly began to upbraid me and criticize me for not passing her the tissues. She became quite panicky and began to accuse me of being callous and uncaring. I responded by saying that I did not know why I had not passed her the tissues at that particular point, but if she could go on talking perhaps we could both understand more about it. What emerged then was material which lent a great deal of specificity to something which we had not been able to crystallize previously. It became clear that her great need for control and for "structure" in her life was based not on a fear of soiling herself, but rather on a fear that she would soil or wet herself *and that there would not be an adult around to clean her up*. This turned out to be the fear which dominated her life. It was a specific fantasy which seemed to have been elaborated during the late anal phase, under the impact of the mother's withdrawal from her because of the birth of the second child. The discovery and working through of this specific fantasy marked the crucial point in her analysis. I do not want to go into any more detail about her material, except to say that I think that I must have picked up unconscious cues from the patient which prompted me to behave in a certain way in her analysis, both to keep passing her the tissues and then to omit doing so. (It would be pure speculation to link the two and a half years of analysis with the age when her anxiety started.) I believe that this patient had forced me into a role, quite unconsciously on her part and on mine, a role corresponding to that of a parental introject, in which I enacted the part, first of the attentive mother and then suddenly that of the parent who did not clean her up. In the session I was not around to make sure that she was clean, just as she felt that, with the birth of her brother, her mother had not been around to clean her, being busy paying attention to the new baby.

Because the length of this presentation is limited I cannot go into this rich topic any further, and in conclusion I shall restrict myself to one or two points. I have suggested that the analyst has, within certain limits, a free-floating behavioural responsiveness in addition to his free-floating conscious attention.

Within the limits set by the analytic situation he will, unless he becomes aware of it, tend to comply with the role demanded of him, to integrate it into his mode of responding and relating to the patient. Normally, of course, he can catch this counter-response in himself, particularly if it appears to be in the direction of being inappropriate. However, he may only become aware of it through observing his own behaviour, responses and attitudes, *after these have been carried over into action*. What I have been concerned with in this paper is the special case of the analyst regarding some aspect of his own behaviour as deriving entirely from within himself when it could more usefully be seen as a *compromise* between his own tendencies and propensities and the role-relationship which the patient is unconsciously seeking to establish. I should add that I do not find the terms "projection," "externalization," "projective identification" and "putting parts of oneself into the analyst" sufficient to explain and to understand the processes of dynamic interaction which occur in the transference and countertransference. It seems that a complicated system of unconscious cues, both given and received, is involved. This is the same sort of process that occurs not only in the aspects of transference and countertransference discussed here but in normal object relationships and in the process of temporary or permanent object choice as well.

REFERENCES

Heimann, P. (1950). On counter-transference. *International Journal of Psycho-Analysis* 31: 81–84.
_____ (1960). Counter-transference. *British Journal of Medical Psychology* 33: 9–15.
Sandler, J., Dare, C., & Holder, A. (1973). *The Patient and the Analyst: The Basis of the Psychoanalytic Process.* London: Allen & Unwin.
Winnicott, D. W. (1960). Countertransference. *British Journal of Medical Psychology* 33: 17–21.

Chapter 8
Countertransference in the Therapy of Schizophrenics

Charles Savage, M.D.

Countertransference is an integral part of the treatment of schizophrenics, perhaps the most important part. Understood, it is our biggest asset, frequently our only guide. Ignored or unrecognized, countertransference may be our biggest stumbling block.

This is hardly a novel thesis. The difficulties occasioned by countertransference were mentioned by Freud as early as 1910, and I think its constructive aspects were implied in his suggestion that the "Physician's unconscious mind (is) able to reconstruct the patient's unconscious" (Freud 1912). Certainly both these aspects were made quite explicit by Paula Heimann in 1950 (after a lapse of 40 years). A great deal of value has been written since then, which unfortunately I do not have the time to review. What I *am*

Presented at the annual meeting of the American Psychoanalytic Association at San Francisco on May 9, 1958, and published in *Psychiatry*, 1985, 24(1): 53–60.

suggesting is that the treatment of schizophrenia leads to counter-transferences which are, both quantitatively and qualitatively of a different order from that found in ordinary analytic practice.

I shall not enter upon the problem whether schizophrenics can be analyzed, and perhaps such a discussion might await an agreed definition of both psychoanalysis and schizophrenia. In my own experience so many parameters are introduced either deliberately or inadvertently in the treatment of schizophrenics that one may raise the question: is this psychoanalysis or psychotherapy? Parenthetically, it is my observation that the introduction of parameters tends to increase countertransference problems.

No agreement as to "what is countertransference?" has emerged from the recent widespread discussions of it. Present day definitions range on a continuum from the rather narrow "the analyst's reaction to his patient's transference," to the extremely broad definitions of the analyst's *total reaction* to his patient (Little 1951, 1957).

Not only is there this continuum but there is also a sharply dichotomous separation of the *obstructive* and the constructive aspects of countertransference as though they were separate entities like good and evil: irrational versus rational countertransference; countertransference versus counteridentification; countertransference versus intuition (the latter facilitating the understanding of the patient, the former blocking it) (Fliess 1953).

It is my contention that the two are genetically and dynamically the same, differing only in the accessibility of these essentially unconscious processes to consciousness.

I should like to take as my starting point Freud's (1910) description of countertransference as arising in the physician as a result of the "patient's influence on his (the physician's) unconscious feelings." I should like to broaden it to include the influence of the therapeutic process on the therapist's unconscious reactions. I have broadened it in this fashion because, especially with schizophrenics, unconscious feelings about the patient may be stirred up by ancillary people including nurses, supervisors, colleagues, or the patient's relatives. I would also consider any person who is involved in the treatment of a schizophrenic, including nurses, administrators, and supervisors, as prey to countertransference problems. Schizophrenic patients are particularly prone to extra-analytic transferences which may be responded to by extra-analytic countertransferences (Savage 1957).

Finally, I must point out that countertransference, as I have defined it, being unconscious cannot be observed directly but can only be inferred from its effects on the conscious attitudes, feelings, perceptions, and behavior of the analyst.

The thesis of my presentation is essentially this:

1. Many problems, anxieties, worries and discomforts beset the analyst in the treatment of schizophrenia.

2. All of these problems may have unconscious (i.e. countertransference) implications for the analyst.

3. The best route to an understanding of the countertransference is by scrutiny of the problems encountered, especially via self-analysis of the analyst's reactions.

4. This in turn leads to an understanding of the patient-doctor relationship and to an understanding of the patient.

5. Therefore problems should be welcomed and studied because of their potential value.

6. More often problems are avoided and defended against by various maneuvers which tend to perpetuate the schizophrenic process in the patient.

Let me give an example of a defense against these problems.

One therapist remarked to his somewhat startled colleagues, "I never have countertransference problems with my schizophrenic patients." And as he went on to describe the treatment of one particular patient, it became apparent why he did not have problems. He had carefully dissected away the libidinal implications of the patient's hallucinations and delusions in a manner vaguely reminiscent of an autopsy report, but he had completely ignored the "I-Thou" relationship. He changed the subject when questions of intimacy and dependency appeared; when these matters became fairly pressing, he fell back on authoritarian directives telling the patient what to do and how he should run his life. This therapist paid a high price for his peace of mind: (1) He did not understand his patient. (2) His patient made no progress.

This example, while not typical, illustrates how countertransference problems can be avoided, but only by mutual repression on the part of both patient and doctor, who must enter into an active, albeit unconscious conspiracy not to disturb the doctor.

Many schizophrenics have had considerable practice in this, having learned to adjust by keeping mother from becoming anxious. The doctor, on the other hand, was being true to an unfortunate tradition: One ought not to have countertransference reactions; they are evidence of technical incompetence and incomplete analysis.

Margaret Little (1957) suggests that countertransference has finally achieved respectability, and a good deal of lip-service is paid to the concept. Yet I am impressed how often presentations that attempt to elucidate some aspect of the patient's pathology via the countertransference arouse massive anxiety, counter-cathexis, denial and abuse in one's colleagues, a fact to which Lucia Tower (1956) has also attested. I believe that countertransference is shunned not from any psychoanalytic prudery but because it is an anxiety-provoking topic. It threatens the medical model of *all* the disease in the patient (a model the parents of the schizophrenic have always been happy to call to his attention), instead of viewing schizophrenia as a disordered relationship to which all parties must of necessity contribute.

Countertransference is admittedly a difficult subject to study, discuss or present, of which the following gives ample testimony. A small group of analysts, including myself, hoping to elucidate some schizophrenic transactions and mechanisms, postulated that the study of countertransference would be a useful vehicle for such an approach. Each of us was intimately associated with some aspects of the psychoanalytic treatment of a ward of schizophrenics. We found that in our dealings with each other, we tended to reflect the transactions of the patients with other patients and staff. By observing mutual interactions, we found that we could tell what was going on with the patient, particularly in the doctor-patient relationship. After nine months this group came to a violent and bitter end. One member became so identified with the patients that he became the bearer of the patients' pathology. Acting out the countertransference instead of discussing it, he withdrew not only from the group of his colleagues, but also from the patients he was treating. Significantly, he announced his decision to the patients, and his colleagues learned of his decision only from them. Having thus disrupted the work of his colleagues and the therapy of the patients, he explained that he had too much other work to do.

I cite this example to demonstrate that discussions of counter-transference are not always innocuous, and that analysts have a realistic if not legitimate cause to avoid them.

I have mentioned that countertransference has both construc-tive and obstructive aspects, its uses and abuses. Examples of its abuses are straightforward enough: analyzing in the patient what really exists in oneself; failing to see in the patient what one does not want to see in oneself; using the patient to obtain substitute gratification. Examples of the uses of countertransference are more recondite and are often referred to in rather vague and mystical language such as "Listening with the third ear," "Diving into the patient's unconscious" (Reik 1949), which refer to the fact that the analyst's unconscious understands that of the patient. This understanding is achieved by what Fliess (1953) would call "transient, trial, identification." The analyst identifies with his patient, experiences what the patient experiences and then evalu-ates it objectively. This process goes on in every analysis, but must be relied on more heavily with schizophrenics because of the peripheral, guarded, symbolic and often non-verbal nature of the schizophrenic communications. Parenthetically, in the analysis of schizophrenics the investment required is so great, the identifica-tion must be so deep in order to understand the patient, that the swing back to the neutral observer position is difficult to achieve and is seldom accomplished *in toto*.

Insights achieved via identification may come in a flash or may follow some moments or months of perplexity and self-analysis. The goal of analysis and training should not be to eliminate countertransference problems but to shorten the time required for their recognition and resolution. The following is an example where countertransference initially blocked but ultimately facili-tated my understanding of a patient. I had been treating a very hostile aggressive chronic paranoid for over a year. Even though he frequently referred to me as a "dewy eyed madonna" and a "sadistic quack," I usually managed to keep my hostility fairly well sorted out. The work seemed to be progressing by fits and starts. However, one day he came in with a torrent of invectives about a toothache and his ill-treatment at the hands of the dentist. I found myself completely baffled and at a loss for understanding. I repressed with difficulty a series of responses which were somewhat less than therapeutic, as for example, "Why did he not talk to the dentist about it?" Even though initially I tended to take his complaint at face value, I found my sympathy waning rapidly and noticed in myself an increasing feeling of extreme annoyance and irritation. "What an ungrateful bastard," I thought. "All I'm doing for him — the least he could do would be to get well or at least not bitch so much." If felt frustrated. I wanted to say, borrowing one of the patient's pet expressions, "Let's quit the horseshit and get onto something useful." Taking refuge behind the analytical silence, I let myself ruminate about the question of my annoyance with him, not an easy thing to do because of the persistent, nagging quality of his complaints. It finally occurred to me that he was subjecting me to considerable oral frustration; he was denying me useful material for analysis. He was not giving me any evidence of progress. He was reactivating all my personal conflicts about oral frustrations. It also occurred to me that he was complaining of the same thing in me, that I was frustrating him in the transference just as his mother had subjected him to severe oral frustration. This turned out to be the case. His toothache disappeared.

My initial reaction had been to join in his paranoid defenses and project all the difficulties first onto the dentist and secondly onto the patient himself. My second impulse was to disparage his complaints, exactly as his mother would have done. I avoided the defense of excessive solicitude and tenderness. This patient did not seem to invite it.

My understanding was completely blocked by my countertransference reaction; otherwise I could have easily arrived at the correct answer by the route of logical analysis. He was, after all, speaking of his difficulties at the hands of another doctor, the dentist. Complaints about another doctor can usually be related to complaints about the analyst. When the patient talks about the analyst, there are inevitably transference implications. Discussion of teeth implies a certain amount of orality, and a complaint of neglect of teeth would imply oral frustration. The transference situation during that period centered largely around his relations to his mother. Therefore, it would not be a great leap to assume he was talking about his oral frustrations with me and his mother. Or the route of symbolic analysis should have led me to Rosen's (1953) parallel case of the man who suffered from intractable toothache which was relieved when it was suggested that he suffered from nursing on a stone breast. My attempts along this line had led me to recall only Reik's (1949) story where a toothache was interpreted as evidence of a concealed abortion. This patient, however, was a male.

Clearly the frustration of my own oral needs reawakened old and not completely resolved problems of orality and led to my retaliating by frustrating him at the oral level, by withholding my understanding and interpretations. Until I understood myself, I was unable to understand him. By becoming aware of my own problem, I was able to become aware of his.

Let us now review some of the problems typically encountered in the analysis of schizophrenics and some of the defenses against them. The majority of the problems may be subsumed under the heading of identification. Let us first consider the inability to identify with the patient. This may stem from three general sources: First, it may lie in the fact that there is so little real mutuality between patient and therapist, as when they come from widely disparate socio-cultural backgrounds, that there is no basis for a common ground. Second, it may lie in the fact that the patient in some way represents some previous significant figure in the doctor's life or a pattern of conflicts and complexes which are rejected and denied by the doctor. Third, it may lie in the doctor's response to the schizophrenic's sometimes immediate rejection of his would-be saviour. The acceptance for treatment of a patient with whom one cannot identify (for whatever reason) is a mistake and guarantees massive countertransference problems.

Such a patient is sure to be rejected by the analyst if he hasn't been already. Early in treatment a pattern of mutual rejection, often reminiscent of the patient–parent relationship, will have been established. The analyst will not understand the patient, will feel anxious at not understanding, and his inability to understand will be increased by his anxiety. Hate and guilt will be mobilized, and the analyst's unresolved or latent reaction to authority figures will be reawakened by the patient. Such a countertransference problem can be worked through only with the greatest of difficulty and tremendous expenditure of time and effort. Where such a problem of mutual lack of identification exists, I would tend to agree with Gitelson's (1952) recommendation of change of analyst, for countertransference problems. Usually changing analysts for countertransference problems is an acting out of the transference and countertransference and such changes are damaging to the narcissism of both parties.

If he cannot identify with the patient, the analyst will encounter difficulties; but identification in turn leads to other difficulties. Ideally, the identification is transient, the analyst alternating between "empathic understanding and detached observation." But the identification with schizophrenics is intense, primitive, and regressive. And it must be so if the analyst is to achieve a true understanding of his patient. But the intensity of the identification and regression make it very difficult, even impossible to swing back to detached observation. The analyst then experiences the patient's intense anxieties, fears, rages, lusts, and conflicts as his own and unless he faces these problems and deals with them directly, he may resort to controlling devices to allay the patient's anxiety (and his own), such as excessive tenderness, devices similar to those employed by the patient's parents. Or he may resort to primitive defenses similar to those employed by the patient, especially paranoid defenses. Some analysts who are most sensitive to the communications of their schizophrenic patients (because of their close identification and their ready awareness of their own unconscious) fall short as ideal therapists because they rely on defenses similar to those of their patient. They tend to distort reality as he does and thus are prone to enter *folie a deux* configurations with him.

Identification in countertransference is both introjective and projective. Introjective identification is, in operational terms, experiencing what the patient experiences; projective identification is equivalent to living vicariously through the patient, particularly gratifying one's impulses through the patient's activity. When projective identification occurs, the countertransference problems are subtler. The patient will act out the unconscious conflicts and impulses of the analyst, in the same way that disturbed children act out the unconscious conflicts and impulses of the parents. It is this propensity of schizophrenics and their analysts that makes essential the close cooperation of analyst and either hospital staff or the family. Otherwise, the analyst may have no way of ascertaining the existence of a countertransference problem, and the patient may be the last one to let him know about it. The problems will then be acted out instead of analyzed. The analyst's introjective identification will make it difficult for him to appreciate the acting out even when he avails himself of corollary data. Often it can be observed only by a supervisor.

In addition to the problems stirred up by identification and the lack thereof, there are a certain number of unresolved unconscious conflicts that the analyst brings to the treatment situation. Foremost of these is infantile magical omnipotence or the manic defense. To some extent, this is almost a requisite for treating schizophrenics. The difficulties in the way of treating schizophrenics appeal to the sense of omnipotence of the analyst; in point of fact the difficulties are so great that a certain amount of omnipotence is a useful commodity. One of the most gifted therapists I ever knew used to seek out the most difficult cases with whom all others had failed. In an incredibly short space of time he would have nude, smearing patients up, dressed, out and going into town on shopping sprees. But then, having demonstrated his omnipotence, shown he was a magic healer, he lost interest in them.

Few of us are so fortunate as to have our omnipotent strivings so handily gratified. More often they are frustrated because the patient's progress is slow, faltering, erratic, and sometimes nonapparent. In these instances where his omnipotent strivings are insufficiently recognized, the analyst may become prone to confabulatory or delusional reports of the patient's progress, delusions sometimes shared by the entire hospital staff and the patient's family, though rarely by the patient. This may lead the analyst to demand more of the patient than the patient is capable, thus repeating for the patient a series of early frustrations and failures. The frustration of the analyst's omnipotent strivings may lead to accumulation of tremendous and often unconscious rage towards the patient.

The inordinate investment of time and energy, coupled with the scant return, often reinforce the analyst's tendency to obtain narcissistic gratification at the patient's expense, by reason of the patient's helpless dependence on him; he may unconsciously need the patient to remain sick, and, while *consciously* enjoining him to growth and development, may, *unconsciously,* not welcome it at all. These conflicting conscious and unconscious messages to the patient that he both grow up and remain a child at the same time place the patient in a pathogenic "double-bind" situation described by Bateson, Jackson, et al (1956).

Frequently the analyst attempts to analyze in his schizophrenic patients that which he has been unwilling or unable to analyze in himself. He finds in the treatment of schizophrenic patients a substitute for his own treatment. The schizophrenic patient, who is in for a long process of reeducation and regrowth, affords the analyst the opportunity to correct in fantasy his own upbringing and to give the patient the gratifications which he (the analyst) was denied as a child. The analyst becomes a Pygmalion making not a Galatea but a super Pygmalion. He becomes a good mother who gives the patient the love he himself did not get.

Another unconscious motive is to take the sting out of schizophrenia. By helping the schizophrenic master his impulses and unconscious, the analyst masters his own. At the same time he can experience vicariously, through the schizophrenic, impulses he does not dare experience in himself. Some therapists treat the schizophrenic out of unconscious guilt which they hope to expiate. This was borne out directly in one individual whose sister was schizophrenic. Unconsciously, he felt responsible for her illness and by treating others attempted to undo it and relieve his guilt feelings. With these not uncommon unconscious motivations clouding the picture, it is not surprising that countertransference problems should arise. But even without them, the treatment situation is such as to make countertransference problems inevitable.

Work with schizophrenics is invariably anxiety-provoking for a variety of reasons, in addition to the anxiety the analyst experiences via identification: there is the sensitivity and perceptivity of the schizophrenic which once had a high survival value for him. As Freud (1922) wrote of schizophrenics, "They let themselves be guided by their knowledge of the unconscious and displace to the unconscious minds of others the attention which they have withdrawn from their own." I recall one patient who greeted his analyst in the following manner: "When I leave the hospital, I am going to make a lot of money. I am going to give it to you so you can get analyzed, get over your homosexuality, and get married." I might add that after a decade the analyst is still single.

There is the intense, stormy, and rapidly fluctuating transference formed by the schizophrenic patient, with its naked demands for love and sexual activity, its violent rages, abuses, and physical aggressions. As Bion (1957) has said with suitable restraint: "The relationship with the analyst is premature, precipitate and intensely dependent." It is all that. It has an intense oral incorporative nature which exhausts the analyst and threatens him with the loss of his identity. Schizophrenics work very hard to make the transference into reality and, by being helpless and dependent and unable to do without him, try to force the analyst to be the good mother; and, by being perfectly hateful, horrid, demanding and ungrateful, try to make him into the bad mother who rejects them. Invariably they are partly successful and the analyst is left with the problem of what to do with his tender feelings, and what to do with his own hateful feelings. Whether the patient should be faced with them is something of which I am not yet convinced. But they must be faced by the analyst. Otherwise, they get acted out at the patient's expense sometimes by physical or spiritual withdrawal, sometimes by physical or spiritual violence. This acting out may take form as an excess of the analytic attitude or overpermissiveness and failure to set proper limits for the patient, or overprotection. Deep interpretations are a good method of cutting the patient down to size, putting him in his place and getting even with him.

Another source of anxiety is the chronic problem of communicating with the patient, with rapid shifting of the communicative set so that one minute there is understanding, the next minute none.

Finally, in working with schizophrenics, there are no real guideposts, no clearly defined rules, no structured field to allay the anxiety, no specific directions except for a few hackneyed phrases such as "interpret process rather than content," phrases of more benefit in alleviating the anxiety of supervisors than in helping the patient's progress.

The hospital is a hotbed of transference and countertransference problems, accentuating all existing ones and contributing new ones of its own. Both patient and analyst are members of the same therapeutic community and come to be closely identified together. The hospital tends to re-establish the family situation for both patient and analyst. Sibling jealousies and oedipal strivings are reactivated in the form of intense rivalries with colleagues and rebellion against both maternal nursing and paternal supervisory figures. For the patient, the family is often reconstituted with the analyst in the role of mother but with nurse and analyst frequently vying for this role. The analyst often arrogates to himself the prerogatives of mother, and, jealously resenting any new attachments the patient may make to the nurses, will actively interfere with these new object relations for the patient's own good, just as the patient's parents had done.

Frequently in the course of treatment the patient, attempting to establish his personal identity, finds himself in conflict with the hospital. Often the analyst identifying with the patient's struggles, cravings, and frustrations will experience the patient's conflicts as his own. When the patient resolves the conflict, as often happens, by leaving the hospital against medical advice, sometimes the analyst also quits the hospital, so intense is his identification. I believe that the Stanton-Schwartz (1954) phenomenon (the precipitation of patient disturbance by covert disagreement of two or more members of the staff) can often be understood in terms of transference–countertransference reactions. One person onto whom the positive transference is projected becomes the good parent, while another onto whom the negative transference is projected becomes the bad parent. The countertransference mirrors the transference, but it is repressed, and the two staff members act out the countertransference against each other and the patient. Each staff member accepts the role assigned to him by the patient and acts it out, each thereby becoming a bearer of one aspect of the patient's psychopathology. The patient then is confronted not with a corrective emotional experience but with the frightening reality confirmation of his own projections. Small wonder that he becomes agitated by this. Small wonder that he is calmed by the resolution of this countertransference difficulty.

One must remember with schizophrenics that the treatment situation must be total no matter how pure the analysis may remain, and inevitably the analyst will have dealings directly or indirectly with the hospital authorities and family, even if only at the rumor level or telephone level. Not only will attitudes stirred up by the patient be projected by the analyst onto hospital staff and family, but often attitudes stirred up by the hospital staff and family will be projected onto the patient.

Work with the families of schizophrenics is extraordinarily anxiety-provoking, more so to my mind than work with schizophrenics themselves. This anxiety carries over into the analytic situation and until resolved makes work with the patient more difficult. The danger lies in becoming so identified with the patient and so provoked with the family that one antagonizes them to the point where they will remove themselves and the patient as well from treatment. Sometimes one takes out one's resentment on the patient.

DISCUSSION

There seem to be essentially three ways in which the analyst's defensive operations may be deleterious to the patient and perpetuate the schizophrenic process. The analyst's own conflicts, often stirred up by the patient, may afflict him with scotomata for similar conflicts in the patient, cause him to be so preoccupied with his own conflicts that he cannot hear or identify with the patient, or the analyst's conflicts may cause him to repress within the patient as well as himself lines of enquiry that are important, or may cause the analyst to analyze in the patient that which really exists in himself. Such errors are the ones most frequently associated with the concept of countertransference. They are the inevitable product of learning to do analysis with schizophrenics. Their resolution may require more personal analysis, but they are as valuable as other bits of countertransference information and are "grist for the mill."

The second way is the employment by the analyst of the same defensive measures used by the patient; this is a direct resultant of the identifications of the analyst with the patient. Regression to primitive levels leads to primitive defenses. The observation by the analyst of his defenses and the awareness of against what he is defending gives insight into the patient's defenses and difficulties.

The third is the employment by the analyst of the same defensive and repressive measures used by the patient's parents. The scrutiny of these measures gives one a clue to the sort of relations which went on between the patient and his parents. The adoption by the analyst of parental measures is a curious phenomenon. The analyst sets about with the intention to enable himself and the patient to understand rather than repeat, to work through rather than reenact the old pathogenic transaction. He wishes to provide a new and corrective ego-ideal for the patient. Yet often he will find himself reacting to the patient as did the parents of the patient, without his having been aware of it.

The patient forces the analyst into the role not of a new and better parent, but the role of the original parent; and the analyst unconsciously accepts this role and plays it. Recently, it has been my good fortune to observe schizophrenic children living in a ward with their parents. I am intrigued with how often and repeatedly the schizophrenic children provoke their parents into behavior which we could consider pathogenic. I am also intrigued that they provoked the staff, including myself, into reacting the same way.

CONCLUSION

The analysis, or psychoanalytic therapy, of schizophrenics leads to many problems. Some of these problems are due to unresolved, primitive conflicts in the analyst which are activated by work with schizophrenics. Some of the problems are due to the analyst's inability to identify with his schizophrenic patient, some are due to his intense identification, some are due to the very nature of the hospital setting, and some are due to the necessity of dealing with the patient's family. The analyst may attempt to avoid these problems by withdrawal, acting out, excessive mothering, denial, avoidance of unpleasant issues, overpermissiveness, acceptance of the patient's distortions or the application of authoritarian measures including drugs and shock. This has a twofold unfortunate effect:

1. The analyst will unconsciously employ the same defenses as the patient or he will utilize the same measures to control anxiety used by the patient's parents, and thus perpetuate a pathogenic transaction.

2. By denying to himself the possibility of understanding his own countertransference, he will lose a valuable source of understanding and communicating with his patient.

The answer to these difficulties is always more self-analysis, and sometimes more personal analysis, though, as I have tried to show, the basis for these problems is not always to be found in the need for more analysis but in the very structure of the treatment situation.

A more helpful suggestion is supervision. Too often supervision is viewed solely as a training function. But this is a shortsighted error. The supervisor should be viewed as the representative of reality who counters the distortions which the analyst's identifications with the patient make inevitable; yet the supervisory situation is far from a cure-all.

Too often the supervisor fails as the representative of reality. Very often the supervisor and analyst reenact the drama between the analyst and the patient without recognizing it. I once observed almost daily for four years a patient in whom the only evidences of progress were the glowing reports of the supervisor.

Perhaps the most useful solution in hospital practice is frequent consultations of the analyst with the rest of the staff. Here, by careful scrutiny of the analyst's problems with his patient and their countertransference aspects, it is possible to understand the patient–doctor relationship and thus the patient. This can *only* be done in an atmosphere which accepts countertransference as a legitimate area of enquiry.

REFERENCES

Bateson, G., Jackson, D. D., Haley, J., and Weakland, J. (1956). Toward a theory of schizophrenia. *Behavioral Science* 1:251–264.

Bion, W. R. (1957). Differentiation of the psychotic from the non-psychotic personalities. *International Journal of Psycho-Analysis* 38:266–275.

Fliess, R. (1953). Countertransference and counter-identification. *Journal of the American Psychoanalytic* 1:268–284.

Freud, S. (1910) The future prospects of psycho-analytic therapy. *Coll. Papers* 2:285–296, London: Hogarth, 1924.

_____ (1912). Recommendations for physicians on the psycho-analytic method of treatment. *Coll. Papers* 2:323–333, London: Hogarth, 1924.

_____ (1922). Certain neurotic mechanisms in jealousy, paranoia, and homosexuality. *Coll. Papers* 2:232–243, London: Hogarth, 1924.

Gitelson, M. (1952). The emotional position of the analyst in the psychoanalytic situation. *International Journal of Psycho-Analysis* 33:1–10.

Heimann, P. (1950). On countertransference. *International Journal of Psycho-Analysis* 31:81–84.

Little, M. (1951). Counter-transference and the patient's response to it. *International Journal of Psycho-Analysis* 32:32–40.

_____ (1957). "R"—The analyst's total response to his patient's needs. *International Journal of Psycho-Analysis* 38:240–254.

Reik, T. (1949). *Listening with the Third Ear.* New York: Farrar, Straus and Co.

Rosen, J. (1953). *Direct Analysis.* New York: Grune and Stratton.

Savage, C. (1957). The diffusion of the transference-psychosis in the treatment of schizophrenia. *Psychiatry* 20:419–421.

Stanton, A. H., and Schwartz, M. S. (1954). The Mental Hospital. New York: Basic Books.

Tower, L. (1956). Countertransference. *Journal of the American Psychoanalytic Association* 4:224–255.

Chapter 9
Countertransference as a Path to Understanding and Helping the Patient

Harold F. Searles, M.D.

A working definition of what I mean by "countertransference" is provided by the first sentence of a lengthy definition in *A Glossary of Psychoanalytic Terms and Concepts,* edited by Moore and Fine, and published by the American Psychoanalytic Association in 1967: "Countertransference: Refers to the attitudes and feelings, only partly conscious, of the analyst toward the patient. . . ." (p. 29). The rest of their lengthy definition is one with which I largely concur, but is unnecessary to reproduce here.

For many years, I have found that the countertransference gives one one's most reliable approach to the understanding of patients of whatever diagnosis. My monograph (Searles 1960) on the

Reprinted from *My Work with Borderline Patients* by Harold F. Searles, 1986, pp. 189–227.

nonhuman environment and many of my previous papers have contained detailed data and discussions of the countertransference in my work with frankly psychotic patients, and this chapter will not attempt to condense those earlier writings.

As an example of the usefulness of the countertransference, as regards the question of whether it is advisable for the borderline patient to use the couch, for nearly 30 years now it has seemed to me that the patient is unlikely to be panicked by this experience if the analyst himself, sitting behind the couch, does not give way to panic.

Comparably, in my work with an ambulatorily schizophrenic woman who had moved from sitting in a chair to sitting on the couch, I found that the next analytic-developmental step, of her becoming able to lie down on the couch, involved a question not merely of *her* being able to adapt to the isolation attendant upon her no longer being able to see *my* face. I came to realize, after she had started lying down upon it but sitting up from time to time to get a look at my face, that my relief at those "interruptions" of her lying on the couch was fully comparable with her own. I had been repressing the feelings of deprivation attendant upon my own no longer being able, while she was lying on the couch, to watch *her* fascinatingly mobile facial expressions.

When a borderline patient who had been sitting in a chair for some months began lying on the couch, I found that during the first session of my sitting behind it I was speaking to her much more than had been my custom. Upon noticing this, my first thought was that I was supplying, empathically, sufficient verbal feedback to her to help her to become accustomed to this new and, for her, much more emotionally isolated situation. Only some time later in this session did I realize that, again, I myself evidently was repressing abandonment-anxiety, and struggling to keep such anxiety repressed and projected upon her.

In the work with the borderline patient, there are several readily-apparent reasons why the realm of the countertransference is so important. I intend to discuss additional, less obvious reasons; but first I shall make brief mention of some of the more obvious ones.

The intensity of the borderline patient's repressed emotions is so great as to make unusual demands upon the emotionality of the analyst. These demands are greatly accentuated by the patient's wide gamut of ego-developmental levels at work in his mode of relating with the analyst, such that the latter finds himself called upon to relate with the patient upon unpredictably shifting levels which vary from relatively mature, healthy-neurotic modes to extremely primitive modes essentially akin to those found in the transference psychoses of frankly schizophrenic patients. Not uncommonly, the analyst feels related with the patient upon two or more of such levels simultaneously.

So much of the borderline patient's ego-functioning is at a symbiotic, pre-individuation level that, very frequently, it is the analyst who, through his own relatively ready access to his own unconscious experiences, is first able to feel in awareness, and conceptualize and verbally articulate, the patient's still-unconscious conflicts. Though these conflicts inherently "belong" to the patient, they can come to be known to and integrated by him only through his identification with the analyst into whom they have been able to flow, as it were, through the liquidly symbiotic transference.

Because the *borderline* patient does indeed seem, during much if not most of our work with him, to be walking a tightrope between neurosis and psychosis, he requires us to face our fear lest he become psychotic, our envy of him for his having this avenue so widely open to him, our hateful desire for him to become psychotic, as well as our ambivalent fear and wish to become psychotic, ourselves.

Because the normal phase of mother-infant symbiosis in him never has been resolved into predominantly individuated ego-functioning, we find that in the transference-symbiosis which naturally ensues over the course of the analysis, we are cast not only as the symbiotic mother in the transference but, equally often and by the same token, as the symbiotic infant. We must accustom ourselves, therefore, to the experiencing of symbiotic-dependency feelings toward the mother-patient such as are only relatively subtly present in our work with neurotic patients.

THE IMPACT UPON THE ANALYST OF THE PATIENT'S SPLIT EGO-
FUNCTIONING

Gunderson and Singer (1975) in an article entitled, "Defining
Borderline Patients: An Overview," provide a helpful survey of
the large literature of descriptive accounts of borderline patients.
Among several features which they found that most authors
believe to characterize most borderline patients, the foremost is
the presence of intense affect. In entering, now, into my more
detailed discussion, I want first to highlight the impact upon the
analyst of the patient's unintegrated ambivalence—or, perhaps
better expressed, the impact upon him of the unintegrated affects
which the patient expresses toward him referable to the splits in
the patient's ego-functioning, such that intensely hateful affects
are not integrated with (and thus modified by) intensely loving
affects, and vice versa.

I cannot fully convey here these impacts, for the reason that I
cannot achieve, at will, such a complete splitting of intense
emotions as prevailed at the level of ego-functioning in these
patients on these occasions; I must elaborate upon the quoted
comments, therefore, with some brief description. One woman
patient said, "I can't tell you how much I love you or how much
of a shit I think you are." In saying, "how much I love you," her
affective tone was one of glowingly unambivalent love; but in
saying only moments later, "how much of a shit I think you are,"
her affect was unambivalently one of hostile contempt. Another
woman, in reminiscing that her mother used to address her as "my
darling rat," conveyed by her tone that her words "darling" and
"rat" had been expressive of forcefully contrasting emotions
without any acknowledgment, in the mother's egofunctioning, of
any conscious conflict between these two images of her daughter.
A chronically schizophrenic woman once said to me, "You should
have the Congressional Medal of Spit." The first seven words of
that eight-word sentence conveyed a heartfelt admiration; but the
last one, said with no break at all in the rhythm of her speech, was
uttered in unalloyed contempt.

The examples of patients' affective expressions which I have just
cited are of expressions which switch instantaneously from loving
to hateful ones. Even more unsettling, oftentimes, is a patient's

expression of highly incongruous emotions simultaneously. Such phenomena comprise a part of what is not only difficult but also fascinating in the work with borderline patients, for one discovers that there are combinations of intense emotions which one had never encountered before within one's conscious memory.

For example, I have come to realize that two of the part-aspects of one of the patients with whom I am working comprise what I experience as an irresistibly funny homicidal maniac. I had long been aware of his quick-tempered fury at any perceived insult, and of his underlying murderousness; but as the work has gone on it has become evident that he possesses also an enormous ability to be funny, giving me at times to feel overwhelmed with the urge to laugh at some of his raging comments, and yet to feel, simultaneously, that it is of life-and-death importance not to let him detect my amusement. On rare occasions with him and comparable patients, I have been seized with a strangled, epileptic-seizure-like laughter, and on some of these occasions have managed successfully, apparently, to disguise it as a cough or somatically-based fit of choking. My underlying terror of detection in some of these instances is lest I be murderously attacked physically or — hardly less frightening — be subjected to a demolishing verbal attack. In a greater number of instances, the terror is lest the outraged patient sever, instantly and irrevocably, the treatment relationship which he and I have built up so slowly and arduously.

In my work with one such patient after another, it becomes evident that the patient's largely-unconscious sadism has had much to do with my finding myself in so tortured a position. Only somewhat milder forms of this same phenomenon are to be found in one's work with a supervisee who, simultaneous with a hawklike sensitivity to any increment of somnolence on one's part, is reporting the clinical material in a soothing tone, or a boring one, or some other tone which drives one almost irresistibly toward sleep.

To return to borderline patients, a woman was reporting a dream in her usual overly-modulated tone which was thoroughly enigmatic as regards emotions, saying, ". . . We were all under some kinda interstellar influence, some kinda unseen force that was controlling things . . . kinda malevolent force hovering around . . ." Meanwhile, as I was writing down the dream, I noticed that each time I wrote the word "force," I had a momentary thought either that it was written "farce" or else that I had to be careful not to write "farce." I sensed there to be an unusual theme, here, of a murderous farce, or a sinister farce. The patient gave a brief chuckle at the beginning of her description of the parts of the dream which I have quoted; but in the main she sounded to be fending off an awed, whistle-in-the-graveyard feeling. Later in this session she commented, without identifiable emotion of any sort, that her former room-mate, years ago in law school, had been electrocuted in a strange "accident." During the years of her analysis, her fear lest she possess an omnipotent destructiveness proved to be one of the major themes of our work together.

To simply mention other unusual affective combinations, I have been struck by the diabolical naiveté of one of my male patients, and by this same patient's ferocious idealizing of me—his idealizing me with ferocity. I have felt one patient to give me a slashing smile upon her walking in from the waiting room, and another (this one far more ill than borderline) to give me a decapitatingly saccharine verbal greeting when I walked into the seclusion room for my usual session with her. Another female patient has often provided me gratification with the caustic warmth of her so-ambivalent responses to me.

I have found this same phenomenon (of strange-seeming combinations of affects) at work in many teaching-interviews I have had with patients who were manifesting pathologic grief-reactions. That is, I have found myself experiencing sadistic urges toward depressed patients who clearly were repressing intense grief; only gradually did my initial shock at finding these sadistic urges in myself, in that setting, give way to an understanding that I was experiencing something of the sadistic feelings which were at work at an unconscious level in the patients themselves, and which thus far had been preventing the further accomplishment of their work of grieving.

Surely some of these instances of patients' giving expression, simultaneously, to so intensely incongruous emotions are manifestations of incongruously non-fitting introjects, within the patient, derived from the two parents; the disharmoniously-wedded parents have counterparts (however much exaggerated or otherwise distorted) in comparably poorly-married parental introjects largely unintegrated in the patient's ego-functioning. But even more pathogenically, neither parent was well-integrated within himself or herself. Thus the mother alone, or the father alone (or both) presumably presented to the child, as a model for identification, the embodiment of intensely incongruent emotionality such as we find in the patient himself. Hence either parent, taken alone, can have been the source (so to speak) of an abundance of non-fitting parental introjects within the patient.

Amusement

In relation to those occasions, which I mentioned earlier, when the analyst finds himself in the grip of amusement which he experiences as crazily incongruous with the more predominant and explicit aspects of his interaction with the patient, I wish to emphasize that, during the childhood of such a patient, some of the most traumatic effects of his family-relatedness derived from his having to maintain under dissociation his essentially healthy laughter. It is this healthy laughter which, more often than not, in the patient-therapist interaction is experienced first by the analyst, and then only after much resistance on the latter's part. Laughter is, after all, one of the precisely most appropriate, most healthy, kinds of response to the crazy things that have gone on in the childhood-families of borderline patients, and that transpire not infrequently during their analytic sessions in adult life.

In the many teaching-interviews I have done, it is usual for there to emerge some occasion, during the interview, for the patient and I to laugh at least briefly together. Not rarely, this is the first time the therapist and other hospital staff-members, for example, have seen such a capacity for humor in the patient. It is rare indeed for me to encounter a patient in whom I am unable, during a single interview, to perceive a sense of humor, no matter how straight-faced or laden with lugubriousness it may be, or manifested in however sadistic or psychotically-distorted a means of expression.

Our traditional training, as well as the mores of our culture, have so schooled us with the rigorous taboo against laughing *at* the poor victim of psychosis that it is difficult for us to realize that some of his most grievous warp, in childhood, derived from the family-wide taboo against healthy laughter, lest such laughter do violence to the so vulnerable sensibilities of the other family members. If we can dare to let our "own" healthy laughter come into the patient-therapist interaction, we can help him to find access to his "own" long-repressed healthy capacities in this regard. Parenthetically, in my many-years-long work with a chronically schizophrenic woman, there are many sessions in which I feel that the only solidly healthy responses she manifests consist in her occasional belly-laughs, unaccompanied by any verbal communications. It is amusement which I share, at such times, however uncomprehendingly in any secondary-process terms.

THE ANALYST'S EXPERIENCE OF TRANSFERENCE-ROLES WHICH ARE BOTH STRANGE IN NATURE AND INIMICAL TO HIS SENSE OF REALITY AND TO HIS SENSE OF PERSONAL IDENTITY

Turning from the subject of the impact upon the analyst of the patient's emotions *per se*, I want briefly to delineate the integrally-related topic of the analyst's experiencing of the strange transference-roles in which he finds himself by reason of the patient's developing transference, at times psychotic or near-psychotic in its reality-value for the patient.

The major roots of the patient's transference reactions are traceable to a stage in ego development prior to any clear differentiation between inner and outer world, and prior to the child's coming to function as a whole person involved in interpersonal relationships with other persons experienced as whole objects. Hence the analyst finds these transference-reactions and -attitudes of the adult borderline patient to be casting him, the analyst, in roles strangely different from those he commonly encounters in working with the neurotic patient whose transference casts him as, say, a domineering father or as a sexually seductive, masochistic mother. Now, instead, the analyst finds the patient reacting to him as being non-existent, or a corpse, or a pervasive and sinister supernatural force, or as God, or as being the patient's mind, or some anatomical part-aspect of his mother (her vagina, for example, or her fantasied penis). My monograph concerning the nonhuman environment (Searles 1960) contains many examples of schizophrenic patients' transference-reactions to the therapist as being one or another of a wide variety of nonhuman entities, and one finds an equally wide range in the work with borderline patients.

Not only the bizarre content or structure of the patient's transference-images of him, but also their near-psychotic reality value for the patient, comes at times formidably to threaten the analyst's own sense of reality and his own sense of identity. For example, I found that one of the sources for my persistent hatred of one such patient was that his intense transference to me as being his highly obsessive mother exerted such a powerful pull upon me toward going back to my earlier, much more obsessive, only partially outgrown self, that I hated him for this. A woman reported, several years along in our work together, that the thought had just occurred to her, for the first time, that perhaps I am *not* crazy. She went on to associate the craziness which, she now realized, she had previously been attributing all along to me, with that which she had perceived in her father since the patient's early childhood. All along I had had to cope, alone, with the patient's persistent but unconscious transference-image of me as being crazy. Another woman, whose childhood had been lived in remarkable isolation from both parents, and who had used to talk with insects and birds, manifested transference-reactions to me as being one or another of these creatures, and I never became able fully to determine whether, even in childhood, the conversations she had had were with real creatures of this sort, or with fantasied ones.

The omnipotent creativity, for good or evil but predominantly for evil, which frankly psychotic patients attribute to their own and the therapist's thought-processes, is to only a somewhat lesser degree true of the borderline patient also. Unlike the frankly psychotic patient, the borderline individual possesses, most of the time, sufficient observing ego so that he does not fully mis-identify the therapist as being someone (or a part-aspect of someone or something) from the patient's real past. But the borderline patient comes, nonetheless, close to doing this. Therefore, the therapist may feel submergedly threatened lest this transference role become, indeed, his—the therapist's—only subjective reality.

A middle-aged woman said in a session several years along in her analysis, during a brief interchange between us as to whom various persons in a just-reported dream were personifying or representing, "People are never to me who *they* think they are. They are who *I* think they are." She said this in a tone of small-child-like grandiosity and without appearing consciously disturbed or threatened. She said it in terms of pointing out to me, or reminding me of, an obvious fact. The charming-little-child quality of this expressed recognition on her part was in marked contrast to the genuinely threatening effects upon me, many times in earlier years when her negative transference had been much more intense and her ability to differentiate between mental images and flesh-and-blood outer reality had been much less well established. During those years I had felt anything but charmed by her reacting to me with the full conviction that I was (to give but one example) a literally stone-hearted witch.

To the extent that a patient is unable to distinguish between the analyst as, say, a mother in the transference-situation, and the actual mother in the patient's early childhood, he is likewise unable to differentiate between *mental images of persons* (i.e., images within his own head) and the corresponding *persons in outer reality*. This is another way of understanding why the analyst reacts to the borderline patient's transference-images of him as being such a threat to the latter's sense of personal identity—that is, as to why the patient's transference-*image* of him, an image which the patient experiences as being so fully and incontestably real, carries with it the threat, to the analyst, that it will indeed fully create or transform him into conformity with that image.

I shall turn again to my work with frankly and chronically schizophrenic patients for relatively unambiguous examples of this point. Each of the following two instances occurred relatively early in my work with such patients, at a time when more areas of my own identity were existing at a repressed or dissociated level than I find to be the case these days in my work with patients. One chronically and severely assaultive woman asked me, at a time when I was conscious of feeling toward her only a wish to help her and a physical fear of her, "Dr. Searles, *why* do you hate me?" She asked me this in a tone of assuming it to be an incontrovertible fact that I hated her, that hatred was the predominant—if not only—feeling I was experiencing toward her, and that all this was something we both had known all along. In response to her question I felt thoroughly disconcerted and at a loss to know what, if anything, to say. I thought that theoretically I must hate her, but was entirely unaware of hating her and—most pertinent for the point I am making here—I felt completely alone, without any ally in her, as regards any attempt on my part to question, with her, whether her view of me was not at all exaggerated, oversimplified, or otherwise distorted.

Another chronically ill woman, who for several years in our work perceived me most of the time as being, in flesh-and-blood reality, a woman, and who was herself the mother of several children, once said to me in very much the same tone as that used by the woman I have just mentioned, "*You*'re a reasonable woman; what do *you* do with a daughter who . . ." She was speaking for all the world in terms of our being two women comparing notes, companionably, about the problems of rearing daughters.

In the neurotic patient it may be that an unconscious *personality-aspect,* such as hostile domineeringness, based upon an unconscious identification with the domineeringness of, say, the father, is projected during the course of the analysis upon the analyst, who is perceived by the patient, meanwhile, as being essentially the same person as before but with, so the patient now perceives him, a hatefully and perhaps intimidatingly domineering aspect. The analyst may sense himself, in response to these developments, to have an uncomfortably domineering personality-aspect, but does not feel his basic sense of his own identity to be appreciably disturbed.

Although such a state of things may be true in psychoanalytic work between a neurotic patient and the analyst, in the borderline patient there is insufficient ego-integration for the unconscious domineeringness to exist as merely a repressed component of the patient's ego-identity. It exists, instead, in a dissociated, split-off state as a largely unintegrated introject derived from experiences with a parent in question. It exists as a separate self, as it were — a component with its own separate identity. Now, when the analyst becomes involved in psychoanalytic psychotherapy with such a patient, he finds that the patient, through projecting this introject upon the analyst, comes not merely to perceive the analyst as being the analyst with a newly-revealed hateful domineeringness. The analyst finds, instead, that the patient becomes more or less fully convinced that the analyst has been replaced by the hatefully and intimidatingly domineering father.

That is, in the work with the borderline or schizophrenic patient, the unconscious affect is encapsulated in, or pervades, an introject-structure which has an identity-value all its own. This affect-laden structure which the patient, to the extent that he is schizophrenic, is convinced *is* the real identity of the analyst has, through its being projected forcibly and persistently upon the latter for many months or even years, at times a formidably shaking effect upon the analyst's own sense of his identity.

But on the positive side, the analyst, through being attentive to the resultant fluctuations in his sense of his "own" personal identity in the course of the sessions with these patients, finds that he possesses a priceless (and, more often than not, previously unrecognized) source of analytic data. In a paper entitled, "The Sense of Identity as a Perceptual Organ," I (Searles 1965a) mentioned that somewhere midway through my own analysis, after I had undergone much change, I visualized the core of myself as being, nonetheless, like a steel ball bearing, with varicolored sectors on its surface. At least, I told myself, this would not change. But by this time, in 1965, I noted that I had lost, long ago, any such image of the core of my identity. In a succession of papers I have described the process whereby my sense of identity has become sufficiently alive to change so that it is now my most reliable source of data as to what is transpiring between the patient and myself, and within the patient. I have described the "use" of such fluctuations in one's sense of identity as being a prime source of discovering, in work with the patient, not only countertransference processes but also transference processes, newly-developing facets of the patient's own self-image and so on; and in supervision, of discovering processes at work not only between the supervisee and oneself, but also between the supervisee and the patient.

For a number of years during the analysis of a young woman I felt, much more often than not during the session, somnolent and much of the time indeed, sensed that her transference to me was, even more, as being comatose, moribund. Many of the sessions felt endless to me. After several years, her transference to me began to emerge into her own awareness through such dreams as this:

> I was at a dinner party. This woman seated across the table from me seemed to fluctuate between being dead and being alive. I was conversing with her and it was almost as though the more involved I became with her, the more dead she would become. That kind of thing went back and forth several times. From a distance she seemed vigorously alive, but up close she seemed lifeless and dull.

Associative connections between that woman in the dream, and myself as a representative of a number of personality-aspects of various persons from the patient's childhood, as well as connections to components of herself which were identified with those emotionally-dead figures from her past, emerged in the subsequent analytic work.

A childless woman, after detailing how moved she had felt at the aliveness of a pair of twin babies she had seen the day before, became somberly philosophical and said, with an undertone of fear and awe in her voice, "There's always the death in the background." I heard this as a clear but unconscious reference to me, behind her, as being death; I said nothing. She went on, ". . . I do have a lot more thoughts about the finiteness of my own life."

More than one patient, of various diagnostic categories, have associated me—partly by reason of their not feeling free to look at me during the session—with those parts of a parent's body at which they had not been permitted to look, during their childhood—with, most frequently, the parent's genitals.

Parenthetically, it seems to me not coincidental that in those so-frequent instances when such transference-responses as those I am citing are prevailing in work with borderline patients for years, the analyst seldom indeed finds it feasible to make effective transference-interpretations. The patient is largely deaf, unconsciously, to verbalized intelligence from an analyst who is powerfully assumed, again at an unconscious level in the patient, to be something quite other than a whole human being.

Further, in a number of patients of varying degrees of illness, I have found that *words*—words from either patient or analyst—are equivalent to *father*, intruding unwantedly into a nonverbal mother-infant symbiosis. This transference-"father" is most significantly traceable to components of the biological mother herself, in these instances of split mother-transference, wherein intense jealousy permeates both the transference and the countertransference. Such jealousy-phenomena are detailed in Chapters 5 and 8 in *My Work with Borderline Patients* (Searles 1986).

The borderline patient's impaired sense of reality is another typical factor which makes the development, and work of resolution, of the transference-psychosis stressful for both participants. Helene Deutsch's classic paper on "as-if" personalities (Deutsch 1942) is highly relevant here. One woman emphasized to me that "I am very different in person from the way I am here." This curious phrase, "in person," seemed to indicate that the analytic sessions possessed for her the reality-value merely of a TV show or a movie, for example. Later in the session she commented that her relationship with her father is so stormy that she sometimes feels an urge to write a novel about it; my own private impression was that, in that relationship, she was indeed living a novel. I have found it commonplace for these patients to emphasize that "in my *life*" or "in my *real* life" they are quite different persons from the way they are in the analysis. Admittedly, an analytic relationship commonly can be seen to be in many ways different from other areas of a patient's life; but these patients refer persistently to the analytic relationship and setting as being not really part of their lives at all. Many times, while reminiscing about events earlier in their lives, they will recall that, "In my *life*, . . ." saying this as though from the vantage point of a very old person whose life is essentially *all* past now or—very often, in my experience—from the vantage point of one who has already died and can therefore look back upon his own life in its totality, as something now behind and quite apart from him.

THE ANALYST'S REACTIONS TO THE DEVELOPMENT OF THE
TRANSFERENCE-BORDERLINE-PSYCHOSIS IN THE PATIENT

Next I shall discuss various emotions which the therapist comes to
experience in consequence of the development of the transference-
borderline-psychosis in the patient, and some of the sources of
those emotions. While the literature is not in full and explicit
agreement that a transference psychosis typically develops in
psychoanalytic therapy with the borderline patient, it seems
generally agreed that he brings into the treatment-relationship a
vulnerability to (or, one might say, a treatment-need for) this
development, and that the emergence of so intense and primitive
a constellation of transference-reactions is at the least a standard
hazard in the therapist's work with these patients. I think it fair
and accurate to say that the borderline patient needs to develop,
and if treatment proceeds well will develop, a transference-
borderline-psychosis in the course of the work.

Certainly in my own work with borderline patients, and in my
supervision of analytic candidates and psychiatric residents concerning their work with such patients, as well as in my study of the
literature regarding psychoanalytic therapy with borderline patients, I find that a transference-borderline-psychosis commonly
develops over the course of the work and needs, of course, to
become resolved in order for the treatment to end relatively
successfully.

My own clinical and supervisory experience strongly indicates to
me that there are certain intense, and intensely difficult, feelings
which the therapist can be expected to develop in response to the
patient's development of the transference-borderline-psychosis. It
may well be that, as the years go on, we shall become able to do
psychoanalytic therapy with borderline and schizophrenic patients
with increasing success in proportion as we become able to accept
that, just as it is to be assumed, as an inherent part of the work,
that the *patient* will develop a transference-borderline-psychosis
or transference-psychosis, it is also to be assumed, as a no less
integral part of the work, that the *therapist* will develop, to, of
course, an attempted limited, self-analytically explorable, and
appreciably sharable-with-the-patient degree — an area of
countertransference-borderline-psychosis or even countertrans-

ference-psychosis in his work with such a patient. It should be
unnecessary to emphasize that going crazy, whole hog, along with
the patient will do no good and great harm. But I believe that we
psychoanalytic therapists collectively will become, as the years go
on, less readily scared off from this work, and better able to take
it up and pursue it as a job of work to be done relatively
successfully, in proportion as we become able to take the measure,
forthrightly and unshamedly, of the feelings we can *expect*
ourselves to come to experience, naturally, in the course of
working with these patients.

Pao (1975) reports his project concerning a schema, devised at
Chestnut Lodge by himself, Fort (1973) and presumably others on
the staff there, for dividing schizophrenia into four subgroups.
Pao, the Director of Psychotherapy at the Lodge, describes that in
the course of this project he interviewed each new patient shortly
after admission. It is of much interest to me that, evidently
without having encountered my (Searles 1965a) paper concerning
the sense of identity as a perceptual organ, his experience led him
to what seems to me the same general direction:

> My emphasis is that the diagnosis should begin with the study of the
> interviewer's own emotional reactions in the interaction between the
> patient and himself. . . . Such personal experience must be supple-
> mented by a careful scrutiny of the patient's background, the course
> of illness, the patient's ability to tolerate anxiety, etc.

I can believe that the time will come, in our work with neurotic
patients, when, just as we now use, as a criterion of analyzability,
the patient's capability for developing a transference neurosis, we
may use as an additional criterion, of earlier predictive significance in our work with the patient, his capability in fostering a
countertransference neurosis, so to speak, in the analyst.

Having said that by way of preface, I shall detail some of the
therapist's expectable feeling-experiences in the course of his work
with the borderline patient.

The therapist comes to feel guilty and personally responsible
for the initially-relatively-well-appearing patient's becoming, over
the months or years of the transference-evolution, appreci-

ably psychotic or borderline-psychotic in the context of the treatment-sessions. It is only in relatively recent years, after many years of tormented countertransference experiences of this sort, that I have come to realize how largely referable is the therapist's guilt and remorse, in this regard, to unconscious empathy with the patient's own child-self. That is, the patient in childhood tended to feel that only he possessed the guilty awareness of how deeply disturbed the mother is and that, moreover, he personally was totally responsible for driving her to the edge of, or even into, madness. The father may have been the more central parent in this regard; but much more often it was, from what I have seen, the mother.

It is garden-variety experience for children in our culture to hear reproaches from a parent, "You're driving me crazy!", and of course I do not mean that such words alone, even with more than a modicum of appropriately maddened demeanor, cause the child any serious and lasting trauma. But the parents of borderline patients have, themselves, more than a mere garden-variety, neurotic-degree of psychopathology; hence it is a formidably serious degree of parental psychopathology for which the child is being assigned, day after day, a totally causative personal responsibility.

The therapist's guilt in this same regard stems partly from his finding, over the course of the work, that the patient's crazier aspects provide him (the therapist) covertly with much more of lively interest, and even fascination, than do the patient's relatively dull areas of neurotic ego-functioning. Although the therapist's conscientious goal is to help the patient to become free from the borderline-schizophrenic modes of experience, privately and guiltily he feels fascinated by these very sickest aspects of the patient, and fears that his fascination with them has led him to foster, to deepen, these most grievously afflicted components of the patient's personality-functioning.

Typically the treatment-process itself, in the work with these patients, becomes highly sexualized, such that the patient reveals newly-experienced and fascinating borderline symptoms in a basically coquettish, seductive manner, while the enthralled therapist struggles to match this priceless material with brilliantly penetrating interpretations. Typically, too, the treatment-process becomes laden with acted-in aggression. For instance, as I have mentioned in a paper written some years ago (Searles 1976a) the therapist, who develops formidable quantities of hatred toward the patient, comes to feel for a time that the only effective "outlet" for his hatred is to be found in seeing the patient suffer from the latter's persistent symptoms.

All these details of the therapist's countertransference have had, so my clinical experience indicates to me, prototypes in the patient's childhood experience with the parent in question. As one simple example, the child could not help deriving gratification, no matter how guilty a gratification, from feeling himself capable of bringing mother out of her depressive deadness into a highly animated and vocal state verging upon madness.

My work with a patient far more ill than borderline has shown me another point relevant for this discussion. She is a chronically schizophrenic woman with whom I have worked for many years. After the first few years of our work she refused to acknowledge her name as her own and, although she has improved in many regards over the subsequent years, it has become rare for her to be conscious of bits of her own real, personal childhood-history such as were relatively abundantly available to her, despite her many already-present delusions, at the beginning of our work. For many years now, one of the harshest of my countertransference burdens is a guilty and remorseful feeling that I personally have destroyed, long since, her only real and sane identity—destroyed it out of, more than anything else, my hateful envy of her for her many and extraordinary capabilities, and for her childhood lived in a setting far different from my own small-town middle-class one.

It is only as she has been improving, recently, to such an extent that some of her psychotic-transference reactions have become clearly linked with newly remembered childhood experiences, that I have felt largely relieved of this burden of guilt and remorse. Specifically, I have come to see that my long-chafing, and often intensely threatening to the point of engendering in me fantasies of suicide, feeling of having destroyed her sense of identity has a precise counterpart in *her*. She had been given to feel, by her mother, that the child had destroyed the mother's so-called real and true identity—an identity based, in actuality, in the mother's ego-ideal as a woman of myriad magnificent accomplishments, above all in the field of dramatics. The mother had been much given to manic flights of fancy, and her fantasied accomplishments were not, to her, so much ambitions thwarted by the patient as a child; she reacted, rather, to the daughter as having destroyed these supposedly actualized accomplishments of hers and, in the process, destroyed the mother's supposedly real, true identity.

THE ANALYST AS UNWANTED CHILD

To return to the discussion of borderline patients *per se*, I have indicated that the therapist is given to feel that he has had, and is having, a diabolically, malevolently, all-powerful influence in the development and maintenance of the patient's transference-borderline-psychosis. But I have found, in my work with a reliably long succession of patients now, that such an experience of myself, in the work, comes in course of time to reveal, at its core, the experience of myself as being an unwanted little child in relation to the patient. It gradually dawns on me that this is who I am, in the patient's transference-relationship with me, as I listen month after month and year after year to the patient's reproaches that all the rest of his or her life is going relatively well these days, with my being the only fly in the ointment. If only he were rid of me, he says more and more explicitly, his life would be a breeze. In case after case, I become impressed, inevitably, with how much the patient is sounding like a mother who is reproaching and blaming her small child, giving him to feel that, had he only not been born, her life would be a paradise of personal fulfillment.

In the instance of my work with one patient after another, the awareness of my unwanted-child countertransference comes to me as an excitingly meaningful revelation and, although its appearance has been made possible only by my having come to realize, more fully than before, how deeply hurt and rejected I am feeling in response to the patient, this phase comes as a relief from my

erstwhile grandiosity-and-guilt-ridden countertransference identity as the diabolical inflictor of psychosis. In some instances,
more specifically, I no longer hear the patient as reproaching me
with diabolically *spoiling* his otherwise satisfactory life, but hear
him saying, as the stronger, parental one of the two of us, that I
as the smaller, child-one am not, and never was, loved or wanted.

All these processes in the patient's childhood regularly involved
his becoming the object, beginning in early childhood or infancy
or even before birth, of transference-reactions on the mother's
(and/or father's) part from her own mother and/or father (or
sibling, or whomever) to the patient. Typically, the more ill
theadult patient is, the more sure we can be that such transference-
responses on the patient's part were powerfully at work remarkably early in the patient's childhood. I have written a number of
times of the schizophrenic patient's childhood in this regard, and
I am aware that a number of other writers have done so. But I feel
that we are only beginning to mine this rich lode of psychodynamics.

Here is, I believe, a prevailing atmosphere in the background of
many borderline patients. Beginning when the patient was, say,
two years of age (or even younger; I do not know just when), his
mother had an unconscious transference-image of him as being,
all over again, her own mother and/or father, in relationship to
whom she had felt herself to be an unwanted child, and whose love
she had despaired of evoking. Now she blames and reproaches her
little son (or daughter) for all sorts of events and situations which
are far beyond his realistic powers to control, as if he were God
Almighty, just as later on, in psychotherapy, the adult patient who
was once this child comes to vituperate against his therapist as
being a diabolical God. During the patient's childhood the mother
does this basically because she unconsciously experiences herself
as being an unwanted child to this transference-"parent" of hers,
who is actually her little child. I sense that as we come to
understand more fully the poignancy of such mother-child relationships, we will discard the crude and cruel "schizophrenogenic
mother" concept (to which I, among many others, devoted much
attention in my early papers) once and for all.

THE ANALYST'S GUILTY SENSE OF LESS-THAN-FULL COMMITMENT TO HIS THERAPEUTIC ROLE

A countertransference-experience which has been long-lasting in my work with one patient after another is a guilty sense of not being fully committed, inwardly, to my functional role of the patient's therapist, despite my maintenance of all the outward trappings of therapeutic devotion. Any thoroughgoing discussion of this aspect of the countertransference would require a chapter in itself, since it has, undoubtedly, so many connections to the patient's primitive defenses of fantasied omnipotence and of splitting, with powerfully idealized or diabolized transference-images of the therapist. It is my impression, in essence, that it is only in proportion as there is a deflation of grandiosity, in the transference and the countertransference, that the therapist can come to feel fully committed to his now human-sized functional role as the patient's therapist. My treatment-records abound with data from earlier phases in the work with, for example, schizophrenic patients who would talk adoringly and loyally of a delusional construct hallucinatorily conversed with as "my doctor," while shutting me out of any functional relatedness with them; but at those rare moments when I would feel he or she was giving me an opportunity, supposedly long sought by me, to step into the shoes of "my doctor," I would quail at doing so.

In this same vein, but in my work with a much less ill female patient, she developed a headache during the course of a session, and in association to this headache reported conjectures about "rage at myself—*at you, maybe my mother* [my italics] . . ." I sensed that she was manifesting an unconscious transference to me as being her mother who was only "*maybe* my mother," which fit not only with my frequent countertransference reaction to her, but also with her childhood experience of a mother who persistently remained tangential to the mother-role, rather than more fully committed to it. It fit also, needless to say, with her own yet-unresolved, fantasied omnipotence, which allowed her to acknowledge only grudgingly, at best, any mother-figure as being "*maybe* my mother."

THE ANALYST'S "OWN" FEELINGS AS COMPRISING LAYER UNDER LAYER OF COUNTERTRANSFERENCE-ELEMENTS

I cannot overemphasize the enormously treatment-facilitating value, as well as the comforting and liberating value for the therapist personally, of his locating where this or that tormenting or otherwise upsetting countertransference reaction links up with the patient's heretofore-unconscious and unclarified *transference-* reactions to him. In other words, the analyst's "own" personal torment needs to become translated into a fuller understanding of the patient's childhood-family events and daily atmosphere. I find it particularly helpful when a "personal," "private" feeling-response within myself, a feeling which I have been experiencing as fully or at least predominantly my "own," becomes revealed as being a still deeper layer of reaction to a newly-revealed aspect of the patient's transference to me.

For a case in point here, I shall turn briefly to my very long work with a previously mentioned chronically schizophrenic woman. I felt on many occasions over the years how seriously disadvantaged I, as her therapist, was in trying to function, since my role in her life precluded my responding to her in the only manner appropriate to her behavior toward me, by administering a brutal physical beating of her such as her mother frequently had given her. Only after many years did I come to realize that, in so reacting, I was being her transference-father; she had come by now to clearly portray me, in the transference, as a diabolical, omnipotent father who controlled from a distance both her and her mother, and who delegated to the mother the physical punishment of the child. His Godlike-aloof role forbade, by the same token, that he dirty his hands with such matters.

A borderline man expressed, during a session after a number of years of work, the realization, at an unprecedentedly deep level, that "You are not my father." What I found fascinating about this were the attendant evidences of still-unresolved transference which revealed to me that, in saying this, although he was consciously expressing the realization that I was in actuality his therapist rather than his father, unconsciously he was expressing the realization that I was his uncle, who had provided most of his fathering to him following the death, early in the patient's boyhood, of the actual father. Experiences such as this have led me, incidentally, to assume that any presumed "therapeutic alliance," supposedly involving relatively transference-free components of the patient's ego-functioning in a workmanlike bond with the analyst, needs constantly to be scrutinized for subtle but pervasively powerful elements of unconscious transference.

SUSPENSE; CHOICE BETWEEN ILLNESS AND HEALTH; THE PATIENT'S ACTING-OUT ON BASIS OF IDENTIFICATIONS WITH THE ANALYST

Suspense is prominent among the feelings of the analyst who is working with the borderline patient—suspense as to whether the patient will become frankly psychotic or will suicide or both; or as to whether he will leave treatment suddenly and irrevocably; or even, at times when the transference is particularly intense and disturbing to analyst as well as patient, as to whether the analyst himself will fall victim to one or another of such outcomes.

In the writings of Kernberg concerning borderline conditions I find much to admire and from which to learn. But one of the major differences between his views (as contained in those writings of his which I have read) and mine is that he does not portray the suspenseful aspect which seems to me so highly characteristic of the analyst's feelings in working with the borderline patient. Kernberg (1957) says, for example, that patients with "borderline personality organization . . . have in common a rather specific and remarkably stable form of pathological ego structure . . . their personality organization is not a transitory state fluctuating between neurosis and psychosis" (p. 3). In a similar vein, he (Kernberg 1972) comments that "Under severe stress or under the effect of alcohol or drugs, transient psychotic episodes may develop in these patients; these psychotic episodes usually improve with relatively brief but well-structured treatment approaches" (p. 255).

Kernberg's writings on borderline states are in part the product of his work in the Psychotherapy Research Project of the Menninger Foundation, and I do not doubt that his experience in that project helps to account for the widely-admired soundness, both theoretically and clinically, of his writings. But in those passages which I have quoted, passages which in their tone are typical of a recurrent emphasis in his work (and, incidentally, passages which I am not contesting here, *per se*, as regards their validity insofar as they go), Kernberg fails to convey how very far removed, indeed, does the analyst feel, in his work, from any such statistician's or theoretician's coolly Olympian view. All too often, for example, the analyst feels desperately threatened lest his patient become frankly psychotic, and the analyst finds little or no reason for confidence that, in such an event, the psychosis will prove transitory.

Any discussion-in-depth of this area of the countertransference would include an exploration of the analyst's envy of the patient for the latter's psychopathology; his hateful wishes to be rid of the patient by the latter's becoming frankly psychotic and hospitalized off somewhere; and his fears of becoming, and wishes to become, psychotic himself. I (Searles 1965) have discussed various among these countertransference phenomena, as regards the work with frankly psychotic patients, in a number of papers.

In my several-years-long work with a woman who showed a borderline personality organization at the outset, I found that she recurrently held over my head, mockingly, year after year, the threat that she would become frankly and chronically schizophrenic. She did not say this in so many words; but her behavior conveyed, innumerable times, that implicit, sadomasochistic threat. In many of the sessions during those years, I felt a strong impulse to tell her ironically that I had felt for years, and still did, that she could become chronically schizophrenic if she would just try a little harder. Essentially, I was wanting at such times somehow to convey to her that this was a *choice* she had. I suppressed this urge each time; but had I given way to it, this would have been an attempt to deal with her infuriating, year-after-year expressions of defiance and mockery and of, above all, the highly sadistic, implicit threat of her becoming chronically psychotic.

The following comments of mine in a paper (Searles 1976) concerning psychoanalytic therapy with schizophrenic patients are in my opinion fully applicable, in principle, to such work with borderline patients also. I wrote there of the crucial issues of *choice*—of the patient's coming to feel *in a position to choose* between continued insanity on the one hand, or healthy interpersonal and intrapersonal relatedness on the other hand. In order for the analyst to help the patient to become able to choose, the former must be able not only to experience, indeed, a passionately tenacious devotion to helping the latter to become free from psychosis, but also become able to tolerate, to clearly envision, the alternative "choice"—namely, that of psychosis for the remainder of the patient's life. I do not see how the patient's individuation can ever occur if the analyst dare not envision this latter possibility. The patient's previous life-experience presumably has proceeded in such a manner and his therapy at the hands of a too-compulsively "dedicated" analyst may proceed in such a manner likewise, that chronic psychosis may be the only subjectively *autonomous* mode of existence available to the patient.

I described further, in that same paper, that an analyst who, for whatever unconscious reasons, cannot become able to live comfortably with the possibility that his patient may never become free from psychosis cannot, by the same token, foster the necessary emotional atmosphere in the sessions for the development of the contented, unthreatened emotional oneness to which I refer by the term therapeutic symbiosis (Searles 1961), a form of relatedness which is of the same quality as that which imbues the mother–infant relatedness in normal infancy and very early childhood. Any so-called individuation which occurs in the patient which is not founded upon a relatively clear phase of therapeutic symbiosis in the treatment is a pseudo-individuation, and only a seeming choice of sanity, with the urge toward psychosis, the yearning for psychosis, subjected to repression rather than faced at all fully in the light of conscious choice. Essentially, at the unconscious level, the patient chooses to remain psychotic.

Although these just-paraphrased passages may be reminiscent of what I have termed the Olympian quality of the passages from Kernberg, most of my writings have emphasized—as I emphasized in the bulk of this recent paper—the struggles which even the experienced analyst must go through, as an inherent part of his countertransference-work with one patient after another, to come to any such harmony with his own formerly so-ambivalent feelings which have been at the basis of his experiencing so much of a threatened suspensefulness.

Along the way, it is especially threatening to the analyst to feel kept in suspense as to whether the patient is headed toward destruction precisely by reason of the latter's functioning loyally as being a chip off the old block—namely, the analyst as perceived by the patient in the transference. That is, the analyst is finding much reason to fear that it is exactly the patient's identification with one of the analyst's qualities, no matter how exaggeratedly perceived by reason of the patient's mother- or father-transference to him, which is carrying the patient toward destruction. Thus the analyst feels responsible, in an essentially omnipotent fashion, for the patient's self-destructive acting-out behavior outside the office. The analyst feels that the patient's behavior vicariously manifests his—the analyst's—own acting-out proclivities.

For example, although I seldom feel inordinately threatened lest any one of my psychiatrist–analysands act out his or her sexual fantasies toward one or another of his or her own patients, I had a more threatened time of it in my work with one analysand. This man was convinced, for years, that I had sexual intercourse with an occasional patient, casually and without subsequent remorse or other disturbed feelings. When, then, he became strongly tempted to give way to his sexual impulses toward one or another of his own current patients, he reported these impulses, during his analytic sessions with me, as being in the spirit of his overall wishes to emulate me as an admired, virile father in the transference. Not to leave the reader in any unnecessary suspense here, I can report that this aspect of his transference became analyzed successfully.

Another example of this same principle is to be found in another paper of mine, "Violence in Schizophrenia" (Searles, Bisco, Coutu, and Scibetta 1975), in which I describe my single teaching-interviews with a number of schizophrenic patients whose histories included seriously violent behavior. In the instance of one particularly frightening man, with whose therapist I worked subsequently in supervision, the role of a threatened suspensefulness, in both the therapist and me, was especially prominent. My paper describes as follows the end of the therapy with this man, who had run away from the sanitarium previously:

He again ran away, was found and taken by his parents to another sanitarium, and ran away from there and joined the Marines without divulging his psychiatric background. Our last bit of information about him was a telephone call to the therapist from an official at an Army prison, stating that this man had stabbed a fellow Marine three times, that his victim was barely surviving, and that an investigation was under way to determine whether Delaney was mentally competent to stand trial. The therapist and I agreed that he had finally committed the violent act which we both had known he eventually would. . . . I want to emphasize the aspect of relief, of certainty, which this clearly afforded me and, I felt, the therapist also. It was as though the distinction between the patient's actualized murderousness and our own murderous fantasies and feelings was now clear beyond anyone's questioning it. . . .

Both the therapist and I, in relating to him, evidently had mobilized in ourselves such intensely conflicting feelings of love and murderous hatred that a regressive de-differentiation occurred in our respective ego-functioning, such that we attributed to the patient our own murderous hatred, and unconsciously hoped that he would give vicarious expression to our own violence, so as to restore the wall between him and us. More broadly put, such a patient evokes in one such intensely conflicting feelings that, at an unconscious level, one's ego-functioning undergoes a pervasive de-differentiation: one loses the ability deeply to distinguish between one's self and the patient, and between the whole realms of fantasy and reality. Thus the patient's committing of a violent act serves not only to distinguish between one's own "fantasied" violence and his "real" violence but, more generally, serves to restore, in one, the distinction between the whole realms of fantasy and outer reality. [pp. 14–16]

Still concerning the matter of the analyst's experiencing suspense, to think of this less globally now (as regards, say, the question of whether the patient will become psychotic or suicide), and more particularly as regards any symptom or personality-trait

or current transference-reaction, I find pertinent the following
note I made half a dozen years ago concerning my work with a
man who manifested a predominantly narcissistic form of ego-
functioning.

> Regarding the therapist's experiencing *suspense*. Thinking back on
> the hour yesterday with Cooper, it occurs to me that, in reacting to
> his projection upon me of his own sadistic unfeelingness, I tend to
> function as distinctly *more* so than I actually feel — partly for the
> reason, as I see it now, of trying to make this issue become clear
> enough so that he can see it and we can thrash it out, analyze it,
> resolve it.
>
> In other words, one of the major reasons why it is so difficult to
> maintain a genuinely neutral position, not reacting in tune with the
> patient's transference, is because it is so very difficult to endure the
> tantalizing ambiguity, the suspense, of the unworked-through trans-
> ference reactions which one can see in the patient, and to which one
> *does* react genuinely. That is, I do experience myself as uncomfort-
> ably sadistic, unfeeling, unlikable and unadmirable to myself in
> reaction to Cooper's transference.

In a paper subsequently, "The Function of the Patient's Realistic
Perceptions of the Analyst in Delusional Transference" (Searles
1972), I described some aspects of my work with a far more ill
patient, in terms both of her delusional-transference perceptions
of me, and of my own subjective experience of what I was "really"
feeling, and communicating to her, in the therapeutic sessions.
That paper mainly emphasizes my discovery, over the course of
years, that again and again and again, seemingly purely-delusional
perceptions of me on her part proved to be well rooted in accurate
and realistic perceptions of aspects of myself which heretofore had
been out of my own awareness.

What was mentioned above, concerning my work with the
narcissistic man, suggests something of why the analyst may
introject (unconsciously, of course, for the most part) some of the
patient's psychopathology, in an attempt to hasten its resolution
and thereby end the feelings of suspense which permeate the
treatment-atmosphere in one's work with so tantalizingly ambiguous a patient.

It has seemed to me that some of these same psychodynamics have applied in a considerable number of instances of my work with patients who have been involved in chronically troubled marital situations wherein there is a chronic, suspense-laden threat of divorce hanging over the marriage. In the course of my work with each of these patients, it has appeared to me no coincidence that, concurrent with especially stressful phases of the analytic work, my own marriage has felt uncharacteristically in jeopardy. My strong impression is that the analyst under these circumstances tends to regress to a level of primitively magical thinking, whereby if his own marriage were to dissolve, this would end the years-long suspenseful question as to whether the patient's verge-of-divorce marriage will, or will not, endure. Whether the analyst were thereby to bring about, vicariously, the disruption of the patient's marriage, or on the other hand to preserve the patient's marriage by sacrificing his own, in either eventuality the tormenting element of suspense in the analytic situation would—so, in my speculation, the analyst's primitively magical reasoning goes—be brought to a merciful end.

DIFFERING KINDS (REPRESSIVE VERSUS NON-REPRESSIVE) OF THE ANALYST'S SENSE OF IDENTITY AS AN ANALYST

Lastly, I want explicitly to discuss a point which has been implied throughout this chapter—namely, that the analyst's sense-of-identity-as-an-analyst must be found in a *kind* of analyst-identity which in major ways is different from the traditionally-striven-for analyst-identity consonant with classical analysis. For the sake of this discussion, at least, it is not an oversimplification to say that classical analysis enjoins the analyst to develop, and strive to maintain, a sense-of-identity-as-an-analyst which constrains him to evenly hovering attentiveness to the analysand's productions, and to participating actively in the analytic session only to the extent of offering verbal interpretations of the material which the analysand has been conveying to him. Such a traditional analyst-identity is neither tenable for the analyst who is analyzing a borderline patient, nor adequate to meet the analytic needs of the patient.

Knight (1953) described that in a relatively highly structured interview, the borderline patient's basic difficulties in ego-functioning tend not to become available for either the patient or the psychiatrist to see and work upon:

> During the psychiatric interview the neurotic defenses and the relatively intact ego functions may enable the borderline patient to present a deceptive, superficially conventional, although neurotic, front, depending on how thoroughgoing and comprehensive the psychiatric investigation is with respect to the patient's *total* ego functioning. The face-to-face psychiatric interview provides a relatively structured situation in which the conventional protective devices of avoidance, evasion, denial, minimization, changing the subject, and other cover-up methods can be used — even by patients who are genuinely seeking help but who dare not yet communicate their awareness of lost affect, reality misinterpretations, autistic preoccupations, and the like. [pp. 102–103]

To be sure, Knight's comments suggest that a relatively free form of analytic-interview participation on the part of the patient is most facilitating of the emergence of the latter's borderline difficulties, and with this I am in full agreement. But his comments suggest, too, that such a patient is unlikely to be helped much by an analyst who himself is clinging, in a threatened fashion, to some rigidly constructed analyst-identity. I hope that this chapter, when taken along with my previous writings concerning countertransference matters, will serve forcefully to convey my conviction that the analyst must far outgrow the traditional classical-analyst identity in order to be able to work with a reasonable degree of success with the borderline patient — to be able, as examples, to utilize his sense of identity as a perceptual organ in the manner I have described here; to enter to the requisite degree into (while maintaining under analytic scrutiny) the so-necessary therapeutic symbiosis; and to be able to preserve his analyst-identity in face of the extremely intense, persistent, and oftentimes strange transference-images which, coming from the (largely unconscious) processes at work in the patient, tend so powerfully to dominate the analyst's sense of his actual identity.

I have seen that various psychiatric residents and analytic candidates who, partly because of a relative lack of accumulated experience, have not yet established a strong sense-of-identity-as-therapist, are particularly threatened by the intense and tenacious negative-transference-images wherein the patient is endeavoring, as it were, to impose upon the therapist a highly unpalatable sense of identity. By the same token, it should be seen that an analyst who is struggling to maintain, in his work with such a patient, a professional identity untainted by such emotions as jealousy, infantile-dependent feelings, sexual lust, and so on, is undoubtedly imposing, by projection, such largely-unconscious personality-components upon the already-overburdened patient. In essence, I am suggesting here that, in the analyst's work with the borderline patient, he needs to have, or insofar as possible to develop, a kind of professional identity which will not be working on the side of the forces of repression but will, rather, be facilitating of the emergence from repression of those feelings, fantasies, and so on which the borderline patient needs for his analyst to be able to experience, on the way to his own becoming able, partly through identification with his analyst, to integrate comparable experiences within his—the patient's—own ego-functioning.

SUMMARY

The countertransference provides the analyst with his most reliable approach to the understanding of borderline (as well as other) patients. The impact upon him of the patient's split ego-functioning is discussed. His experience of transference-roles which are both strange in nature, and inimical to his sense of reality and to his sense of personal identity, are explored; in the latter regard, the value of his sense of identity as a perceptual organ is highlighted.

There are detailed some of the analyst's reactions—his guilt, his envy, and so on—to the development of the transference-borderline-psychosis in the patient. The analyst finds that, underneath the patient's transference to him as being an omnipotent, diabolical inflictor of psychosis, is the patient's transference to him as being an unwanted child.

The analyst's guilty sense of less-than-full commitment to his therapeutic role is described briefly, as is the general principle of his finding, time and again, that what he has felt to be his "own" feelings toward the patient include layer under layer of responses which are natural and inherent counterparts to the patient's transference-responses and -attitudes toward him.

The prominent role of suspense is discussed at relative length, and the related issue of choice between illness and health. The phenomenon of the patient's acting-out on the (partial) basis of unconscious identifications with the analyst, and the impact of this phenomenon upon the countertransference, are mentioned.

Lastly, the significant role, in the countertransference, of the analyst's sense of identity as an analyst is discussed, and it is suggested that the borderline patient needs for the analyst to have, or insofar as possible to develop, a sense-of-identity-as-analyst which will be enhancing predominantly of derepression, rather than repression, of countertransference attitudes and feelings.

REFERENCES

Deutsch, H. (1942). Some forms of emotional disturbance and their relationship to schizophrenia. *Psychoanalytic Quarterly* 11:301–321.
Fort, J. (1973). The importance of being diagnostic. Read at the annual Chestnut Lodge Symposium, October 5, 1973.
Gunderson, J. G., and Singer, M. T. (1975). Defining borderline patients: an overview. *American Journal of Psychiatry* 132:1–10.
Kernberg, O. (1972). Treatment of borderline patients. In *Tactics and Techniques in Psychoanalytic Therapy,* ed. P. L. Giovacchini, pp. 254–290. New York: Science House.
_____ (1975). *Borderline Conditions and Pathological Narcissism.* New York: Jason Aronson.
Knight, R. P. (1953). Borderline states. *Bulletin of the Menninger Clinic* 17:1–12. Reprinted in *Psychoanalytic Psychiatry and Psychology,* ed. R. P. Knight and C. R. Friedman, pp. 97–109. New York: International Universities Press.
Moore, B. E., and Fine, B. D., Eds. (1967). *A Glossary of Psychoanalytic Terms and Concepts.* New York: American Psychoanalytic Association.
Pao, P-N. (1975). On the diagnostic term, "schizophrenia." *Annual of Psychoanalysis* 3:221–238.

Searles, H. F. (1960).; *The Nonhuman Environment in Normal Development and in Schizophrenia*. New York: International Universities Press.

_____ (1965). *Collected Papers on Schizophrenia and Related Subjects*. London: Hogarth. New York: International Universities Press.

_____ (1965a). The sense of identity as a perceptual organ. Presented at Sheppard and Enoch Pratt Hospital Scientific Day Program, Towson, MD, May 29, 1965. Reprinted in Concerning the development of an identity. *Psychoanalytic Review* 53:507–530. Winter 1966–1967.

_____ (1972). The function of the patient's realistic perceptions of the analyst in delusional transference. *British Journal of Medical Psychology* 45:1–18.

_____ (1976). Psychoanalytic therapy with schizophrenic patients in a private-practice context. *Contemporary Psychoanalysis* 12:387–406. Reprinted in *Countertransference and Related Subjects—Selected Papers,* pp. 582–602. New York: International Universities Press, 1979. Paraphrased passages are from pp. 597–598 in latter volume.

_____ (1976a). Transitional phenomena and therapeutic symbiosis. *International Journal of Psychoanalytic Psychotherapy* 5:145–204.

Searles, H. F., Bisco, J. M., Coutu, G., and Scibetta, R. C. (1975). Violence in schizophrenia. *Psychoanalytic Forum* 5:1–89.

Chapter 10

Countertransference Enactments

Theodore J. Jacobs, M.D.

I would like to begin this paper with a story. It concerns a colleague of some renown who, though great in reputation, was extremely small of stature. One day this analyst, who stood barely five foot three inches tall, received a telephone call from a man who wished a consultation. The appointment was made and at the arranged time the new patient arrived at the office. About to enter the waiting room to greet him, the analyst suddenly stopped at the threshold and, momentarily, stood transfixed. There in front of him was a Paul Bunyan of a figure, fully six foot eight inches in

Reprinted from the *Journal of the American Psychoanalytic Association,* 1986, 34(2). Many of the concepts in this article were presented at the Regional Conference of Psychoanalytic Societies of Greater New York at Princeton, New Jersey, June 8–10, 1984, as part of a panel discussion chaired by Dr. Edmund Slakter.

height, weighing perhaps two hundred and sixty pounds, and wearing cowboy boots and a ten gallon hat. For several more seconds the analyst looked at him in silence. Then, with a shrug of his shoulders and a resigned gesture he motioned towards his office. "Come on in, anyway," he said.

This opening phrase carried with it worlds of meaning for both analyst and patient and highlights a fact that, though well understood, is sometimes overlooked; that from the very outset of treatment, transferences are activated in the analyst as well as in the patient. Whether overt or disguised, dramatic or barely perceptible, the analyst's transferences may exert a significant influence not only on his perceptions and understanding but on the particular form and manner in which the patient's transferences emerge. Conveyed in tone and gesture as well as in words, these reactions may be expressed in ways more subtle than obvious; in the barest of nods, the most minimal of smiles; the scarcely audible grunt or in the slightest variation in words of greeting or of farewell.

The analyst's countertransference reactions, however — and I am using the term here to refer to those influences on his understanding and technique that stem both from his transferences and from his emotional responses to the patient's transferences — may be expressed in ways that are even more covert; as aspects of his well-accepted methods and procedures. When they take this form countertransference reactions are intricately intertwined with and embedded within customary — and often unexamined — analytic techniques as well as within the attitudes and values that inform them.

The way in which we listen; our silences and neutrality; the emphasis we place on transference phenomena and interpretation of the transference; our ideas concerning working through, termination, and what constitutes a "correct" interpretation; these and many other facets of our daily clinical work may, and not infrequently do, contain within them concealed countertransference elements.

It is this aspect of countertransference that, by means of several clinical examples, I would like to focus on in this paper. I do so because it seems to me that our understanding of the phenomena of countertransference can be enhanced by consideration of some of its subtler as well as its more obvious expressions.

It is the latter aspects, its noisier and often dramatic forms that, for the most part, have received attention in the literature. Illustrative in this regard are some of the statements made by Annie Reich who, in her article *Empathy and Countertransference* (1966) remarks that "countertransference pushes the analyst to act out in a positive or negative way." The affects stirred up in him, she says, "carry the full charge of repressed impulses suddenly bursting out from the depth. Thus they lead to real action, to over-strong emotion or to the opposite, to rigid defenses or blank spots" (p. 352). And later in this article she describes the not uncommon situation in which the analytic material touches on some specific problem of the analyst's, precipitating in him an inappropriately strong response.

"In all relevant situations," she states, "the intensity of conflict interferes with understanding. Sublimation fails. Real action, over-strong emotion, misunderstanding, blocking, etc., occur. Where minimal amounts of energy should lead to thought, that is to trial action, real action occurs" (p. 355).

Such responses on the part of the analyst are, of course, not rare. Much that we call countertransference behavior can accurately be described in these terms. Because reactions of this kind impinge quite directly on the analytic work and constitute obvious sources of difficulty, it is understandable that when, in the fifties, the problem of countertransference began to attract the attention of analysts it was such phenomena that became the focus of interest. Even today the idea of countertransference, for many colleagues, is synonymous with overt actions and with an identifiable piece of acting out on the part of the analyst.

Typical of the kind of material that one hears at case conferences — when the issue of countertransference is mentioned at all — is the revelation made recently by a colleague well known for his candor.

"By mistake I ended one session three minutes early," he reported, "and I became aware then of how intensely frustrated this patient was making me. In fact, I was in a fury. She reminded me of the stepsister I could never get along with. She is the same kind of controlling, manipulative woman. After I realized my error, I did a piece of self-analysis which has helped me avoid a repetition of this problem. Now," he added with a grin, "I usually begin sessions a couple of minutes late."

While such reports are unquestionably valuable, they refer to only one aspect of countertransference—that characterized by overt and rather obvious actions on the part of the analyst. In this regard they may be compared to a view of acting out that includes in such behavior only gross motor actions. This perspective, as Boesky (1982) has pointed out, constitutes a limited way of conceptualizing the highly complex and diverse behaviors that come under the heading of acting out. For some patients acting out will be expressed not in motion but in immobility; not in words, but in silence. For others, acting out may be conveyed in subtle vocal qualities; in the pitch, tone, and rhythms of speech as well as in syntax and phrasing. For phenomena of this kind Boesky has used the term, actualization, so as to distinguish them from the more obvious kinds of motor actions that are commonly associated with the term "acting out."

A similar distinction may be made with regard to countertransference phenomena. Oftentimes it is not his overt actions, including even troublesome lapses of control, that are the source of the analyst's greatest countertransference problems, but the covert, scarcely visible, yet persistent reactions that pervade his manner of listening and responding.

This idea is not a new one. To the contrary, in recent years a number of authors, writing from quite different perspectives, have focused on the manifold, and often subtle, ways in which countertransference reactions may influence the analytic process. Langs (1975c), emphasizing the importance of the framework and boundaries of the therapeutic setting, points out that the way in which these ground rules are managed implicitly conveys to the patient a great deal about the analyst's intrapsychic state.

In another vein, Arlow (1985), discussed indicators of countertransference reactions. These include not only blind spots with regard to specific material and parapraxes concerning such matters as billing and appointments, but certain reactions of the analyst's that occur outside the consultation room. Among these are recurrent thoughts about the patient, often accompanied by feelings of depression or other mood changes, a repetitive need to talk about the sessions, and the appearance of the patient in the manifest content of the analyst's dreams.

Stein (1981) has stressed the importance in analytic work of analyzing the positive, or so-called unobjectionable part of the transference. Not uncommonly, he points out, there is hidden behind this transference picture powerful competitive and negative feelings as well as an idealization of the analyst. Uncritical acceptance of the old analytic maxim that the positive transference should not be interpreted unless it becomes a resistance may contain within it a well rationalized countertransference reaction. Oftentimes it is the aim of such reactions both to sustain the hidden gratification afforded the analyst by the patient's positive view of him and to avoid confrontation of the aggression that lies behind the surface attitude.

Focusing on the patient–analyst interactions that comprise the essence of analytic work, Sandler (1976) has pointed out that in analysis each party seeks to impose on the other an intrapsychic object relationship. Responding to the patient with spontaneous actions as well as with affects and associations, the analyst employs a "free-floating responsiveness" that complements his "free-floating attention." While invaluable in providing cues to nonverbally transmitted communications from the patient and the analyst's response to them, these reactions may also contain significant countertransference elements. Unless these are grasped by the analyst, he may find himself simply accepting the role imposed on him by the patient and joining him in a piece of mutual acting out.

Writing from a Kohutian perspective, Ernest Wolf (1979) has noted the regular occurrence in analysis of mini-countertransferences. These are inevitable failures of empathy and understanding on the part of the analyst based on momentary countertransference reactions. While such reactions are the source of temporary disruptions in the established analytic process, in Wolf's view they also provide an opportunity for patient and analyst alike to gain insight into the precise nature of these disruptions and their transference meanings.

Joyce MacDougal (1979) has pointed out that the use of ordinary analytic technique in the cases of individuals who have suffered traumatic experiences in the preverbal period and for whom silence and abstinence are experienced as fresh traumas not infrequently contains countertransference elements. She writes:

> Like all other human beings we as analysts have difficulty in hearing or perceiving what does not fit into our pre-established codes. Our own unresolved transference feelings here play a role since the garnering of analytic knowledge has been accomplished and deeply impregnated with transference affect and thus tends to carry an in-built resistance of its own, making it difficult for us to hear all that is being transmitted. We tend to resent the patient who does not progress in accordance with our expectations or who reacts to our efforts to understand as though they were hostile attacks upon him. These problems added to our personal weaknesses, provides us with a delicate task. [p. 301]

In what follows I will also discuss the question of analytic technique and the way in which countertransference elements may be concealed within our standard, well-accepted, and quite correct procedures. In citing case examples, however, my focus will not be on the severely traumatized patient or the more disturbed one, but on those individuals whose symptoms and character problems make psychoanalysis carried out in an unmodified way clearly the treatment of choice.

Some years ago, after I had begun analytic work with a man of considerable artistic talent and ingenuity, I discovered in myself an unusual phenomenon. I noticed that despite having listened to Mr. K. for better than four months I had not missed a word that he had spoken. This, I must confess, was for me a situation worth reflecting on for I was quite aware of a tendency when tired, conflicted, or anxious, for my attention to drift in the direction of my own associations rather than those of the patient. This had not happened with Mr. K. and I was on the verge of considering myself cured when I gave some thought to the way that, in fact, I had been listening to him. Then I realized that in listening so alertly, so carefully, and with such rapt attention, I had done nothing more than trade one symptom for another. My listening had taken on a special quality that now I recognized as familiar. It contained within it something akin to awe and I realized that although I had missed nothing, neither had I offered much in the way of interpretation.

I became aware, too, that there occurred in my visual associations to Mr. K. a frequently recurring theme; this involved the depiction of an orator or public speaker holding forth before an entranced audience. It did not take much more detective work for me to understand what had been happening. I had been listening to Mr. K., as, for years, I had listened to my father holding forth at the dinner table and, like the two-thousand-year-old man, expounding his personal view of world history. Long after dessert was served, I would sit transfixed listening to him spin tales of biblical times and of the *tsouris* experienced by Rabbi Joshua, later known by the name of Jesus. It was his show, and if I spoke at all it was simply to ask for more details—the equivalent of my interventions years later with my patient.

Mr. K.'s talent for storytelling and his transference wish for me to play the role of appreciative audience had transported me back four decades. I was listening as I had listened as a boy of ten; silently, intently, half-mesmerized. Only later did I realize that the particular way in which I listened was serving an old and familiar purpose; to keep from my awareness the negative and competitive feelings that I was experiencing toward the performer on stage.

Like the rather extended silences that, in this case, I found myself slipping into, silence in the analyst not uncommonly contains elements of countertransference. Familiar to all of us are the silences that reflect anger, boredom, depression, and fatigue. Familiar too are the silences of confusion, of retaliation, and of momentary identification.

Less well recognized as a potential conveyor of countertransference feelings is the kind of silence that, as analysts, we strive to achieve as part of our analytic instrument; the silence of empathic understanding. Precisely because this attitude is so important to us, so much emphasized, and in reality so valuable in our work, countertransference elements that on occasion may be concealed within it are easily overlooked.

This fact was brought home to me in the course of analytic work with a middle-aged professional woman. During one session in particular I became aware in myself of unusually strong feelings of empathy. In that hour I was able to see what Mrs. A. saw, experience what she experienced, feel what she felt. It was with considerable surprise then, that after the patient had left the office I noted in myself some irritation with her and the thought that what she had told me was only one side of a complex story.

This reaction caused me to reflect on the material of our hour and, with the patient out of the room, once again to associate to it. It was then that I realized that the scene that Mrs. A. had depicted was entirely familiar to me and that in my adolescence I had played one of the central characters. Distraught over an argument with her husband, Mrs. A. had been unable to sleep. She waited up until her teenage son had come in from an evening out, and then talked to him at some length of her distress. He had listened and been understanding as I had been when, under similar circumstances, my mother had confided in me her hurt and anger over my father's behavior.

Now as I listened to Mrs. A. and imagined the scene she was depicting I had, unconsciously, become again the son at the kitchen table listening to and sharing his mother's upset. I had become the good listener, the empathic listener, but also the listener who had to conceal from himself some feelings of resentment at what he was hearing. It was only after Mrs. A. was gone that I, like the adolescent who, when alone, can experience certain emotions that do not surface in a parent's presence, became aware that my responses during the hour were only one side of a complex countertransference reaction. The other side, the resentment I felt over Mrs. A.'s presenting herself as the helpless victim and her husband as the brutish aggressor, had been defended against as similar emotions had been defended against years before: by the upsurge of the strongest feelings of empathy.

For many colleagues the experiences in childhood and adolescence of being an empathic listener to parents or other family members has played a role of importance in their choice of vocation. It is not a rare occurrence for the memories of these experiences to be evoked in the analytic situation. Then silently, outside of awareness, the analyst's usually valuable empathic responses may contain within them enactments of those memories. Enactments which, subtly, can alter and distort his perceptions and understanding.

Neutrality, too, may become invested with countertransference reactions. The analytic idea of neutrality is a highly complex one. It involves not only a way of listening that receives with impartiality material deriving from each of the psychic agencies and a technical approach that eschews the resolution of conflict through influence in favor of interpretation, but it implies in the analyst a state of receptivity that can accomplish these goals. The proper use of neutrality as a technical measure requires in him a considerable degree of inner "neutrality"; that is, the achievement of a state of mind in which those ego functions necessary for analytic work are not impaired by conflict. The relationship between these two forces of neutrality, its outer one which is an integral aspect of analytic technique and the inner one which defines one of the psychological conditions for the employment of that technique, has not been focused on in discussions of the issue of neutrality. It is, however, tensions and disharmonies between these two aspects of the analyst's neutrality that, not infrequently, underlie its countertransference distortions.

I found such a situation to have developed during the analysis of a young attorney. This was a man of outward charm and inner rage. So well concealed was his anger, however, that he appeared to all the world to be quite simply a man of utmost graciousness and wit. To his qualities of keen intelligence and sophistication, was added a persuasive tongue, so that Mr. C. was known for his ability to attract clients. This talent he utilized in the analysis in playful, witty, and seemingly good-humored efforts to get me to render judgments on one or another of the fanciful—and invariably self-defeating—schemes and projects in which he was forever engaged.

In the face of Mr. C.'s charm and persuasiveness I remained admirably neutral—or so I thought. Repeatedly, if not doggedly, I identified and interpreted his central inner conflicts; his obvious oedipal rivalry and his unconscious guilt as well as certain pre-oedipal attachments—all with no effect whatever on him. Not for many months was I able to confront Mr. C. directly either with the destructive impact of his behavior on his personal and professional life or with his aggression in the analytic situation.

The reason for this was simple. Aggression in Mr. C., though deep and pervasive, was so well concealed, so covertly expressed, that for some time I was not consciously aware either of its

presence or of the strong counter-aggression that it was stimulating in me. In a vague and not easily defineable way, I felt
uncomfortable with him, and I began, therefore, in sessions to pay
attention to my autonomic responses. With regularity I found,
when working with Mr. C., that my heartbeat was rapid, my
mouth dry, and my guts feeling tense and knotted. It became
increasingly clear to me that these were bodily signs of concealed
anger occurring in response to the covert anger directed at me.

Because of this state of affairs, I was unable to attain a properly
"neutral" (that is, relatively conflict-free) inner receptivity. Since I
was not consciously aware of this situation, but in some intuitive
way, perceived it, I unconsciously overemphasized the outer
aspect of neutrality, its technical side. I became, as it were, not
only a neutral analyst but a determinedly neutral one. Afraid in
the face of Mr. C.'s persuasiveness—and the aggression that lay
behind it—to lose my stance of neutrality, I lost what Sandler has
termed the analyst's free-floating responsiveness. In this case that
meant the ability to confront Mr. C. more directly with his
behavior both within and outside the analytic situation.

Reflection on my responses to Mr. C. led me to a memory that
helped clarify some of the more specific countertransference
reactions involved. As a youngster I had great admiration for an
after-school sports group leader who, for a time, became for me a
father surrogate. Bright, witty, and ingenious, he was also something of a provocateur with his charges. In ways that were both
humorous and vexing, he would tease the boys about aspects of
their dress or behavior. Increasingly I became angry at this leader,
but because he was emotionally important to me I concealed my
feelings both from him and myself.

It was not until, for quite other reasons, that I left the group,
that I realized how large a role aggression on both sides, mine as
well as his, had played in our relationship. No doubt Mr. C.'s
behavior in the analytic situation, which in many respects was
similar to that of the group leader and other important figures of
my childhood, aroused in me a familiar pattern of response. It was
this response, with its emphasis on attempting to quiet an inner
disturbance through greater emphasis on outer neutrality, that led
to its inappropriate use.

Central to the question of working through, all analysts would agree, is the matter of repetition. It is the repetition of interpretations, first in one situation, then in another, that permits a patient to take the necessary steps from insight to the resolution of conflicts.

Scrutiny of the analyst's use of repetitions, however, and the patient's response to them may reveal an interaction between patient and therapist that is quite different from that taking place in the usually conceived process of working through. Not uncommonly a familiar scenario has developed. The analyst offers an interpretation which in one way or another is resisted. He interprets again, and once again the patient's resistance rises up to meet the intervention. Consciously aware of the need for repetition to foster working through, the analyst once more repeats his interpretation—only this time more insistently. Again the patient offers resistance—only this time more stubbornly. I need not go on to complete the picture. Within the framework of what appears to be a necessary, if painstaking, process of repetition and the gradual working through of resistance, a formidable, if unconscious, battle has been joined. As a result of the arousal of infantile conflicts in both parties—analyst as well as patient—the process of repetition becomes a hammer blow against an iron door. The result, unless this transference-countertransference interaction can be identified and effectively interpreted, is the kind of stalemate that often characterizes such struggles in childhood.

Even in situations in which the process of working through gradually takes place, the interaction between patient and analyst may bear the hallmarks of similar parent–child relationships. The analyst interprets and the patient accepts perhaps a fraction of his offering. Further interpretations may lead to the acceptance of additional fractions. No doubt this is what is meant by fractional discharge. Under favorable circumstances this situation may continue until the patient's mouth has opened wide enough for the analyst to slip in a few spoonfuls of his special nourishment.

Much has been written in the analytic literature on the process of termination and the complex emotional responses that it evokes in analyst and patient alike. Less discussed has been the issue of the decision to terminate and how this decision is arrived at.

Not infrequently the idea of terminating is first broached by the patient, though this is not invariably so. For some patients, this

decision is reached when particular goals have been met, motivation to continue has slackened, or a certain plateauing has
occurred in the analysis. For others the idea of terminating has
clear transference meanings and is related on the one hand to
feelings of rejection, anger, disappointment, or frustration or, on
the other, to anxiety over victory and success. Such situations are
well known and require no elaboration here. What has not been
studied with equal intensity are those situations in which the issue
of termination arises as the result of covert, often unconsciously
transmitted cues that pass between the participants in the analytic
situation. These, in turn, are the manifestations of subtle and
easily overlooked, but critically important transference-countertransference interactions. The following examples may clarify the
kind of situation that I have in mind.

For some years I had been working with Mr. R., a middle-aged
businessman whose deliberate and weighty verbal style was ex-
ceeded only by the ponderousness of his thought processes. He
was not an easy man to listen to or to analyze, and at various times
in the treatment I had the thought that in in the face of his
rock-ribbed obsessional defenses my interventions were little more
than small arms fire careening off a fortified concrete bunker. For
more than nine years I had persisted, however, partly out of
stubbornness, partly out of pride, but also because I detected each
year grindingly slow but tangible progress in self-understanding
and in the mitigation of troublesome symptoms.

About halfway into the tenth year of treatment, the patient
rather suddenly brought up the idea of termination. He had been
thinking, he said, and he believed that he had gone about as far as
he could in his analysis. Although certain problems remained, he
was much improved. Since, as far as he could tell, things were
pretty much at a standstill, he doubted if he could expect many
more gains by continuing on.

For a number of reasons I was surprised by this turn of events.
To begin with, Mr. R. was not a man who usually took the
initiative in making decisions. Passivity was deeply rooted in his
character and I had long been convinced that when it came time
for termination to be discussed it would be I who would have to
raise the issue. Furthermore there was nothing in the recent
material that suggested that Mr. R. had, in fact, been thinking

about termination. It is true that the analysis was proceeding with the speed of a hippo moving upstream and in the past few weeks the resistances had been unusually tenacious, but this situation had existed before and I had not been thinking about termination. Or had I? I began to wonder.

In any case I now gave much thought to the idea of ending and it seemed to me that Mr. R. was probably right. In all likelihood we had gone as far as we could. There was no question that in many ways Mr. R. was better, and as for the rest, well, analysis had at least given him some tools to work with. I was on the verge of saying just that to my patient and setting with him a mutually acceptable termination date when something gave me pause. The rather abrupt way in which termination arose and my ready agreement with Mr. R. made me uneasy. Deciding to end in this way did not seem quite right and I decided to wait a bit and to review more clearly the material of the week prior to Mr. R.'s raising the question.

As I did so I remembered one session in which I had been particularly frustrated. On the basis of what seemed to me to be clear-cut material I had made an interpretation connecting certain aspects of Mr. R.'s behavior in the transference to ways in which his mother related to him. Not only did the patient refute the interpretation out of hand with a barrage of sarcastic rejoinders, but in that session he could accept nothing else that I offered. I recalled feeling tense and angry and in the face of his assault had lapsed into silence. I recalled also that in that hour, and in a subsequent one I had been aware of experiencing a fleeting visual memory that involved my former analyst. This memory centered on a case conference at our Institute which I had attended and at which my former analyst was a discussant. Although at the time that it arose I was aware that such a memory must constitute a meaningful response to the analytic material, I could make nothing of it and so let it pass.

Now I returned to that memory and let myself think freely about it. What came to mind was something I had forgotten. In connection with the case presented at the conference, a patient who had been in analysis for quite a number of years, my former analyst had made the remark that "If you have not broken through after nine years of analysis, perhaps you had better re-think the value of continuing." The memory I'd had of that meeting was clearly a shorthand reference to that statement. In the face of Mr. R.'s stubborn and frustrating resistances I was, in effect, telling myself, "Your own analyst would not continue in such a situation. He would advise you to quit. Perhaps you had better listen!"

How I managed to communicate to Mr. R. my feeling that we were at an impasse and that there was no point in going on is in itself an intriguing question. I had said nothing to Mr. R. about ending and consciously was not thinking in those terms. What I realized in reviewing the situation, though, was that in response to the powerful resistances I had recently encountered a certain despair had set in and I had begun to withdraw. I spoke less, and when I did my tone was somewhat muted. I was aware, too, that a certain quality of fatigue, if not exasperation, had crept into my voice.

Always sensitive to the slightest hints of rejection and by nature a counter-puncher, Mr. R. had reacted to these clues in a way that was entirely characteristic for him. He struck back by being the first to propose termination and, by that means, sought to reject me before I had a chance to send him away.

The analysis did not end at that point but, in fact, went on for another two years during which time Mr. R. made more progress than he had in the previous nine. Together, however, we had come within a hair's breadth of terminating the treatment. Had we done so, the decision to end would have seemed on the surface entirely reasonable. It would have been initiated by a patient who had been in analysis for nine years, who had made substantial progress in a number of areas, but whose treatment had now reached a plateau. And it would have been agreed to by his hard-working analyst who had taken him a fair distance and who now recognized on clinical grounds that further progress was unlikely. That a countertransference factor was, in fact, the determining one might very well have gone unrecognized. How often, one wonders, does the decision to terminate come about in a similar manner?

Of primary importance in our technique is the matter of transference interpretation. The current well-accepted view that such interpretations are the only mutative ones has led in some instances to a way of listening that may be called listening *for* the transference. While such a focus in listening may be most valuable in detecting what Gill has termed the experience of the relationship, it may also prove problematical. Not only may the analyst's listening processes be restricted, and, in the extreme case, even deformed by so narrow a focus, but the analyst's less than subtle reactions to transference material may lead to its more abundant appearance. It may happen, too, that there is formed between patient and therapist a defensive collusion that has as its unconscious purpose the exploitation of the transference so as to avoid the emergence of other anxiety-laden material.

Such was the case with Mrs. G., a clever and sophisticated woman who oriented herself to others by picking up in them the slightest behavioral and verbal cues. During a difficult time in her life, when her husband had become acutely ill, she brought in material that contained within it detectable, though quite concealed, references to her analyst.

Though it took a hawklike alertness to the barest hints of transference to dig out these nuggets, I was able to do so and was rather pleased at being able to interpret certain transference feelings that had not previously surfaced.

Only after this period had passed and Mrs. G.'s husband had recovered did I become aware of how patient and analyst had utilized this transference material. Terrified that her husband would die and unable in the analysis to face this possibility, Mrs. G. had, unconsciously, made use of her knowledge that I invariably reacted with interest to transference material by feeding me bits and pieces of it as a decoy. For my part, Mr. G.'s life-threatening illness had reactivated some painful memories concerning personal losses which I, too, was eager to suppress. By joining with my patient in a particular kind of detective game called "locate the transference," I had colluded with her in doing just that. At this time in the analysis the central issue was not the subtleties of the transference — as important as these were — but Mrs. G.'s inability to face the reality of death; a reality that her analyst was also quite willing to avoid.

Finally, I wish to say a few words about the issue of correct interpretations. Although one of our primary goals as analysts is to offer interpretations that are correct, the extent to which our interventions are, in fact, accurate is not always easy to assess. The commonly held view that a correct interpretation will regularly elicit in the patient material that confirms it requires some rethinking in light of contradictory clinical evidence.

Every analyst has had the experience of making interpretations which, while later proven to be correct, are initially met with responses that are not obviously corroborative. Familiar are the reactions of silence, of incredulity, of anger, of denial, of awe, of protest, of depression, or, in some cases, reactions characterized by an increase of symptoms.

This state of affairs suggests that we may need to inquire further as to what it is that constitutes a correct interpretation. On what level of meaning is its correctness to be judged? Is it solely the cognitive-denotative level, the overt meaning of the analyst's intervention and the resonance of his words with the preconscious of the patient? Or must we include also the meta-communicational level, the covert message hidden behind and within the analyst's words? If this is the case, how do these two levels relate to each other and to the "correctness" of an interpretation? Can an interpretation be correct on one level and not on another? If so, will a patient experience the intervention as being correct or must both levels resonate with the analogous ones in himself in order for him to have the inner experience of an interpretation being true?

Clearly these are complex and relatively unexplored areas that will, in the future, require further investigation. For the moment, however, I must limit myself to the briefest discussion of a patient's negative response to a "correct" interpretation.

When I first began to see her, Mrs. L. was a woman in her late thirties who, since the age of four, had sought reparations for the sudden loss of her mother. Full of rage, she had clung to and tortured three husbands before taking on her analyst. In all of these relationships she threatened repeatedly to leave the men in her life but never did so. Instead it was they who, weary and battle-scarred, threw in the towel.

Her threats to end the analysis were no less frequent. Quite regularly, after excoriating me for not getting her out of her present unhappy marital situation, she threatened to get rid of me, too.

Although for the most part I was able to maintain my equanimity in the face of Mrs. L.'s attacks, on occasion I found it difficult to do so. During one session in which, once again, she threatened to leave treatment, I offered an interpretation aimed at bringing to the fore one of the genetic determinants of the repetitive pattern in which she was engaged.

She was treating me, I said, the way she treated her husband, her husbands before him, and, in childhood, her feared and hated stepmother. Although she had told me many times that she was leaving treatment, in fact she seemed very frightened to do so. She acted as though I was the only analyst in the city and in this attitude she was responding to me as though, in fact, I was her stepmother. With her mother gone she could never follow through on her ever-present plan to leave her stepmother as this woman had become the only mother she had.

The patient's response lingers in memory. She became tearful and agitated, accused me of wanting to get rid of her, and felt totally hopeless.She sank into a depression that lasted for several weeks and, for some months thereafter, was quite wary of any interpretation that I might offer her.

The cause of Mrs. L.'s reaction was quite clear. She had understood correctly her analyst's message. The manifest interpretation was probably correct enough but it was not these words which reached her. It was my true meaning. Responding with anger to her sustained provocations, I had reacted in the way that, in reality, her stepmother and her husbands had; they had invited her to leave. Because this countertransference reaction was so unacceptable to me, so contrary to a helpful intervention, I had most likely blocked it from conscious awareness. It found its way out, however, not in the formally correct overt interpretation, but in the covert one that served as a vehicle for the expression of my countertransference feelings.

Reactions such as Mrs. L.'s raise interesting questions about our patients' negative responses to our interpretations. No doubt some of these responses constitute aspects of the classical syndrome of the negative therapeutic reaction in which the issue of unconscious guilt often plays a central role. Others, however, may derive from quite different sources. Among these are those negative responses that represent accurate and intuitive readings of the analyst's hidden communications. In such instances we have to be alert to the possibility that aspects of the very interpretive process itself may, imperceptively, have become an enactment. And it is just such subtle and well-concealed enactments on the part of the analyst, that, in many cases, constitute the greatest source of countertransference difficulty.

SUMMARY

In this communication I have focused on one aspect of the problem of countertransference: its relation to analytic technique. In doing so I have wished to call attention not to the more obvious forms of countertransference that have been commented upon by previous writers on the subject, but to its subtler ones.

The overt, noisier, easily recognizable face of countertransference is well known to us in the form of slips, omissions, symptomatic acts, and more or less clear-cut pieces of acting out. Its other face is its muted one. Often well camouflaged within the framework of our traditional, time-tested techniques, this aspect of countertransference may attach itself to our way of listening and thinking about patients, to our efforts at interpretation, to the process of working through, or to the complex issue of termination.

Less recognizable than its more boisterous counterpart and in some respects less tangible, this side of the problem of countertransference is no less important. For it is precisely those subtle, often scarcely visible countertransference reactions, so easily rationalized as parts of our standard operating procedures and so easily overlooked, that may in the end have the greatest impact on our analytic work.

REFERENCES

Arlow, J. (1985). Some technical problems of countertransference. *Psychoana-lytic Quarterly* 54(2):164–174.
Boesky, D. (1982). Acting out: a reconsideration of the concept. *International Journal of Psycho-Analysis* 63:39–55.
Langs, R. (1975). The therapeutic relationship and deviations in technique. *International Journal of Psychoanalytic Psychotherapy* 4:106–141.
MacDougal, J. (1979). Primitive communication and the use of countertransfer-

ence. In Epstein, L., Feiner, A. (eds.). *Countertransference.* New York: Jason Aronson, pp. 267–303.

Reich, A. (1966). Empathy and countertransference. In Reich, A. *Psychoanalytic Contributions.* New York: Int. Univ. Press, 1973, pp. 344–360.

Sandler, J. (1976). Countertransference and role-responsiveness. *International Review of Psychoanalysis* 3:43–47.

Stein, M. (1981). The unobjectionable part of the transference. *Journal of the American Psychoanalytic Association* 29:869–891.

Wolf, E. (1979). Countertransference in disorders of the self. In Epstein, L., Feiner, A. (eds.). *Countertransference.* New York: Jason Aronson, pp. 445–469.

Part III
Questioning Countertransference

Unless otherwise credited, all the remarks directly and indirectly quoted in the following six chapters were made at workshops and discussion groups during The Regional Council Conference of the Psychoanalytic Societies of Greater New York in June of 1984. Unfortunately, it was not always possible to determine from the tapes of these sessions who the speakers were and thus to credit them individually. The author thanks them as a group for their contributions to this discussion of countertransference.

Chapter 11
Is Countertransference a Meaningful Term?

COUNTERTRANSFERENCE AS A FAULTY CONCEPT

One consequence of the new emphasis on countertransference is that a number of analysts have begun to question the usefulness of the concept itself. Some believe it is so flawed that it should be discarded entirely, while others want either to broaden or to narrow its definition.

Charles Brenner is one of the strongest advocates of discarding the concept. According to Brenner, countertransference is a completely inadequate term, which, like a debased coin, no longer has any sure value. The concept purports to make distinctions: between conscious and unconscious, between pathological and normal, and, in the view of some, between obstructive and constructive. Yet in Brenner's view, the distinctions that it makes are largely spurious. He offers as an example the implied distinction between normal and pathological. Yet normal psychic phenomena, he believes, do not differ in their autonomy from pathological phenomena; that is, both are related to instinctual conflicts originating in childhood. Therefore, any effort to frame a controlling concept on the basis of such a difference is doomed to confusion.

The presumably pathological elements of the countertransference are, we are told, to be dealt with through self-analysis. But, Brenner notes, this neat formula does not really operate in practice. To begin with, the feelings for which self-analysis is invoked are probably in most cases quite normal—part of being alive, part of what the analyst simply has to work on. Furthermore, self-analysis is a highly imperfect procedure. Brenner quotes another analyst's remark that the real trouble with self-analysis is the countertransference. In Brenner's view, self-analysis is limited by its dependence on whatever sources of difficulty the analyst locates within himself. The most the analyst can hope for is that in treatment he will, with some frequency, be able to spot problems that have been uncovered in his own analysis. Self-analysis, then, is no panacea.

Nor is it usually clear, when an interference arises in treatment, that self-analysis is the answer (or, for that matter, that the interference is coming from the analyst). In every analysis there is a vast assortment of interferences, ranging from the temporary to the ubiquitous and from the trivial to the serious and the very serious. Until he unearths enough data from the patient, the analyst cannot know with certainty whether self-analysis is the remedy for a given interference. Sometimes self-analysis will solve the problem; on other occasions, time alone seems to clear up the difficulty. In any case, by the time the analyst has enough information, the problem may well have passed.

A more fundamental difficulty, Brenner points out, is differentiating between countertransference and noncountertransference phenomena. Our present state of knowledge, he claims, suggests that any differences are merely quantitative. Those reactions that for clinical purposes we call countertransference—that is, reactions that more or less interfere with the analyst's ability to analyze—are no more intimately related to childhood instinctual conflict than the reactions that make possible, indeed motivate, the analytic work. In other words, what we call countertransference is a compromise-formation like any other and is determined not just by the analyst's reaction to the patient but by all the compromise-formations the analyst has used throughout his life.

Many analysts, including Brenner, believe that infantile wishes can never be truly relinquished, no matter how strenuously they are opposed by our adult thoughts. Everyone, analyst as well as patient, is subject to the constant battle between these forces. How the issue will be decided in treatment depends on a wide range of factors. Hence it is impossible to isolate any one of the analyst's struggles as countertransferential. It may be that the conflict in question derives from the analyst's substitution of the patient for some object from his childhood, and/or from numerous other psychic phenomena as well. Given these confusions, Brenner argues that the term is simply unhelpful and should be discarded.

William Grossman is another analyst who regards countertransference to be a severely limited concept and he would like to discard it. Commenting on Brenner's ideas about derivatives, Grossman notes that ordinarily the analyst does not directly experience countertransference phenomena as reactions to the patient. Rather, these phenomena help form the analyst's motivation for his work and keep functional his relationship with the patient. If the analyst has adequately understood his infantile motivations for becoming a therapist, these impulses will not be directly gratified by treatment, nor will they directly influence it. And in the absence of such gratification, the concept of countertransference becomes, in this context, irrelevant.

Grossman also claims that the very fact of development argues against the kind of instinctual constancy implied in the notion of countertransference. Development means that once a compromise-formation exists, it operates differently in relation to conflictual and nonconflictual issues. The nature of the conflict changes with the development and transformation of the original impulses. This observation implies neither that conflict is absent nor that the ego is free from conflict, but merely that the independent variable changes. Given these facts, then, Grossman, too, feels that the concept of countertransference becomes too vague to be helpful, and that the term should be scrapped.

A Question of Terminology and Meaning

Harold Blum also finds countertransference to be a faulty concept, but he recommends that we keep it and simply try to pay closer attention to its meanings. Noting that in psychoanalytic theory old terms never die and rarely even fade, he speculates that the attachment analysts have to their terminology may itself be a sign of transference or countertransference. In his view, analysts even fail to notice when a basic term acquires a new meaning over several generations, as has happened with transference, acting out, and countertransference.

Consequently, while some analysts may wish to substitute another term for countertransference, their chances of gaining the assent of their colleagues are poor. The old term will probably be with us for a long time. Perhaps the best approach, then, is to be aware of the different ways in which we apply it in different contexts. For example, when first formulated, countertransference referred to the direct, irrational reactions that the patient's transference stirred up in the analyst. Blum suggests that if we remember that countertransference incorporates both this meaning and the subsequent idea that some of these reactions are neurotic, then we can sidestep the confusion created by more totalistic definitions.

Yet even if we exercise such care, it is doubtful that any one term will ever satisfy our need to categorize and classify every different response now included under the rubric of countertransference. The training situation illustrates the problem. In Blum's opinion, we cannot attribute to countertransference all the errors of the young candidate or of the senior analyst during this process. Obviously, they also arise from other sources. Certainly many errors and inappropriate interventions probably occur because of misjudgments rather than countertransference. No analyst, however experienced, is immune to making mistakes of this sort, for our education always remains ongoing, our knowledge incomplete.

Faced with such a multitude of determinants, the analyst sometimes finds it impossible to determine the appropriate intervention. Often it is only much later in the treatment that he understands how wrong he was in a certain situation. And perhaps equally often he discovers his countertransference to have been only one source, albeit an important source, of technical error. In other words, countertransference is in most instances, a component of error, not a global explanation of it.

Another delicate matter relating to our nosological notions about countertransference is the patient's conscious or unconscious response to the analyst's attitudes. Blum cites the example of a patient who had "felt" for some time the passive-regressive withdrawal of her analyst, who "seemed" to her silently hostile. These feelings crystallized one day when he forgot that she had an appointment and locked her out. In this instance, the patient's fantasies of victimization apparently contained some truth.

But was it the sole truth? According to Blum, some analysts would say that it was. But in seeing the transaction between the patient and her analyst in this way, they are really altering the theory of transference so that transference becomes almost a present phenomenon — a reaction to the analytic situation as it exists in the present — rather than a repetition of the past. In Blum's opinion, an analyst accepting this view loses sight of the connection between the patient's present feelings and infantile past. In the case of the locked-out patient, he fails to see that she was a masochistic character *before* she ever entered treatment and that her interaction with the analyst was influenced by her tendency to exploit any sadistic inclinations in others.

APPLYING NEW TERMINOLOGY TO A NECESSARY CONCEPT

Whereas Brenner, Grossman, and, to a lesser extent, Blum, express strong reservations about the concept of countertransference, it is not without its defenders. **Martin Silverman,** for example, finds much value in the term as long as it is narrowly defined. In his view, countertransference should be limited to the "introduction, usually without conscious awareness or almost without conscious awareness, of derivatives of incompletely resolved unconscious conflicts within the analyst, in response to what is occurring in the treatment situation." Silverman warns that if we do not narrow its meaning in this way, the term will become, and in the view of people such as Brenner, already has, the receptacle into which anything and everything gets thrown.

One problem that Silverman addresses is that the term does *not* cover all the analyst's responses to the patient. For example, a complicating factor in the child analyst's life is that he must deal not only with his patient, but also with the patient's parents. Sometimes the double load can be exhausting, causing reactions that, however strong, are nevertheless not necessarily counter-transferential. The child analyst also has to deal with attacks and provocations more primitive than those the usual adult patient presents. When a child kicks the analyst in the shin or throws a toy at him or rubs a wet lollipop into the new couch, the analyst will be hard pressed not to feel some hostility, though again this is not, strictly speaking, countertransference. To label such responses to the patient, Silverman suggests the term *emotional reactions*.

This new term could also be useful not just for child analysts but also to describe the response to an adult patient's onslaught of raw aggression. It might also cover the analyst's reaction to the ordinary stresses of life. (The relationship between countertrans-ference and reality issues will be taken up in Chapter 14.) Naturally, such stresses will evoke responses that influence treat-ment. Some of these responses will be countertransferential; others, uncomplicated by unconscious conflict, would be more aptly described simply as emotional reactions.

In sum, Silverman feels that not everything coming from the analyst and interfering with the treatment is countertransferential. He also argues against moving facilely in our focus and terminol-ogy from the analyst's transferential reactions to those of the patient. Of course the patient's transference of unconscious neurotic wishes and strivings onto the analyst is of central importance in the analytic process, yet the tendency of analysts to slip over from trial (empathic) identification into transferring their own unconscious strivings onto the patient is so crucial that to abandon the term that describes this transition would be a grave mistake. Thus, Silverman suggests *emotional reactions* as a term complementary to countertransference, one that would cover those reactions of the analyst that lie *outside* the countertransfer-ence.

At recent conferences, *emotional reactions* has also been offered as a possible substitute term for countertransference. Employed in this way, the term would describe the full range of the analyst's responses, rather than just those that are the counterpart of transference. In terms of their impact on treatment, these responses range from the neutral (or perhaps beneficial) to the grossly obstructive. In between are occasional feelings of irritation and hostility as well as more uncertain reactions that may become a permanent part of the analysis. As we have seen, the analyst may find it hard to determine which of these reactions are countertransferential and which not. He might resolve some of this confusion by breaking down his emotional reactions into different categories, such as feelings of hostility, sexual fantasies, and so forth. The analyst might even set aside a specific time to evaluate his feelings and actions as precisely as possible. Then he might try to fit these reactions into the proper category instead of dismissing them casually with, "Oh, that's a countertransference response — I'll get to it later."

For example, another analyst — not the one cited by Blum — locked a patient out "by mistake." Luckily, the whole session was not lost. The therapist's first fleeting thought in the remaining time was that he had committed a countertransferential act, and he made a mental note to think about this when driving home that night. In rethinking what had happened, he remembered that he had done the same thing to other patients at other times in his career. Accordingly, he concluded that his "mistake" represented an "emotional reaction" — in this case a tendency based on a response to patients in general — rather than a countertransference response to this particular patient's transference.

Distinguishing between various kinds of emotional reactions might be of use in respect to another aspect of what we now call countertransference. We are referring here to the idea that countertransference may be related to the genesis of interpretation — that is, that the countertransference may constitute a "hunch," pointing in the direction of the interpretation, which is itself a response to the material. By calling both this hunch and the interpretation it initiates "emotional reactions" and distinguishing between them, we might clarify some of our responses. For example, one analyst described his reaction to a patient's provocative remarks by saying, "I wanted to spank her." This was an interpretation *in statu nascendi,* and seeing it as an emotional reaction rather than as countertransference might have enabled the analyst to say to the patient at that moment (he did not), "You are behaving in this way because you want me to spank you."

Another term that has often been suggested as a substitute for countertransference is *counterreaction,* or the analyst's reaction to the patient's emotional reactions. This proposal is based on the observation that many of the analyst's responses derive from his own unique personality and character traits. For example, some analysts are afraid of their patients' aggression. When a patient responds to an interpretation with a flow of aggressive material, the analyst will have a defensive counterreaction, intervening to cut the patient off before he can express these feelings in depth.

Some other terms that have been put forth as possible substitutes for countertransference consider the analyst's transference, for transference is an inevitable part of any discussion of the adequacy of countertransference as a clinical term.

Transference, or reaction to a person in the present on the basis of who, in your past, that person represents for you, is not unique to the analytic environment. It occurs in every object relationship. What is special about the treatment situation is that the therapist's responses to the patient's wishes, defenses, and superego reactions usually differ from those of anyone else in the patient's past and present life. By analyzing these transference reactions, the analyst gives the patient the chance to become aware of the internal conflicts disturbing him. This knowledge should then enable the patient to resolve those conflicts in new, less destructive ways. However, just as the analyst often has difficulty deciding whether a response is countertransferential, he frequently has problems determining which of the patient's responses are transferential. But in clarifying this matter for himself, he can use his conclusions to help the treatment.

For example, a new patient repeatedly came ten minutes late for his sessions. After four days of this, the therapist became irked by the patient's behavior and called it to his attention. The patient responded by saying, "I'm always late. I've been late my whole life." Thus his behavior was not necessarily transferential, as initially thought, but was more likely a manifestation of a character trait.

Having made this distinction, the therapist could then trace the patient's habitual lateness to conflicts with the object concerned in its formation. By changing this neurotic symptom into a recognizable conflict, related to a particular object and drive, therapist and patient were able to analyze the behavior. If, however, the therapist had simply reacted to the immediate fact of lateness and not gotten the historical background, the behavior could easily have been labeled transferential.

The same approach is applicable in deciding whether a reaction is countertransferential. If an analyst rigidly adheres to a time schedule, he is probably not acting countertransferentially. He simply has certain character traits, and this is one of them. We know this because he behaves in the same way with all his patients. The analyst has to analyze his own traits, trace them to his neurotic conflicts, and work on them. If he is a candidate in supervision, the task is made easier, for the supervisor will pick up these disturbances and tell him to talk them over with his analyst. But when the analyst runs his own practice, with no one there to supervise him, he must depend on himself to do the necessary self-analysis. His predicament and the way he works it out bears some resemblance to the situation of the patient, who tries to work out *his* neurotic conflicts with the analyst. The following example of an analyst's evaluation of his countertransference shows some of the difficulties inherent in this task.

The analyst had treated a man for ten years. After this time, he decided that the patient had not progressed sufficiently, so he transferred him to another analyst. In analyzing his countertransference, the first analyst isolated as critical factors the patient's extreme masochism and his profound wish for unusual closeness. The patient was an identical twin. He had a need for a very close relationship with his sibling and, by extension, with his analyst. The analyst found this need too great a burden. Furthermore, the patient's masochism was such that he would have stayed in analysis forever. During the entire treatment, he rarely expressed a wish of his own. The analyst pointed out to him his masochistic submissiveness, with no effect. All the patient wanted was simply to continue the analysis. Incidentally, he revealed that in the latency period he and his twin brother had practiced a sadomasochistic spanking game, with the patient as the masochistic partner. In any case, the analyst finally decided that the man might fare better with someone else. (As it happened, the second analyst, many years later, confided to the first analyst that he too saw this patient for ten years and then, doubting his own effectiveness, sent him on to a third analyst.)

Another problematic consideration is the variability of counter-transference, and transference plays a role here as well. The same transference operations may elicit different responses in different analysts. For example, one analyst may work effectively with a patient's seductiveness while another may have great difficulty with it. In addition, an analyst may respond in a certain way at the start of treatment before the patient has any significant transfer-ence, and differently at a later stage after the transference has gelled. The analyst's behavior changes because the patient's trans-ference, as it forms, elicits in him responses derived from his own past. It is for describing these latter responses that the term "transference of the analyst" has been proposed as an alternative to countertransference. The value of this term is that it does not exclude the analyst's compromise-formations; indeed, it indicates that his response occurs primarily because of what the transfer-ence evokes in him. The particular nature of each analyst's compromise-formations will dictate his particular responses, in-cluding countertransference, to a transference.

Still another proposed substitute for countertransference is the analyst's "instinctualized transference." Its proponents contend that by reducing the reaction to its earlier form, this term would permit us to recognize more easily that both positive and negative transference can interfere with treatment. Using such a term would also focus our attention on how countertransference can benefit the treatment one moment and not the next—a truth that analysts have not recognized until recently. Perhaps we might go even further and employ the term "instinctualized countertrans-ference" rather than "instinctualized transference."

Another proposed approach, one that does not entail new terminology, is that we look for the countertransference in our judgments of how the patient is doing. As one proponent of this approach puts it, "It seems that when we are analyzing, we have to ask ourselves, 'What are we really analyzing? Are we analyzing the patient's character structure or his conflicts?' If something gets resolved during the analytic process and we say the patient is 'doing well,' does this mean he is resolving a neurotic conflict that may be more akin to a transference-countertransference phenomenon, or are we saying that he is doing well because his character is somehow changing and expanding?" In other words, what is getting resolved may be, in part, the countertransference, and this may be the source of our judgment that the patient is "doing well."

PERIPHERAL ISSUES

Critics of countertransference have also raised a number of peripheral issues relating to its general meaning. One concerns "psychological processes," which we may in certain instances define as countertransference. These processes go on constantly in the patient–analyst interaction. Some of them, however, do not interfere with treatment and therefore lie outside countertransference defined as a negative force. With this in mind, it might be more helpful to distinguish between the processes that interfere with treatment and those that do not, rather than put them under the same rubric.

Another peripheral issue concerns nonverbal communications, such as the analyst's tone of voice and body movements when he makes an interpretation or other comment to the patient. These too may be signs of countertransference. The effect of such communications on the patient is difficult to assess. Yet as most analysts have noted, an interpretation can be offered in a calm, didactic manner with no apparent effect, whereas if the same interpretation is later given in a more emphatic or affect-laden tone, it can produce the desired result.

The problems involved in the use of the term *counter-transference* have led a number of analysts to make up their own definitions. **Charles Socarides,** for example, sees countertransference as "any untoward reaction to the patient that impedes the healing functions." He illustrates how he uses this definition in analyzing his own countertransference operations:

One evening I was pressed by family matters when a patient called and asked to change her appointment. I answered her brusquely, though I did switch the hour. Later that same evening something came up that made it impossible for me to keep the newly scheduled appointment. So I phoned the patient back and said I was sorry but I had to change the appointment. She answered me sharply, saying, "Well, how come?" and hung up. In thinking over our two conversations, I realized that my original response had been too curt. My reaction to her request was not in keeping with my therapeutic role. For whatever reason, I had lost sight of the analytic situation. Once I had this insight, I thought of something about this patient that could relate to my countertransference. She was a very talented young woman who had run out of money, and I had agreed not to charge her until she found work. This situation may have accounted for my abrupt tone, which she had picked up. After all, I had spent thousands of dollars worth of time on her, which she might never be able to pay for. I would still call this countertransference even if I hadn't acted on it, for I felt she was somehow behaving ungratefully. But I wouldn't have *resolved* the countertransference if I hadn't asked myself what was going on between us and then realized that I had acted in an untoward way, momentarily burdening her with an untherapeutic manner.

Clearly, no agreement exists as to the meaning of countertransference. Just as each individual countertransference experience is unique, so we seem to have many unique approaches in conceptualizing the phenomenon. The substitute terms that have been suggested, together with the "personal definitions," only dramatize the difficulty of arriving at a consensual terminology. Perhaps the most conclusive thing we can say at present is that countertransference concerns those personalized emotional responses each analyst makes to a broad range of individual patients in a wide variety of situations during various phases of treatment. While in themselves neither inherently positive or negative, these responses can promote or hinder the therapeutic process, and it is from this effect that they derive their value, and ultimately their meaningfulness.

Chapter 12
Countertransference and Empathy

EMPATHY'S ROLE IN TREATMENT

In almost every analysis, empathy and countertransference seem so entwined that it is difficult to separate them. Are they in fact separate phenomena? It is my belief that they are and that part of the analyst's task in treatment is to untangle them and clarify their relationship to each other.

We have already discussed various theories of countertransference and its effect on treatment, but what is empathy and what role does it play in the same process? Empathy is one person's partial identification with another person. In the therapeutic situation, the analyst's empathy consists of his ability to project his own personality onto that of the patient in order to understand him better. As is implied in this definition, empathy is partly a countertransferential reaction. Yet whereas the analyst's countertransference can occasionally be inhibitory and even destructive to treatment, it is usually his empathy, along with intuition, that leads to insight.

Or does it? Sometimes the matter is more complicated, as when the analyst has a positive empathic response that is also a negative countertransference.

> A patient was presenting material related to childhood friends who had abandoned her. The general mood of the session had been positive, although in discussing how these friends now avoided her, the patient became dejected. As she talked, the analyst found himself fantasizing about a meeting that he was going to have that evening with some of his own childhood friends. His happy anticipation of his reunion, coupled with his good feelings about the patient, produced a positive emotion that could be called empathic in the sense that he was on the same axis as she: both were reacting to feelings about old friends. But the analyst's affect led to no insights about the patient. In fact, it inhibited the process at that moment, by preventing him from understanding her feelings. In other words, the empathic response contained a negative counter-transferential element, for it was not based on a positive identification with her feelings of sadness, but instead narcissistically reflected the analyst's own personal reality.

How can we summarize what happened here? Both countertransference and empathy are products of development, each rooted in different stages. And the former, as the more primitive response, can block the latter. That is, conflicts related to childhood drive derivatives can prevent the analyst from feeling with the patient. According to Brenner, no analyst, even if he has been successfully analyzed, is immune to this. "Successful analysis," in his view, means that conflicts find more normal outcomes, more normal compromise-formations. But they do not disappear. And there is always the chance, with the analyst as well as the patient, that the psychic balance will shift, causing undesirable and even pathological compromise-formations to emerge.

COUNTERIDENTIFICATION

An important link between empathy and countertransference is *counteridentification,* whereby the analyst both identifies with the patient and at the same time pulls back from that identification so as to view the patient's conflict with objectivity. Empathy is based on counteridentification; indeed, it is counteridentification that permits our empathy to be therapeutically useful. But counter-identification is also a component of countertransference, and if it operates imperfectly, whereby that objectivity is not achieved, then the analyst's negative countertransferential reactions can cause his empathy to diminish or even vanish altogether. When this happens, he may become vulnerable to additional negative countertransference reactions. And these in turn, if he fails to analyze them, may lead him to countertransferential acting out.

The distinction between countertransferential thought and action is critical. For one thing, it is easier to analyze thoughts than acts, and more importantly, it is easier to stop them before they do harm. An analyst, for example, may have a patient whose artistic or financial success he envies. If he recognizes and accepts these feelings in himself, seeing them as natural and human, they will probably have little negative impact on the way he analyzes the patient or behaves toward him. But if he does not exercise this kind of self-intervention and his envy becomes act, that is, he displaces his envious feelings to the patient, he may set treatment back considerably.

This applies, of course, not just to envy but to the full range of countertransferential emotion. A clinical example of the struggle between empathy and countertransference may be useful here.

An analyst had a patient who shortly before the end of each hour would invariably glance at the clock on the table and say, "I see there are only a couple of minutes left." Hence the analyst never had the chance to say, "We have to stop now." The analyst sensed the patient's need to control the situation by controlling the time. The analysis had already revealed numerous other examples of this patient's anal-sadistic, authoritarian, and power-related conflicts. Yet something stood in the way of the analyst's empathizing with the patient's need. Instead, he found himself, one day, beating the patient to the punch by calling the end of the hour before the patient did — with the result, as he discovered after the patient left, that the session was cut short by a good five minutes. The analyst was puzzled and chagrined by his own behavior, and when the same sequence of events repeated itself a few days later, he became even more upset. Why had he done this? Through self-analysis he found the reason: it was not that he wanted to get rid of the patient, but rather that *he* had to be the one to control the situation. This observation led him to think about his childhood rivalry with his younger brother, who, like this patient, was highly assertive and competitive. He then realized that the patient and he were engaged in a similar power struggle. With this recognition, he was able, at an appropriate moment, to speak neutrally to the patient about his (the patient's) need for control—something he couldn't do in his own sibling rivalry. Here, until he analyzed himself, his negative countertransference had blocked his empathy and with it the emergence of an interpretation.

LINKING EMPATHY TO COUNTERTRANSFERENCE

The link between objective countertransference and empathy has not been stressed by American analysts. It is our British colleagues—Heimann, Klein, and Little—who have emphasized it. They even go so far as to define countertransference as the ability to empathize with or intuitively understand the patient. Moreover, unlike most American analysts, the British feel that a properly analyzed therapist cannot misunderstand a patient. The patient's unconscious projects his wishes onto the analyst, whose own unconscious then responds to them, without any substantial interference. Many American analysts have difficulty accepting this. They would be more inclined to agree with Jacob Arlow's remark that if the analyst does the right thing with a patient, he attributes it to his empathy, but if he does the wrong thing, he attributes it to his countertransference.

A number of American analysts do, however, speak of empathy in relation to "transience," and thereby indirectly connect it to countertransference. In their view, the analyst's empathy originates in certain transient identificatory processes attuned to what the patient is experiencing or fantasizing at the moment. Countertransference is then seen as empathy stuck in time: it does not fade, but remains fixed, or nontransient. For example, every time a particular patient arrived for a session, her analyst experienced an intense feeling of her sadness. At first he believed that he was responding to some element or quality in her that manifested itself even before she lay down on the couch. Eventually, however, he changed his mind and saw this feeling as a sign of countertransference, for through self-analysis he had become aware that he was responding not to the patient's words, gestures, or behavior, but to some fixed constellation within himself.

EMPATHY: THE CENTER OF THE ANALYST–PATIENT RELATIONSHIP

Some analysts place special emphasis on the reality and importance of the analyst's empathy. Ralph Greenson (1960, 1970), for example, extensively discusses the "real relationship" between therapist and patient, a connection, he insists, with empathy at its center. Many analysts, he notes, have problems dealing with such a relationship, probably because they are afraid of their own positive countertransferential capability. But if they permitted themselves such responses, they might avoid the trap of assuming that their transference interpretations are simply neutral descriptions of the patient's behavior. In Greenson's opinion, the analyst has to know himself and his patient very well in order to determine with certainty that he is dealing with a transference and not a realistic reaction. Differentiating between the two is made more difficult by the analyst's blind spots, or his failure to recognize painful characteristics within himself. Another complicating factor is that he and the patient may assign different values to various traits. Given these confusions, Greenson concludes that most transference interpretations are actually highly subjective judgments — a fact which avoidance of empathy prevents many analysts from understanding.

Greenson also emphasizes that empathy is a two-way process: While the analyst is trying to understand the patient, the patient is trying to understand the analyst. The patient's strivings in this regard should not be underestimated. It is true that he never comes to know the analyst in the same way that the analyst knows him. Still, everything the analyst does — the way he opens the door, greets the patient, makes an interpretation or keeps his silence — reveals something about himself, and from these signs the patient comes to know him.

Greenson suggests that this real relationship should include, when necessary, indications of compassion for the patient. For example, the analyst should show the patient that he feels for him in the event of an extraordinary misfortune, such as a death in the immediate family. These expressions do not have to be elaborate or intense. In contrast to the analyst's usual reserve, mere ordinary responsiveness will make an impression on the patient.

Greenson believes that another situation in which the analyst might express special sympathy is the last hour before a lengthy separation like the summer break. He should never end this session as though he were seeing the patient the next day. If he does, the patient is likely to regard him as unfeeling, or at least out of contact with what is really happening between them. This perception will then impede the development of the trusting relationship necessary for a productive analysis.

According to Greenson, the benefits of empathy extend to the very core of the therapeutic process. In his view (see Part I), the final resolution of the transference neurosis depends largely on its replacement by the real relationship between analyst and patient. In other words, the analyst's interpretations, by themselves, will not resolve the patient's neurosis. They need to be supplemented by the patient's realistic and genuine, albeit limited, connection to the analyst. Those analysts who believe that treatment consists solely of making interpretations may actually be using such interpretations as a defense against their own connection to the patient.

We have discussed Greenson's ideas at length because of their relevance to the subject of this chapter. For a central component of a realistic and genuine analytic relationship is the capacity to respond to and deal with countertransference in such a way that it does not interfere with our ability to empathize with the patient. Freud's image of the analyst as mirror no longer seems valid.

Chapter 13

Revealing Countertransference to the Patient

Ever since Ferenczi, analysts have been debating the advisability of revealing to patients any information that does not constitute an interpretation. On one side are a small number of purists who believe that no matter what the patient asks, or why, they should only respond, "What are your thoughts about that?" in order to reach behind the question's manifest content to the fantasies informing it. In their view, the therapist who explains that he has to cancel a session because of a cold or who answers the patient's inquiry about whether he is married, has children, or owns a country house is offering an object lesson on how *not* to conduct an analysis. Any such disclosures will more or less put an end to serious treatment since, by permitting real data from his own life to invade the treatment situation, the analyst blocks the emergence of the patient's fantasies about him and hence of the patient's unconscious life.

On the other side are the analysts who would agree with the reservations expressed by Greenson that too often psychoanalysis becomes adversarial. We tend to forget the inequalities of the analytic situation. The patient is asked to reveal all of himself; the analyst is trained to expose as little of his personal self as he comfortably can. To be sure, we do not want our personality traits to intrude upon the patient's transference reactions; but we sometimes seem to use nonresponsiveness and interpretations because they are safer and easier to us, not because they are best for the patient. For these analysts, the issue is not whether to reveal anything to the patient, but what to reveal and when to reveal it. It is on this problem of self-revelation and disclosure that this chapter will focus.

Many analysts acknowledge that they feel quite uneasy when personal material seeps into sessions — a discomfort that, in some cases, stems from a feeling that the disclosure was counter-transference-based.

One analyst experienced regret after revealing a personal matter to a patient. Even though, at the time, the comment had seemed to him to mesh with where the patient was emotionally, the analyst later decided that this revelation, like others he had previously made, was a mistake. It really had to do with the degree of regression the patient was then experiencing: "If I became a little frightened by how regressed he was when he demanded to know something about me, then I tended to reveal more than I felt I should have, and also to question his degree of pathology and wonder whether he was a suitable analytic case. As result, my tendency recently has been not to reveal anything personal."

For another analyst, a single experience was particularly instructive about the way he responded to patients' material. During a session, this analyst found himself deeply absorbed by a patient's fantasies about her Prince Charming, to the point where he too seemed to be undergoing an important experience. He was on the verge of remarking that the rescue fantasy was common among men too (an implicit admission of his own arousal) when a mental alarm bell went off. "What are you so excited about?" he asked himself. "Something odd is going on here. You'd better watch your reactions." When the patient continued fantasizing about her Prince

Charming, he silently admonished himself, "Be careful; you're not the one who is going to rescue her. She will have to work out her own rescue." This insight released him from being inside the patient's story. Now he could either acknowledge his countertransference in some way or make an interpretation that might help the treatment.

In describing this episode later, the analyst saw it as an illustration of why analysts should be careful in responding personally to the patient's material: "No matter what you do, something is going to happen. If you deserve it, you're going to be caught, because the patient has no choice but to try to use whatever is available to establish a transference situation in which his initial strivings can be lived out instead of analyzed and given up. So you always have to watch out, be careful, see where the analysis is heading and what the possibilities are." As these remarks imply, if the analyst is lax, he may find himself pushed into making revelations.

BREACHES OF THERAPEUTIC CONDUCT

Still, certain situations do pose particularly perplexing choices for the analyst who is uncomfortable with the issue of self-revelation. For example, what should he do if he dozes off during the session and awakens to discover that the patient either knows what has happened or has guessed something is wrong? Upon being awakened by the patient, some traditional analysts have remained silent, whereas other analysts have explained to the patient that their falling asleep was a response to his wish to put them into a stupor. Perhaps such analysts would do better to apologize for behaving badly before making any interpretations. If they do not, the patient may correctly perceive any attempt at interpretation as a stratagem on the part of the analyst for minimizing his lapse. In Greenson's view (and it is one I share), it is not an apology, but the absence of an apology, that in this case will interfere with the treatment process. By failing to be honest, the analyst introduces hypocrisy and oppressiveness into the treatment process. Moreover, in general, the analyst should apologize to a patient when his behavior causes unnecessary hurt. Otherwise, he is showing both impoliteness and disrespect (Greenson 1971).

When an analyst's long-term behavior seems to constitute a breach of therapeutic conduct and he does not apologize, the entire analysis may collapse.

> A patient left her therapist precisely because he refused to acknowledge her realistic complaints about his behavior. Throughout the therapy, the analyst had demanded that she adhere to the rules of classical analysis. She had to report her dreams in such and such a way, associate to them in such and such a way, pay her bill only in the manner he laid out, and so forth. As a result of his rigid and intricate rules, she felt continually dominated, harried, and uncomfortable. Her sense of oppression deepened as she saw him flagrantly disregard rules governing his own conduct. For example, he had accepted her for analysis even though he had previously treated a close relative of hers; sometimes, too, he ate his breakfast during the session. During the four years of treatment, the analyst never acknowledged either *his* behavior or *her* feelings about it. At the end of this time, fed up with the lack of progress, she left.
>
> In her second analysis, the patient commented on this interaction: "I saw myself there as a bad girl who was not doing her job. We talked a lot about my resistances, and I always tried to please him, do a good job, be a good patient. But I really felt I was getting nowhere. I never perceived any empathy for me. I felt I was working and trying to get better for him, not for myself." Much of the early part of the second analysis consisted of repairing the damage done by the first.

This kind of acting out and avoidance behavior on the part of the analyst is more common than one would hope.

> One woman, also in a second analysis, reported that her first therapist routinely read the newspaper and also occasionally ate his lunch during her sessions. One day the patient timidly made reference to his newspaper reading and asked if he could listen to her at the same time. The analyst replied that he could do several things simultaneously. His response both intimidated and infuriated her. She became so angry that she wanted to rise from the couch, snatch the paper from his hands, roll it up, hit him over the head with it, and walk out. Instead, she did nothing. Eventually, she left the

analysis without ever having displayed her legitimate anger. Once again, the analyst's refusal to confront the patient's justifiable anger had resulted in therapeutic disaster.

Both these cases are complicated because they each involved two analyses. The second analyst must be cautious in judging whether his predecessor was right or wrong; he does not, nor can he ever, know the other treatment situation fully. He can, however, arrive at some judgment on the basis of the material in the current treatment.

What happens when the analyst does apologize for some error or analytic breach? The results vary.

One analyst had a patient who either fell asleep or was sleepy during sessions. Once, however, when the patient was awake, the analyst drifted off himself. On awakening, he apologized. The patient responded by expressing relief that the analyst hadn't "pushed" the responsibility of his falling asleep onto him and had actually felt comfortable enough to doze. The patient's mother had always pressured him and he resented this. The analyst, both in his lapse and in his apology, showed that he would not act in the same bullying way.

Another analyst who fell asleep during a session had a different experience. When the patient complained, the analyst apologized, explaining that he had taken an antihistamine and that it had made him sleepy. The patient replied grudgingly, "I hope you feel better." After the session, the analyst reconsidered his behavior. On the one hand, he still felt that it was right to apologize; on the other hand, he vowed that, no matter how sick he was, he would never again take a drowsiness-inducing medicine during a workday. The experience had simply been too uncomfortable for him.

But what happens when the patient unfairly accuses the analyst of improper or annoying behavior? For example, one patient angrily ordered her therapist to stop taking notes when in fact he was not writing anything. He then had the choice of defending himself — a form of self-revelation — or of asking for the patient's thoughts about his alleged action. He opted for the latter. If, however, he had simply said, "I wasn't taking notes. Why do you think I was?"

this might have been no great mistake. Indeed, such a response could even be beneficial, for the patient, at this stage in his or her treatment, might need the reassurance of an apology for one reason or another. The important thing in making such a revelation would be the linking of it to the question about the patient's response to the alleged action. If this is done, the patient will probably not be inhibited in expressing his feelings. However, the analyst must make sure that a "defensive" remark on his part does not stem from anxiety over the patient's anger.

PATIENT SEDUCTIVENESS

Another situation that raises questions concerning disclosure is seductiveness on the part of the patient.

> One charming and highly attractive patient had been for some time acting in a sexually provocative way with her analyst. For his part, he noticed that he was trying to be witty and affable during their sessions. Finally, one day when she had been more forward than usual, he said, "I feel that you are trying to elicit in me a sexual response. There is no question that I can feel these feelings. But wouldn't it be more useful to talk about your need to stir them up with men whom you see as authority figures? In saying this, I hope you will see that I am not rejecting you, but trying to help us understand you better."

Here the analyst had taken the risk of tacitly acknowledging his personal response to the patient's seductiveness, while at the same time trying to employ it in making an interpretation. In doing so, he wanted the patient—who beneath her polished surface felt extremely insecure about her femininity—to perceive that she was a woman capable of arousing a man sexually and at the same time for her to feel protected against her equally powerful fear of seducing the analyst. The wisdom of the analyst's maneuver was confirmed by the patient's next remark. "I don't know why," she said, "but before I came here today, I felt a little tense. Now I'm so relaxed."

Self-revelation is not the only issue raised by seductiveness. Some analysts, in the face of a seductive patient, are not attracted but instead made angry or anxious — feelings which can lead them to question the appropriateness of their interpretations. The general feeling is that before doing anything, an analyst in this situation should ask himself, "Why do I feel this way?" This pause for reflection may save him from deriving his interpretation from the countertransference.

What happens if the analyst, outside the context of an interpretation, reveals to the patient that he has seductive fantasies about him or her? This is not something that analysts readily admit to. It may come out, however, during a second analysis.

An analyst confided to his female patient that he was so attracted to her that it was interfering with treatment and that in fairness to her, he felt she should see another therapist. The patient, who had trusted this analyst — indeed, he had helped her through a number of difficult situations — felt furious and betrayed. In this instance, disclosure, it seems, served more to assuage the analyst's guilt than to promote the therapeutic process. It was, at the very least, nonproductive. Could he have not worked with these feelings, and used them to help the patient? Perhaps he might then have discovered that his countertransference was in some measure related to seductiveness on her part, which, instead of analyzing, he had simply reacted to.

Extra-analytic Circumstances

In some cases, extra-analytic circumstances may call for a disclosure from the analyst. For example, if he is in mourning and his depression is coloring his responses, he might well make some reference to his loss. Otherwise patients may easily misinterpret his reactions, relating them to the analytic material. Or a patient, having read about the death in the newspaper, may express sympathetic feelings. Here, too, the analyst may find it best to acknowledge these expressions by some personal comment.

Mourning is only one instance in which strong personal feelings on the part of the analyst may become apparent to the patient. As much control as the analyst tries to exert, that control is never perfect; the patient, on occasion, will pick up the analyst's anxiety or depression. And if the patient expresses a strong response to the analyst's emotion and seeks verification that what he is responding to is real, the analyst might cautiously confirm his perception. Is there anything to guide him in deciding on the appropriateness of such a response? I would say that if he feels confident in his judgment, he can at times make a disclosure.

PATIENT PROVOCATIVENESS AND NEEDINESS

A patient's praise of a former therapist may provoke an analyst into a response other than an interpretation. Analysts report that they often feel angry or seduced by such remarks. Should they reveal these feelings to the patient? Most advise against this. If the treatment is to progress, the analyst should in this case use his feelings only as grounds for interpretation. Likewise, when patients complain about the analyst's attitude toward them (e.g., "You're not interested in me"), most analysts would agree that any self-revelation is out of place. Here the analyst should try simply to obtain the patient's associations. Later he should ask himself whether the patient's complaint is in any way justified and, if so, what the countertransferential factors are and how they can be resolved.

Certain kinds of patients, such as bulimics and anorexics, constantly try to provoke the analyst into a response. To this end, they miss sessions, distort, and lie to the point where their analysts repeatedly feel angry or frustrated enough to want to get rid of them. With this type of patient, should one respond personally or stay with interpretation?

One such patient repeatedly angered her analyst, though he never mentioned this to her. One day she said, "Doctor, there are times, particularly when I hear you lean forward, when I have fantasies that you're going to hit me." When the analyst said nothing, she continued, "It reminds me of the German nurse my mother hired when I was three, who beat my younger brother and me. My mother came home one day unexpectedly and found her hitting us and fired her." At this point, the analyst decided to intervene and told her about the reactions she stirred in him. In the following session she reported a dream in which she had shouted at herself. For some time she had sensed the analyst's irritation at her provocations but had said nothing; now her dream, along with her associations in the previous session, clearly revealed this understanding to both of them.

Here the analyst seems to have acted appropriately in confirming the patient's reality.

Another related question is whether the analyst should ever give the patient a word of encouragement when he deserves or appears to need it. Although making a remark like "You seem to be taking charge of the money situation" does not strictly constitute a personal revelation, it is a departure from interpretation. Except for analysts who strictly adhere to the rule of never revealing anything to the patient, most do find themselves occasionally providing a little positive reinforcement. Some say they do so when the patient appears to require this kind of support in order to continue the painful work of looking at his primitive self.

MAINTENANCE OF THE ANALYTIC FRAME

Another matter of concern involving self-disclosure has to do with the frame. As the Balints first acknowledged (1939), the way the analyst furnishes his office can be self-revelatory. Many analysts, in keeping with the reveal-nothing rule, choose the most neutral furnishings possible, while others surround themselves with the furniture they like and put up their favorite paintings and photographs. (Freud, whose consulting room was filled with his beloved artifacts, was clearly in the latter camp, whatever his stated policies on disclosure.) How should we approach this matter? Here I think that what makes the analyst personally comfortable should be the criterion, as no analysis will proceed well if the analyst is ill at ease in the environment he has created.

Even when self-revelation appears appropriate, many analysts feel that it should be restricted to the acknowledgment of small, clear-cut lapses such as billing or scheduling errors. Otherwise, the treatment may become contaminated, for, if excessive, the analyst's self-revelations will lead to confusion in the therapy. Most of the time, the analyst should use his personal reactions to ask himself, "Why does the patient evoke these feelings in me?" For example, one analyst described a treatment in which, in response to promptings from the patient, he was repeatedly tempted to compete with past and present objects in her life, including her husband, parents, and previous analyst. He never revealed these feelings to her, however, an approach which he later concluded was entirely correct. It would have been easy, he remarked, to be swayed by her point of view, to enter into her seduction, as a way of expressing "my own wish for her to love me, and with that, my own grandiosity and needs." He added that sometimes analysts may find it difficult to accept that "certain patients may have had parents who were much better parents than we are to them."

This brief discussion has focused on those situations in which the analyst is directly confronted with the question of whether to reveal countertransference reactions. Naturally, the same question will arise indirectly at many other points in treatment. My own view is that if an analyst has thoroughly analyzed his countertransference, he will be reasonably comfortable with both the patient and himself. As a result, he will also feel reasonably comfortable about what he reveals or does not reveal. The following example shows how such an analyst skillfully coped with an embarrassing situation that had the potential for self-revelation.

The analyst arrived at his office one morning, made some coffee, and in the process spilled some of it on himself, leaving a large brown stain on his shirt, tie, and jacket. The first patient was due in fifteen minutes. Fortunately, it was summer, and the analyst was wearing the kind of clothing that could be rinsed out and dried quickly. Indeed, before the first patient's arrival, he managed to dry the shirt sufficiently so that he could wear it, although the jacket and tie were still too wet to be put back on. The patient walked in, glanced at him, and said nothing. The analyst suppressed his urge to apologize. The silence deepened. The analyst waited, in profound discomfort, for he felt it was improper to appear so seductively undressed.

The analyst was aware that he was experiencing countertransference feelings. Clearly, he was displacing his infantile, exhibitionistic anxieties onto the current situation. With this in mind, he continued to be silent. Now the patient began talking about his anger toward his son, who was interested only in blondes. (The patient's own preference was for brunettes.) The son had invited a "gorgeous blonde" from his college home for the weekend. At his son's request, he had invited this young woman to visit his office because she was interested in his line of business.

The analyst sensed that the patient was anxious about his feelings toward the "gorgeous blonde" to whom he was "not attracted," and the patient soon confirmed this. After briefly shifting to other subjects, the patient admitted to having a fantasy that the young woman would appear at his office wearing a jump suit and high heels. Throughout the visit she would giggle a lot, just as she had over the weekend. The atmosphere of his office was sober and serious, and the thought of her presence there was unsettling.

As the session progressed, the analyst began to note his own preoccupation with the idea that the patient was fleeing from his son's "blonde" because he feared identifying with her and admitting to himself his sexual interest. (The patient had a deep identification with women because of his close childhood attachment to his mother.) Simultaneously, the analyst became increasingly aware that he himself was repressing material associated with improper clothes.

Only as he watched the patient's back recede from sight did the correct interpretation come to him: The connection between himself and the "blonde" in the patient's productions, the unsettling but sexually attractive inappropriate clothing in the sober and serious office. Why had he missed it? The timing of the interpretation confirmed the existence of a countertransference response; that is, he made it only after the patient had left. Although consciously the analyst had been looking for information about improper clothing, unconsciously he had blocked any reference to it because of his own anxiety about his clothes. At the patient's next session, the analyst did not mention his countertransference. It was enough that he knew of it.

Chapter 14
Reality Issues
and Countertransference

THE ANALYST'S REAL-LIFE TRAUMAS

When the analyst experiences anxiety during the treatment process, how does he know whether this is the result of reality issues or of the countertransference? Reality issues include both chronic and acute circumstances in the analyst's life. If someone in his family has died or is ill, or if he himself is ill or in financial trouble or in the middle of a divorce, this may well interfere with his free-floating attention and his ability to concentrate and empathize. Reality issues also increase his vulnerability to countertransference. For example, an analyst whose teenage son has been in trouble at school may have a patient who evokes his rescue fantasies. These in turn may relate to some earlier episode in the analyst's life. Until his son's troubles, he may have kept these fantasies in check. But now, under the pressure of worry about the child, he may find himself actively trying to rescue the patient.

Yet we must exercise caution in drawing connections between real events and the way analysts treat their patients. For one thing, invariably, no stimulus elicits a specific response. We can never predict how a particular analyst will react at a particular time to an outside situation. Real-life trauma summons up certain persistent unconscious reactions, and the analyst will have to make an adaptive compromise-formation in response. Obviously, his successful compromise-formations will enhance the treatment, whereas his unsuccessful ones will interfere with it. But the compromise will vary with the analyst.

When faced with a disturbing reality situation, some analysts become more involved in their work in order to distract themselves.

> One analyst had a child who needed surgery. The analyst was very worried about the operation, and particularly about the anaesthesia. On the surface, he seemed unaffected by these concerns. If anything, his busy daily schedule grew even more hectic. Only later did it dawn on him that, when confronted with patients for whom castration or suffocation anxiety was a particular problem, he became much more active in trying to relieve their fears. By changing his analytic pattern from that of passive listener to active interventionist, where nothing in the patients' material justified this, he had switched the focus from these patients' fears to his own. Moreover, almost every one of the patients in question noted the difference, with varying degrees of disturbance. His hyperactivity was, in effect, a negative countertransferential response brought about because some of his patients had the same anxieties as he.

Some analysts feel that it is counterproductive to dwell too much on the analyst's reactions to real-life events and how these reactions, and characterological traits, relate to the countertransference. According to this argument, nobody, not even the analyst, can attain complete maturity. Like everyone else, the analyst is a human being with unconscious, unresolved conflicts, and like everyone else, he struggles with his problems and tries to solve them as best he can. Yet if he focuses overscrupulously on every nuance of his responses to the patient, searching for links between his realistic concerns and negative countertransference, then the inquiry into the patient's unconscious will break down.

On the other side are those who argue that the analyst's reactions to real-life events, together with his character traits, can easily become interwoven with his neurotic tendencies, and that unless he searches very carefully for the solutions to these problems, they will interfere with treatment.

For example, some analysts seem to be angry with all their patients. Unaware of the origins of this characterological anger — their dislike of being analysts — and perhaps even of its existence, they tend to use their patients unanalytically. If the analyst is angry, for this or for any other reason, patients will often pick up on it. This should come as no surprise when we consider the kind of people who choose to undergo analysis, for they appear to be characterized by a capacity to understand others as well as themselves. They also have their own individual ways of presenting their problems. (This is another reality the analyst must deal with.) One speaks quickly; another, with labored slowness. One constantly dissolves into tears; another is prone to nervous giggling. These very idiosyncrasies, meshing with the analyst's unresolved conflicts, can at times impel him to react countertransferentially, especially with anger, and when unchecked, this anger may turn exploitative. For example, in response to a patient whose slow speech makes him impatient, the analyst may unconsciously retaliate and start the sessions late, thus causing the patient to be angry too. By recognizing the many conscious, and where possible the unconscious, components in the treatment and relating them to his reactions to real events, the analyst can avoid such traps.

CONFUSION AMONG VARIOUS TREATMENT MODALITIES

Another reality issue has to do with the tendency on the part of today's therapists to offer many different kinds of treatment. Some of us, for example, may move in a given workday from psychoanalysis with one patient to educational psychotherapy with a second to supportive psychotherapy with a third. Such crossing-over can cause problems, for I believe that some therapists do not distinguish carefully enough among the various treatment modalities, and particularly between psychoanalysis and its derivatives. If the therapist is not sufficiently clear as to the specific operations appropriate to the form of therapy he is administering, this increases his chances of behaving with negative countertransference. (I should add that therapists are not the only culprits here. Analysts also confuse modalities.)

When countertransference arises in such a situation, some people would say that it is the countertransference that is causing the confusion of modalities. I think, however, that in many cases the reverse may be true. That is, the confusion of modalities, due primarily to inappropriate training, is disturbing the treatment and that the countertransference is a response to and signal of this treatment disturbance. Consider, for example, an analyst who is treating a psychotic patient. Since this particular patient usually has minimally intact ego functions, he requires supportive therapy instead of intensive insight therapy. The analyst, however, may use insight therapy because he prefers this technique, with its opportunity for deeper interpretations and because the analyst may feel more comfortable with it. One might say that here the analyst is acting out of countertransference; he is angry because he is not really comfortable with supportive psychotherapy. But there is also the possibility that he is simply unclear as to the boundaries between insight therapy and supportive psychotherapy. In any case, the unclarity of technique will mobilize great anxiety in the patient, and whatever the role of countertransference before, it is likely to come into play now.

To avoid repeating mistakes such as this, the analyst need not necessarily subject himself to a close analysis of the countertransference. Rather, he should subject himself to further study of the different treatments and their specific techniques. Some people have expressed doubts as to whether therapists *can* switch back and forth comfortably between various kinds of therapy in their daily practice. I think they can, but they must be well versed in whatever therapies they are using.

THE ANALYST'S REALISTIC CONCERN

Certain cases on their own may generate realistic worry in the analyst. I, for example, had a patient, a jeweler, who was licensed to carry a gun, and frequently, as he lay on the couch, I could see the tip of the holster above his ankle. The feelings I had at those moments I would not attribute to countertransference.

Another analyst took on a patient who he knew had just received a suspended sentence for a major white-collar crime. During the treatment, it came out that the patient was also heavily in debt to the Mafia. When the patient interrupted treatment to go on trial for a second crime, the analyst experienced a feeling of relief. Subsequently, having received another suspended sentence, the man began therapy with a second analyst. Soon, however, he called the first analyst and asked if he might return to him. The analyst pondered the request and then politely refused. The man, he concluded, simply made him feel too uncomfortable. Was this countertransference? After some self-analysis, he decided it was not. He actually liked this patient, even though the man was a psychopath with strong manipulative tendencies. What disturbed the analyst was that the patient constantly acted out, to an extent that the analyst felt he could not be dealt with analytically. For example, the patient had already lost several million dollars through various business deals. These considerations convinced the analyst that the reality of the situation had dictated his decision.

Despite this conclusion, others have suggested that instinctual conflicts and their derivatives might play a role in the analyst's reactions to criminals. In their view, treating criminals will naturally invoke childhood conflicts, and these reactions can in turn become countertransferential. Others, like Brenner, do not think that a patient's having a Mafia connection automatically generates countertransference. Brenner does see the analyst's reaction in this case as a compromise-formation, in which childhood instinctual conflicts and their derivatives play an important part. "The analyst" he says, "cannot help responding in this way; that is how he is. He is not going to escape from his conflicts any more than the rest of us." However, because an analyst's response to such a patient is a compromise-formation, this still doesn't mean that he should take the man back into treatment.

Another reality situation that can interfere with the treatment is the seductiveness of either the patient or the therapist. If the therapist is seduced—that is, if he has an affair with the patient—

then he is responding not just to reality but also to the counter-transference. And in doing so, he is creating a new reality situation, one that is bound to destroy the treatment.

Besides assessing the real situation, is there any way to judge whether the analyst's emotional response is reality-based or countertransference-based, or to make the distinction clearer? Some analysts believe that we should differentiate only between the patient's transference and his characterological modes of behavior and limit the term *countertransference* to responses to the former. In this case it might help if we defined the transference more carefully. All of us have noted that a variety of the patient's transferences develop at the beginning of treatment and that only some of these will turn out to be actual transference neuroses. Perhaps, in a parallel manner, we should distinguish among the various countertransference phenomena that emerge. This would make the ultimate identification of our "countertransference neuroses" more clear cut.

Other analysts, like Silverman, as we have seen (Chapter 11), suggest the term *emotional reactions* to cover all those responses to the patient that are not countertransferential. This is perhaps a useful distinction, not only because it helps separate the counter-transference from the reality issues presented by the patient, but also because it separates the reality issues connected to the patient and those connected to the analyst. For example, an analyst who is unhappy in his private life may behave in a depressed manner to all his patients. Here he may be said to be reacting characterolo-gically instead of to the patient's transference or to realities presented by the patient.

In considering reality issues, I have stressed the influence personal matters can have on the analyst, and therefore on the treatment. But professional concerns can also affect his therapeu-tic behavior. One analyst, for example, raised the question of whether or not the emotional impact of insurance policies (third-party payers and/or malpractice) comes under the heading of countertransference. He described a recent meeting in San Diego, attended by the presidents of the various analytic societies, in which a representative from one of the insurance companies brought the audience up to date on current malpractice statistics involving cases against analysts. Among the bases for such suits, he cited sexual involvement with patients, misprescription of drugs, and patient suicides. As the analyst pointed out, this raises some questions for those who treat seriously ill patients, such as the suicidal or those under medication. Would these analysts' realistic concern about legal liability color their perception of the patient? We might, in fact, consider this concern to be a form of countertransference.

But is it? Some analysts disagree, saying that insurance coverage is a practical and realistic matter. In their view, every analyst should have malpractice insurance to cover all psychotherapeutic activities, including analysis. Naturally, if these analysts prescribe drugs, even occasionally, they should be covered for that too.

As this brief discussion has shown, reality factors do not exist in a closed compartment, sealed off from the unconscious. Almost any reality issue can reawaken childhood conflicts. In the compromise-formations that both the patient and the analyst make in response to this mix of reality and memory, we may discover many of the central transferential and countertransferential transactions of the analysis.

Chapter 15
The Fit between Patient and Analyst

Until recently, the question of analytic fit was only infrequently discussed in the literature. With the emergence of countertransference as an issue, however, a number of analysts have begun to explore the question of whether some of us work better with certain patients and, conversely, whether some patients do better with certain analysts.

My own opinion is that the unique specificity of the analyst's character structure and unresolved neuroses dictates that he will help some individuals more than others, and still others not at all. It is this combination of factors that will affect not only transference and countertransference but also, and perhaps more so, the analyst's success in establishing a "real relationship" with the patient, which, as Greenson has suggested, is essential to the resolution of the transference neurosis.

Some analysts may find these ideas hard to accept. Yet why

should we believe ourselves capable of analyzing everybody seeking help? In truth, many people seeking treatment are simply unanalyzable, no matter who the analyst or how great his skill. Perhaps in our narcissism we are threatened by the thought that we cannot work equally well with everyone.

An analyst once treated a twin. The therapy took a rocky course, leading him to conclude that among the causes for poor progress was that *all* twins were basically unanalyzable. As he later realized, this was not an altogether unwarranted conclusion, but when he made it, it was based on wounded professional pride.

If we cannot treat everyone, how do we decide whether the person sitting across from us in the consulting room is one of the ones we *can* treat? After an initial meeting or two, we might decide, "I'll take on this young woman—she's a person I'd like to work with." Or perhaps, if there is any reason for hesitation, we might say to ourselves cautiously, or bemusedly, or even a little defiantly, "Well, what *if* this man's a Mafioso? I still don't dislike him." We may discover in ourselves an affection for scoundrels, or at least for some scoundrels. If we consider the matter, I think most of us will admit that when we accept someone as a patient, we do so not only because of an initial positive response to the person, and because we deem him analyzable, but also because some quality in him resonates in us.

LIKING

Is "liking" an essential element of the patient–analyst fit? Is it a countertransferential phenomenon? One therapist vividly remembers his first exposure to countertransference and its effect on fit. At the time, he was a child psychiatry fellow in a dynamic and eclectic, though not really analytic, clinic. One day a staff member confided to him that she selected her patients on the basis of personal liking. Whenever she disliked or was neutral about a child, she simply referred him to another therapist. With one child in particular, she had marvelous results. In discussing the case, she talked about her great affection for this child. Watching her work, the young resident began to think more deeply about the importance of liking one's patients. Some years after establishing his own practice, he finally concluded that it was possibly nonproductive for analysts to bind themselves to patients they swiftly and instinctively "like," for these feelings may change, and may continue to change throughout the therapy. This is not, in fact, an uncommon practice and many analysts can confirm the truth of this. They will take on a patient they do not like as much as another and then find themselves becoming increasingly fond of him. Or, initially, they may find a patient very attractive and then come to like him less as the treatment progresses.

Personally, I believe it is not essential that we like a person in order to treat him. Nor, by the same token, should our initial dislike of someone automatically disqualify him for treatment, although it may not make for an ideal or even preferred fit. What we describe as initial liking or disliking of a patient is partially based on attitudes (transferences) formed through childhood conflicts and experiences. These feelings, in other words, are part of an immediate and possibly countertransferential transference, and as such, they are likely to diminish. With some of my own patients, I seem to progress more toward boredom than dislike. Many other analysts report a similar response. There may be a number of reasons for this boredom, their applicability varying from analyst to analyst. In any case, perhaps the ideal treatment circumstance is that in which the analyst neither likes nor dislikes a potential patient, but feels neutral, accepting, and curious. Such a position, with perceptions unclouded by bias, would enable us truly to get to know the patient.

When we say we like a patient, then, we are really talking about an extremely complex issue. What do we mean by this? Are we curious to know something about the patient? Or do we want to understand more about the character type he represents? Our interest could, like so many countertransferential phenomena, derive from our own childhood conflicts, such as voyeuristic aims. As we sit listening to the patient describe his sex life, are we still trying to find out what is happening in our parent's bed? Do we like to see, or relieve, suffering? When we expose ourselves to the torment of others, are we sustained by our wish to help them or by a secret pleasure that it is they, not we, who are suffering? Or is it both? Each analyst has his own personal answers to such questions. Some of those answers may involve sexual feelings of which the analyst is only incompletely, if at all, aware and which may turn out—if he remains blind to their existence—to be a problem in the treatment.

During the early stages of most supervised therapies, it becomes obvious to the supervisor that the treating analyst's initial feelings of like or dislike are partially a function of reciprocity—that is, they are based in part on the patient's immediate transference reactions to the therapist. Like the other initial responses we have discussed, this "returned" liking or disliking tends to diminish with time. As it recedes, however, it is usually replaced by a related form of reciprocity: the analyst's response to the patient's progress. Most analysts feel more warmly toward patients who are doing well than toward those who seem to make no progress. Here I am speaking not about passionate feelings of like or dislike, which the analyst would probably be conscious of, but of subtle attitudes toward the patient which, enduring over the course of treatment, may indicate the presence of transference, counter-transference, or other problematic emotional reactions.

Given that it may appear in such circumstances, is countertrans-ference the predominant causal agent of these feelings, and hence of the therapeutic stalemate? It is unquestionably true that a persistently unanalyzed countertransference can obstruct the de-velopment of a workable analytic fit. Yet I wonder which is typically the cause and which the result. Might not the analyst's unconscious negative feelings be signaling that something has gone sour in the therapeutic relationship?

Nevertheless, a number of analysts cite countertransference as the chief reason that the treatment goes awry. Their views may be summarized as: If the analysis is not going right, if we are not receiving the response we expected to reach in our interpretations, if material is not developing in the way we anticipated, or is developing in ways we don't know how to cope with, such as the patient's unexpectedly walking out of treatment, this is when we should begin to look at our countertransference.

The same analysts describe countertransference as a "grab bag of things that have gone wrong." I myself remain unconvinced that any one concept such as countertransference can encompass all the things that may have gone wrong in the treatment. Many other factors may be at fault—noncountertransferential aspects of the analyst's psychology, extra-analytic forces (e.g., an economic recession), and still other forces whose origins are entirely obscure.

Still, it is clear that countertransferential reactions can undermine treatment, and therefore we must keep our eye on the countertransference *before* things go wrong. Indeed, sometimes the sense that treatment is going *well* — and one sign of this is the analyst's increased liking for the patient — is a signal for the analyst to exercise caution. For example, one therapist realized that he was looking forward with some eagerness to his sessions with a patient. Upon analyzing these feelings, he discovered that the patient aroused in him many pleasing sexual fantasies. Once he became aware of this countertransferential response, he was able to use it interpretively.

CHARACTER TRAITS

A number of analysts also caution that analytic fit is harder to evaluate when the therapist remains unaware of his own character traits, such as rigidity, or its opposite, overflexibility. Though ordinarily we make a distinction between character traits and countertransference, there are times when the operation of a character trait can be a manifestation of countertransference. The following account by a young candidate in training analysis illustrates this point.

One day the candidate arrived for his appointment, was welcomed by his analyst, lay down on the couch, and began free-associating. Gradually, he became aware that his associations were drifting to the topic of time. After ten minutes, he had an almost irresistible urge to glance at his watch. He did not look, but he mentioned his desire, for he was an obedient patient who revealed all his thoughts. When the analyst said nothing, the candidate could no longer restrain himself and looked down at his watch. "My God," he exclaimed, "I'm an hour early. This isn't my hour. What time do you have?"

"I have the same time as you," the analyst said.

Utterly confused, the young man stood up. "I'm awfully sorry," he said, "I'll come back tomorrow," and he walked out. Thinking over what had happened, he became increasingly angry at the analyst for allowing him to have the session at the wrong hour. Still disturbed, he went to a friend in the same building and told him the story. The friend was also in analysis with this analyst. His friend listened silently and then said, "Now I understand! I was going downstairs for my hour, the hour you took. I saw you in the waiting room and figured we must have switched hours and I had forgotten about it."

His friend's remarks only fueled the candidate's irritation with the analyst. He began his next session by saying, "How could you have just sat there yesterday and let me take Joe's hour and expect him to take mine? I'm furious. Why did you do it?"

The analyst said, "When you came in, I thought you and Joe had switched hours and that I had forgotten about it." This explanation in no way appeased the patient, and it was some time until the therapy got back on course.

In this encounter, the analyst's unconscious overflexibility strained the fit between himself and his patient. The incident also underlines once again the importance of our examining carefully every single interruption in the treatment.

Periodically, almost every patient will draw the analyst into a transference-countertransference reaction. As in the case above, the analyst may not notice or act upon it. But if the therapist does analyze his feelings, he will discover his countertransference. Only then will he begin to clarify this aspect of his relationship with the patient. Afterward the analysis may proceed peacefully until a similar disruption occurs, for every treatment veers off course from time to time. As I have emphasized, these are precisely the moments when the analyst should rigorously continue his self-analysis and try to become aware of his feelings and thoughts so as to further, rather than upset, the therapeutic relationship.

GENDER

Can all analysts work equally well with patients of both sexes? Probably not. Certain male analysts, like certain males in general, are threatened by overaggressive women, and others by oversubmissive women. Such analysts should think carefully before accepting female patients with these particular qualities. Even though the analyst may be well analyzed, the fit between him and the patient may still be poor.

What about the patient's feelings about men and women analysts? Will these affect fit? During consultation with a woman therapist, a successful actress said that she was convinced that she could seductively manipulate any male analyst to such a degree as to impair his therapeutic effectiveness. For this reason, she was adamant that her next therapist be a woman. She had already seen and left two male analysts, both of whom, according to her account, had shown severe countertransferential acting out in response to her seductiveness. On the surface, these reality situations supported her belief that she might do better with a female therapist. This woman did in fact subsequently enter therapy with a female analyst, with whom she has not yet disrupted the treatment through her seductive acting out. One might ask, however, whether a female analyst, precisely because she probably will never be exposed to the full intensity of this patient's sexual blandishments, can help her to resolve her conflicts. In this instance, the better fit would clearly have been a male analyst who could handle the patient's seductiveness without countertransferential acting out.

Another issue concerning the relationship between gender and fit involves homosexual patients. Will all heterosexual male analysts be able to work well with patients whose homoerotic conflicts cause them to transfer intense libidinal feelings onto the therapist?

In this context, it is interesting to note the reactions of candidates who work with homosexuals. A number of supervising analysts have experienced discomfort in the training analysis of such candidates. As one such analyst observes: "I find that they (candidates) seem to take pleasure in giving repetitive accounts of homosexual activity." When these candidates narrate such stories to the supervisor, he often, if not generally, will have a counter-transference reaction. This is not surprising in view of the fact that many of us are poorly versed in the treatment of homosexuality.

Another analyst who has treated homosexuals says that they often launch severe attacks on the therapist, accusing him of having caused their perversion. Homosexual patients are also prone to expressing suicidal thoughts, at the same time repressing homicidal wishes toward the analyst. Such tendencies threaten the fit and make it difficult for the analyst to help these patients work through and understand their fixation to early phases of separation-individuation. This is a particularly challenging area for future investigation of fit, and one that, because of anxieties regarding our own homosexual impulses, we may not have gone into as much as we should. A preliminary observation is that, to begin to fit with such patients, the analyst must ascertain to what extent sexual preference issues are part of the pathology for which they have sought help.

PERSONALITY AND CULTURE

I was asked for a referral by the overtly rebellious, yet secretly cowed, son of a prominent analyst. In thinking about whom I would recommend to him, I vacillated between a rather gentle, modest analyst and a strong, aggressive, and highly successful practitioner who resembled the young man's father. Most of my questions, I realized, related to a more fundamental concern: Would this young man fit best with an analyst who, by virtue of his personality and status, could more readily provoke an intense transference, which might in turn provoke countertransferential responses? Such a question seems to challenge the very concept of fit. We often think of it in terms of similarity or at least complementarity of personalities, but perhaps the critical issue should be how strong a transference-countertransference crossfire is likely to be set up between a given patient and his analyst. Countertransference responses, we should not forget, provide us with some of our most vital data.

The analyst should carefully and honestly consider matters of culture in determining whether he and a prospective patient can establish a good fit. Can a white, middle-class analyst comfortably take as a patient a black man who has been reared in a totally different environment? Some analysts would be attracted, others frightened, by the difference. As a professional community, we have perhaps narrowed our treatment population too much. Yet is it not possibly a sign of arrogance to take into treatment someone whose life circumstances we might have great difficulty identifying with? Or should we assume that whatever is universal in the human experience will transcend cultural barriers? Whatever the answers, I believe that the questions themselves need to be confronted more forcibly.

THE PATIENT'S EXPECTATIONS

There is a final consideration, one that we've already implied. The patient or potential patient also has some concept of fit with the analyst. Sometimes this is unconscious, but at other times the patient is looking for something quite specific in the analyst. For example, during an interview, a young woman asked the male analyst if he was married. He replied that he was not. The woman then said that she wanted a married therapist, because forming a lasting partnership was one of her goals in entering therapy. After the interview, the analyst realized that his anxieties about his unmarried state had prompted him to answer her question with a personal disclosure (see Chapter 13) rather than to probe more deeply into why his marital status was so important. While it is generally true that if the analyst thinks the fit is correct, so does the patient, it might be said that patients also have some "instinct" for correct fit.

The fit between patient and analyst is a real but subtle matter. It is incumbent upon us to examine the factors that make us comfortable or uncomfortable with a patient. Such feelings arise in every treatment and probably originate in the interaction of transference and countertransference phenomena. One hopes that the analyst can recognize his contribution to these problems, analyzing them first for their meaning to him personally and then for their effects on the patient. It is when this process occurs and the difficulty is resolved that we see analytic progress, which is the real test of analytic fit.

Chapter 16
Countertransference and Money Issues

PAYMENT OF FEES

Before he retired, an analyst referred a patient whom he had treated for eight years to a younger colleague. The patient was fairly wealthy, yet despite this fact, and the fact that analytic fees had generally risen during this period, the analyst had continued to charge him a low fee. When the patient interviewed his prospective new analyst, he asked about fees. The analyst gave him a figure fifteen dollars higher than what he had been paying the first analyst, and the patient readily agreed. In reporting the results of the consultation to the referring analyst, the new therapist mentioned the fee he had requested. The older man sighed and said that for several years he had wanted to raise his fees but had wavered because of his impending retirement.

This anecdote illustrates some of the anxieties and hesitations that beset patients and analysts in relation to fees. These issues are charged; for both participants in the therapeutic transaction, these practical concerns relate to vital emotional experiences from the past.

There is no one right or wrong method in dealing with fees. What is critical is that the analyst be alert to any break in the treatment contract and monitor well his reactions. For countertransference can interfere with his ability to handle such situations in therapeutic ways.

ADJUSTING THE PAYMENT SCALE

Certainly, we must take into account that all patients do not have the same financial status. Some are very wealthy, others comfortable; still others can barely come up with the requisite amount each month. Such differences can be equalized in some measure by a sliding payment scale. It should be kept in mind, however, that sliding scales are a fertile breeding ground for transference and countertransference.

One analyst described the case of a patient who started out at a fee of 30 dollars, which was 20 dollars less than the analyst's usual fee. When the patient got a job that paid better, he himself initiated raising of the fee to 50 dollars. Later, when his income increased again, the fee was raised to 70 dollars, although, again, this was below the analyst's fee at that point. After several years at this fee level, the patient mentioned certain facts that took the analyst by surprise. He realized that the patient now made over $225,000 a year. The patient added that he was buying a larger house and that his business was booming. Yet he was still paying a reduced fee, and the analyst made no move to adjust it.

The analyst described his reasons: "Two things were clear to me. He was a twin and close to his brother. Out of his negative, oedipal, passive, feminine, submissive attitudes, he would have liked nothing better than to settle into an interminable, lifelong analysis with me, in which he paid to let me take care of him and let him take care of me. This is what I wanted to be very careful to avoid. Even before, during our earlier fee discussions, it was evident to me that if I pounced on him and demanded that he pay the normal fee, I would be gratifying his wish for an anal rape, with all of its implications.

Also, I would be acting out with him his wish for us to take care of each other, instead of analyzing it. All along, there had been a tendency on his part to creep along very slowly, going nowhere, moving around in little circles, waiting for me to step in and say, 'You have to take care of this, you have to take charge of that.' I was not about to do that.

"Eventually, on his own, after almost another year of working, he realized that behind this provocation — which is what it really was — lay his wish for me to attack him. He wanted me to fight with him and rip the money from him. Behind this wish was his wish to pay me, to give money, instead of giving up his infantile yearnings and strivings. And behind that, yet another level, was his oedipal wish to take care of me. There was, as well, a maternal transference. As a boy he always wanted to be the lord of the manor and take care of his mother.

"He wanted to take care of his brother too, for that came up after we worked out all of this. He mentioned he would be the one to take care of his brother forever. This was partly reaction-formation and partly the wish for that attachment and togetherness.

"After about ten months of analyzing this, he became much more assertive. He said recently his company was rapidly expanding and was buying another company. He told me about a meeting with the owner of the other company. The two of them were very far apart in their negotiations. Finally my patient said, 'Now look, Mr. X., we are so far apart, we ought to stop. You know we are not going to pay what you want. Your company's not worth that much. I think we ought to break this off.' And the other man said, 'Wait a minute. Hold on. Let me think it over. I'll get back to you, with a different offer,' and he walked out of the room. Whereupon my patient's father, who was present, turned to him and said, 'Who are you? I don't know you. You're a different person.' My patient has taken more charge of his life. He eventually did suggest raising the fee. He asked what my minimum fee was and I told him it was 80 dollars. He said, 'I'm going to pay you ninety.'

"We're now in the termination phase. But looking back, I think the fee business went exactly the way it should have gone. If I had said, 'Look, our agreement at the start was in deference to your circumstances at the time. Now that your circumstances have changed, we should reconsider the fee,' the treatment would have dragged on for years. I didn't see what difference it would make to me in the long run if we raised the fee at two months, six months, eight months. It was more important that he struggle with this and that we analyze it, rather than just cutting it off."

Here there were good analytic reasons to delay raising the fee to the appropriate level. In general, however, I think that when a patient whose fee has been adjusted downward registers a considerable increase in earnings, the analyst is almost obligated to readjust the fee, not only as acknowledgment of the new financial reality and in fairness to himself but also as a sign of respect for the patient. A therapist who, either from insecurity or other conflictual reasons, hesitates to request a higher fee may not only be implicitly deprecating the patient's success; he also may inhibit the patient from expressing anger or other feelings related to money matters and even to the analysis itself.

A different kind of difficulty arises when the analyst, in an effort to meet increased costs, needs to raise his fee but cannot do this because the patient can't afford it. The analyst may then respond with certain countertransferential feelings, such as resentment of the patient's situation—feelings which may in turn lead him unconsciously to weaken his efforts on the patient's behalf. On the other hand, if, despite the patient's difficulty, he goes ahead and requests a higher fee, it may negatively affect the patient's perception of him and thereby harm the treatment. In weighing these matters, we should try to remember that analysis succeeds best where the working climate is optimally comfortable for both parties. The analyst must take into account the patient's situation, but the patient, though certainly to a lesser degree, since he knows far less about the analyst than the analyst about him, must also respect the situation of his therapeutic partner.

REDUCING FEES

Another issue arises when the patient runs out of money during the course of the treatment. When Freud's "Wolf Man" encountered severe financial problems, Freud not only stopped charging him but also loaned him money. I know of several analysts who have done the same on occasion. I, too, have, in several instances, reduced my fee or changed a payment schedule.

In reducing fees, I definitely had some countertransferential fantasies. I felt that I was giving scholarships to my "students." And I had certain expectations as well. One of these was that, although these patients' failure to pay was causing me no financial distress, I did not want them to take advantage; in fact, I expected them to work harder out of gratitude. Despite these countertransference reactions, I found, in general, that my reduction of fees moved the treatments forward, presumably because, in part, the patients involved interpreted it as an effort to help them. Also, I found that they were still able to express anger toward me, although this too depended on what treatment phase they were in. As for whether the fee reduction increased their dependency on me, this varied also, again according to the treatment phase and also to the nature of their personal conflicts. Sometimes the very fact of the fee reduction served to bring forward the issues of dependency and manipulative exploitation that were inherent both in the patients' financial situations and in their responses to my concession to them.

MISREPRESENTATION OF FINANCIAL STATUS

Another, though rarer, question has to do with the patient who misrepresents his finances. How should the analyst respond?

In presenting himself to me, a man in his late thirties complained of his inability to hold down a job. On the basis of this and other information, I offered him a reduced fee. The therapy began, but something about it was odd, for during the first year or so I frequently experienced an uneasy feeling that there were gaps in his associations, as if he were avoiding some material. Imagine my surprise when, upon entering a midtown department store during the holiday season, I saw my patient, loaded with shopping bags, exit from the same store into a chauffeured Rolls Royce that had his initials on the license plate. At our next session, I matter-of-factly described what I had seen. He broke down and cried. When he stopped, he expressed his extreme embarrassment and guilt, and also his relief about being found out. His imposture, it turned out, was a character trait; he hid his wealth, he said, in all social situations where it was unknown, for he was afraid that people would be interested in his money, not him. Once I understood the circumstances of his duplicity, any anger that I had at being conned immediately disappeared. Indeed, this discovery proved a turning

point in the analysis. Because I showed no negative countertransference disguised as moral judgment, we were able to go on and
examine what led him to this pattern.

Among the monetary issues that arise during therapy, payment for
missed sessions is one of the most irritating to the patient.
Analysts have different ways of dealing with this matter. Some
follow a strict practice of accepting neither personal nor natural
disasters as excuses for nonpayment. If a patient misses a session
because of a funeral, or if he has a board meeting he cannot
postpone or cancel, he still has to pay. I have even heard of
instances where a blizzard blanketed an area, making it impossible
for the patient to keep his appointment, yet the analyst refused to
schedule a make-up session or reduce the end-of-the-month bill.

Other analysts recognize that, just as emergencies arise in their
own lives, causing them to cancel an appointment, the same will be
true for their patients on occasion. These analysts respond more
flexibly to their patients' difficulties, scheduling another hour if an
emergency causes a cancellation or even, as one analyst did,
offering telephone sessions during a transit strike. In the latter
instance, the analyst decided that the patient's precarious emotional state made any interruption in the treatment ill advised.
Subsequent events proved the correctness of this evaluation, as
therapeutic trust perceptibly deepened almost immediately afterward. Unlike the man's parents, the analyst had proved flexible
and understanding, and the patient noticed and appreciated the
difference.

In commenting on this case and on the missed-appointment
issue in general, another analyst remarked, "When we look at this
question practically, the number of times such crises take place
during the average analysis is not going to change the economic
lifestyle of either the patient or the analyst. Accordingly, if we,
too, closely approximate the authoritarian childhood environment, we are creating an atmosphere that infantilizes the patient
and may possibly, I won't say always, lead to making the situation
unanalyzable."

Besides these issues, which can affect all therapists, child
analysts have their own special money problems, foremost among
them being the fact that it is not the patient, but his parents who

pay for the therapy. This—together with the fact that it is normally not the patient but the parents who have decided on the need for therapy—can diminish the patient's incentive to change. And if change comes slowly, this can diminish the parents' incentive to pay. Moreover, if the parents cause difficulties with payment, the analyst must be watchful lest he take out any anger he may feel on the child.

A number of money issues arise during every treatment. In order not to contaminate the therapy with negative countertransference, the analyst needs to exercise care and honesty with his responses. However discomforting money issues may be, by not confronting them we show both ourselves and our patients disrespect.

Afterword

One reason analysts hesitated for so many years to explore countertransference may be found in their sublimations, the principal one being sexual curiosity. We must remember that the impulse to expose usually, if not always, coexists with its opposite, the impulse to observe. As analysts, we have had much practice in working with our sublimated voyeuristic curiosity, but it has been at the expense of repressing our impulse toward self-exposure. We were, and are, careful not to exhibit ourselves to patients—an abstention essential to treatment. Yet in our discussions of professional questions we must beware of carrying this caution to the point of rigidity, where it ceases to be a virtue.

In recent years we have experienced a cultural change that has affected our attitudes toward the "sin" of exposure. The change began in the late 1960s, with the general directive to "let it all hang out." This new emphasis on self-revelation has probably made us more prone to expose ourselves in our discussions about counter-transference in meetings and in papers. Obviously, we can misuse this new ability to be open, as when we reveal something to the patient in the interest of truth that harms the treatment. Truth may be what one tells one's friend just before he becomes an enemy. But I think we also have to be aware of our conflicts about exposure and how they may prevent us from truly understanding the analytic process.

In this book I have tried to stimulate an heuristic interest in countertransference — its relationship to the psychoanalytic situation, to treatment processes, and to various elements of technique. What interests me is how these relationships affect therapeutic outcome. When the patient acts lovingly, responsively, and pro-ductively, we may say that he is showing positive transference. But, can we say that when the analyst believes that treatment is progressing well and discovers in himself positive feelings and fantasies about the patient, this is positive countertransference? And do these conditions promote treatment success? It is my hope that the questions raised in this book will prompt further study.

References

Balint, M., and Balint, A. (1939). On transference and countertransference. *International Journal of Psycho-Analysis* 20:223–230.

Benedek, T. (1953). Dynamics of the countertransference. *Bulletin of the Menninger Clinic* 17:201–208.

Bleger, J. (1967). Psycho-analysis of the psycho-analytic frame. *International Journal of Psycho-Analysis* 48:511–519.

Breuer, J., and Freud, S. (1936). On the psychic mechanism of hysterical phenomena. In *Studies on Hysteria,* pp. 1–13. New York: Nervous and Mental Disease Publishing Co.

De Forest, I. (1942). The therapeutic technique of Sandor Ferenczi. *International Journal of Psycho-Analysis* 23:120–139.

Deutsch, H. (1926). Occult processes occurring during psychoanalysis. In *Psychoanalysis and the Occult,* ed. G. Devereux. New York: International Universities Press, 1953.

Feiner, A. (1977). Countertransference and the anxiety of influence. In *Countertransference,* ed. L. Epstein and A. Feiner. New York: Jason Aronson, 1979.

Ferenczi, S. (1919). On the technique of psycho-analysis. In *Further Contributions to the Theory and Technique of Psychoanalysis,* pp. 177–189. London: Hogarth Press, 1950.

_____ (1920). The further development of an active therapy in psychoanalysis. In *Further Contributions to the Theory and Technique of Psychoanalysis,* pp. 198–217. London: Hogarth Press, 1950.

Fliess, R. (1942). The metapsychology of the analyst. *Psychoanalytic Quarterly* 11:211–227.

Freud, S. (1909). Five lectures on psychoanalysis. Delivered on the occasion of the celebration of the twentieth anniversary of the foundation of Clark University, Worcester, Massachusetts, September 1909. *Standard Edition* 11:3–55.

_____ (1910). Future prospects for psycho-analytic therapy. *Standard Edition* 11:141–142.

_____ (1912). Recommendations to physicians practicing psychoanalysis. *Standard Edition* 12:111–112.

Fromm-Reichmann, F. (1950). *Principles of Intensive Psychotherapy.* Chicago: University of Chicago Press.

Gill, M. (1979). The analysis of the transference. *Journal of the American Psychoanalytic Association (Suppl.)* 27:263–288.

Giovacchini, P. (1979). Countertransference with primitive mental states. In *Countertransference,* ed. L. Epstein and A. Feiner. New York: Jason Aronson.

Gitelson, M. (1952). The emotional position of the analyst in the psycho-analytic situation. *International Journal of Psycho-Analysis* 33:1–10.

_____ (1962). The curative factors in psycho-analysis; the first phase of psycho-analysis. *International Journal of Psycho-Analysis* 43:194–205.

Glover, E. (1927). Lectures on technique in psychoanalysis. *International Journal of Psycho-Analysis* 8:311–338.

Greenson, R. (1960). Empathy and its vicissitudes. *International Journal of Psycho-analysis* 41:418–424.

_____ (1971). The "real" relationship between the patient and the psychoanalyst. In *The Unconscious Today,* ed. M. Kanzer, pp. 213–232. New York: International Universities Press.

Grinberg, L. (1957). Projective counteridentification and countertransference. In *Countertransference,* ed. L. Epstein and A. Feiner. New York: Jason Aronson, 1979.

_____ (1962). On a specific aspect of countertransference due to the patient's projective identification. *International Journal of Psycho-Analysis* 43: 436–440.

Hann-Kende, F. (1933). On the role of transference and countertransference in psychoanalysis. In *Psychoanalysis and the Occult,* ed. G. Devereux. New York: International Universities Press, 1953, 1970.

Heimann, P. (1950). On countertransference. *International Journal of Psycho-Analysis* 31:81–84.

Issacharoff, A., and Hunt, W. (1978). Beyond countertransference. *Contemporary Psychoanalysis* 14:291–310.

Jones, E. (1953). *The Life and Work of Sigmund Freud,* pp. 223–225. New York: Basic Books.

Kernberg, O. (1965). Notes on countertransference. *Journal of the American Psychoanalytic Association* 13:38–56.

Klein, M. (1946). Notes on some schizoid mechanisms. *International Journal of Psycho-Analysis* 27:99–110.

Langs, R. (1978). *The Listening Process.* New York: Jason Aronson.

Little, M. (1951). Countertransference and the patient's response to it. *International Journal of Psycho-Analysis* 32:32–40.

———(1957). "R"—The analyst's total response to his patient's needs. *International Journal of Psycho-Analysis* 38:240–254.

Lorand, S. (1946). *Technique of Psychoanalytic Therapy.* New York: International Universities Press.

Low, B. (1935). The psychological compensation of the analyst. *International Journal of Psycho-Analysis* 16:1–8.

McDougall, J. (1979). Primitive communication and the use of countertransference. In *Countertransference,* ed. L. Epstein, and A. Feiner. pp. 267–303. New York: Jason Aronson.

Mahler, M., and Furer, M. (1963). Certain aspects of the separation–individuation phase. *Psychoanalytic Quarterly* 32:1–14.

Menninger, K. A., and Holzman, P. S. (1958). *Theory of Psychoanalytic Technique.* New York: Basic Books.

Money-Kyrle, R. (1956). Normal concepts of countertransference and some of its deviations. *International Journal of Psycho-Analysis* 37:360–366.

Racker, H. (1953). A contribution to the problem of countertransference. *International Journal of Psycho-Analysis* 34:313–324.

——— (1957). The meanings and uses of countertransference. *Psychoanalytic Quarterly* 26:303–357.

Reich, A. (1951). On counter-transference. *International Journal of Psycho-Analysis* 32:25–31.

Reich, W. (1933). *Character Analysis: Principles and Techniques for Psychoanalysts in Practice and Training.* 2nd ed. New York: Orgone Institute, 1945.

Schafer, R. (1959). Generative empathy in the treatment situation. *Psychoanalytic Quarterly* 28:342–373.

——— (1985). Wild analysis. *Journal of the American Psychoanalytic Association* 33:275–299.

Searles, H. (1958). The schizophrenic's vulnerability to the therapist's unconscious processes. *Journal of Nervous and Mental Disease* 127:247–262.

——— (1975). The patient as therapist to his analyst. In *Tactics and Techniques in Psychoanalytic Therapy,* vol. II: *Countertransference,* ed. P. Giovacchini, pp. 95–151. New York: Jason Aronson.

Sharpe, E. (1930). The technique of psychoanalysis. *International Journal of Psycho-Analysis* 2:361–386.

Spotnitz, H. (1963). The toxoid response. In *Active Psychotherapy,* ed. H. Greenwald, pp. 49–62. New York: Jason Aronson, 1984.

Stern, A. (1924). On the countertransference in psychoanalysis. *Psychoanalytic Review* 2:166–174.

Strachey, J. (1934). The nature of the therapeutic action of psychoanalysis. *International Journal of Psycho-Analysis* 15:127–159.

Tower, L. (1956). Countertransference. *Journal of the American Psychoanalytic Association* 4:224–255.

Winnicott, D. (1949). Hate in the countertransference. *International Journal of Psycho-Analysis* 30:69–74.

Index